Objects of Desire

Also by Beryl Schlossman

Joyce's Catholic Comedy of Language

The Orient of Style: Modernist Allegories of Conversion

Angelus Novus

Objects of Desire

The Madonnas
of Modernism

BERYL SCHLOSSMAN

CORNELL UNIVERSITY PRESS

ITHACA AND LONDON

First published 1999 by Cornell University Press

Printed in the United States of America

Library of Congress Cataloging-in-Publication Data
Schlossman, Beryl
    Objects of desire : the madonnas of modernism / Beryl Schlossman.
       p.   cm.
    Includes bibliographical references and index.
    ISBN 0-8014-3649-4 (cloth : alk. paper)
    1. Modernism (Literature)   2. Literature, Modern—20th century—History
and criticism.   3. Literature, Modern—19th century—History and criticism.
4. Literature, Modern—Classical influences.   5. Virginity in literature.
6. Desire in literature.   7. Women in literature.   8. Love in literature.   I. Title.
PN56.M54S36   1999
809'.9112—dc21   99-32826

Cornell University Press strives to use environmentally responsible suppliers and materials to the fullest extent possible in the publishing of its books. Such materials include vegetable-based, low-VOC inks, and acid-free papers that are recycled, totally chlorine-free, or partly composed of nonwood fibers. Books that bear the logo of the FSC (Forest Stewardship Council) use paper taken from forests that have been inspected and certified as meeting the highest standards for environmental and social responsibility. For further information, visit our website at www.cornellpress.cornell.edu.

Cloth printing 10 9 8 7 6 5 4 3 2 1

FSC FSC Trademark © 1996 Forest Stewardship Council A.C.
      SW-COC-098

Contents

Illustrations

Acknowledgments

For the generous support that enabled me to complete the research and writing of this book, I would like to express my gratitude to Carnegie Mellon University for a Falk Award in 1993 and for Faculty Development Awards in 1994 and 1996. I thank the Center for Advanced Studies of the University of Virginia for a fellowship from the Andrew Mellon Foundation in 1988 and 1989. I also thank the Fulbright Foundation and, especially, Pierre F. Collombert, Director of the Franco-American Commission for Educational Exchange, for a Senior Research Grant to Paris, France, in early 1998. My research there was sponsored by the *Institut des Textes et Manuscrits Modernes,* Centre National de Recherche Scientifique (C.N.R.S.). I am grateful to Daniel Ferrer, the former Director of I.T.E.M., for his invitation to pursue my research under the auspices of the Institute, and for access to its collections.

For reproductions and permissions, I wish to thank the Estate of James Joyce, the National Gallery of Art in Washington, D.C., the Metropolitan Museum of Art in New York, the Louvre Museum, the *Réunion des musées nationaux* in Paris, and the Museum of Carthage, in Tunis.

Early drafts of several chapters have appeared as follows: "Retrospective Beginnings," *James Joyce Quarterly* 29:1 (1991): 85–101; "*Che vuoi?* Don Giovanni and the seductions of Art," in *James Joyce 2, "Scribble" 2: Joyce et Flaubert,* edited by Claude Jaquet and André Topia. Paris: Minard, 1990, 133–153; "(Pas encore!)—Flaubert, Baudelaire, and Don Giovanni," *Romanic Review* 82:3 (1990): 350–367; and "Figures Transfigured: Madonnas of Modernism, Altars of the Sublime" in *Ulysse à l'article: Joyce aux marges du roman,* edited by Daniel Ferrer, Claude Jaquet, André Topia. Tusson Charente: Du Lérot, 1991, 221–254. With slight changes, chapter 6 appeared as "Tristan and Isolde or the Triangles of Desire: Jealousy, Eroticism, and

Poetics" in *Genetic Studies in Joyce: Probes,* edited by David Hayman and Sam Slotes. Amsterdam and Atlanta: Rodopi, 1995, 149–178. In somewhat different form, parts of chapters 1 and 7 respectively were accepted to appear in *Joyce and Language,* edited by Laurent Milesi (Cambridge: Cambridge University Press) and in the collected papers from the Eighteenth James Joyce Colloquium in May 1997 at the *Institut des Textes et Manuscrits Modernes* (C.N.R.S.) in Paris, edited by André Topia and Daniel Ferrer.

BERYL SCHLOSSMAN

Objects of Desire

INTRODUCTION

Taking the Veil

Madonna
1. a former Italian style of address equivalent to *madam*.
2. (M-) the Virgin Mary; "Our Lady"; also, a picture or statue of the Virgin; as, Raphael painted many *Madonnas*.

—Webster's Dictionary

HAMLET: Do you think I meant country matters?
OPHELIA: I think nothing, my lord.
HAMLET: That's a fair thought to lie between maids' legs.
OPHELIA: What is, my lord?
HAMLET: Nothing.
OPHELIA: You are merry, my lord.

—Shakespeare, *Hamlet*

Love is at the center of modern literature, and the texts of modernism locate its cultural contexts all over the map: on the street, in the movie theater, in religious devotion, in social history, in theology, and in popular entertainment. Love enters a mix of "high" and "low" culture where the sublime faces the obscene and passion confronts violence. The phenomena of love inform culture and haunt its subjects with temptations and taboos. The media project images of the feminine as an icon of desire and as a vessel of pure love: from videos of the performer Madonna luridly displayed in peepshow mirrors and bullfight scenes to the international mass mourning of Lady Di, who seems to have been revered as much for her designer frills and yachting parties as for her public relations centered in compassion, the fiction of the feminine subject reflects the images of the Madonna. In spite of feminism and other cultural challenges to traditional gender roles, love remains a woman's job. The figures that I am calling madonnas of modernism are female characters featured in secular modernist works as subjects and objects of desire.[1] The path of love that these characters take includes resonances of mariolatry (the cult of the Blessed Virgin Mary), mystical spirituality, and the cult of virginity (an investment of sacred powers, taboos, and social values across cultures).

A provocative ambivalence characterizes the Western cult and culture of love. As the unique feminine object of adoration in Christian culture, the Virgin provides some refuge for the subject who has accepted the taboo placed on desire; at the other extreme, the sacred is denied and the feminine object is torn from her pedestal. No longer "alone of all her sex," the Virgin is consumed, finally, in the mid-nineteenth century at the libertine altar of desire when Flaubert's Don Juan resurrects her with his love. Ambivalence rules in this deathbed

---

[1] Joyce's oeuvre and its innovations within high modernism are central in the critical, theoretical, and new philological writings of David Hayman. See *Joyce et Mallarmé: 1. Stylistique de la suggestion,* and *2. Les Eléments mallarméens dans l'oeuvre de Joyce* (Paris: Lettres Modernes, 1956); *"Ulysses": The Mechanics of Meaning* (Englewood Cliffs, N.J.: Prentice Hall, 1970; *Re-Forming the Narrative: Toward a Mechanics of Modernist Fiction* (Ithaca: Cornell University Press, 1987); and *The "Wake" in Transit* (Ithaca: Cornell University Press, 1990). Other major theoretical work on Joyce and modernism includes the following: Jacques Derrida, *Ulysse grammophone* (Paris: Galilée, 1987); Jean-Michel Rabaté, *James Joyce: Portrait de l'auteur en autre lecteur* (Petit-Roeulx: Cistre, 1984); idem, *Joyce upon the Void* (New York: St. Martin's Press, 1991); idem, *James Joyce* (Paris: Hachette, 1993). Based at the research center of I.T.E.M. (C.N.R.S.), directed until 1998 by Daniel Ferrer, genetic studies of Joyce have produced a number of indispensable publications and series. See Daniel Ferrer, "La Scène primitive de l'écriture," in *Genèse de Babel: Joyce et la création,* edited by Claude Jacquet (Paris: CNRS, 1985), 15–35; idem, "The Freudful Couchmare of /\ d: Joyce's Notes on Freud and the Composition of Chapter XVI of *Finnegans Wake,*" *James Joyce Quarterly* 22, no. 4 (1985): 367–82; idem, "Circé ou les regrés éternels," *Cahiers de l'Herne 50: James Joyce,* edited by Jacques Aubert and Fritz Senn (Paris: L'Herne, 1985), 341–58; idem, "Archéologie du regard dans les avant-textes de 'Circé,'" *La Revue des Lettres Modernes, James Joyce, "Scribble" 1* (Paris: Minard, 1988): 95–106; same author with Derek Attridge, *Post-Structuralist Joyce* (Cambridge: Cambridge University Press, 1984). See also Phillip F. Herring, *Joyce's Uncertainty Principle* (Princeton: Princeton University Press, 1987); André Topia, "'Sirènes': l'expressivité nomade," *La Revue des Lettres Modernes, James Joyce, "Scribble" 1* (Paris: Minard, 1988): 69–94; the collections of essays in the following: *Genèse de Babel* (cited above); the series entitled *Revue des Lettres modernes, James Joyce* (Paris: Minard, 1988–); *'Ulysse' à l'article: Joyce aux marges du roman,* edited by D. Ferrer, C. Jacquet, and A. Topia (Tusson: Du Lérot, 1991); *Cahiers de l'Herne 50: James Joyce,* edited by Jacques Aubert and Fritz Senn (Paris: L'Herne, 1985).

scene which is rendered as a tryst in a boudoir. Sacred and profane, adored and debased, the resurrected woman represents the Virgin as the object of true love, while her moment of passion recalls the debasement of Donna Elvira, seduced and jilted in the convent. For Don Juan, the libertine lover, nothing is sacred, because he is interested only in consuming beautiful objects. But in the end, according to Flaubert's notes for "Une Nuit de Dom Juan," Don Juan's ultimate object of passion is the virginal mystical Madonna: "[Don Juan] finissant par désirer la sainte Vierge [[Don Juan] ends up desiring the holy Virgin]." The impact of the Madonna as a feminine object beyond all others is not limited to religious worship: the cult of love overflows the boundaries of the sacred.

The eroticization of the virginity of feminine love objects is evidence of the repression that Freud saw as the source of the object's debasement. In this context, the cult of the Blessed Virgin Mary is symptomatic of the modern shift away from the valorization of sexuality that Freud locates in antiquity:

> The most striking distinction between the erotic life of antiquity and our own no doubt lies in the fact that the ancients laid the stress upon the instinct itself, whereas we emphasize its object. The ancients glorified the instinct and were prepared on its account to honour even an inferior object; while we despise the instinctual activity in itself, and find excuses for it only in the merits of the object.[2]

The lover's valorization of virginity anticipates the debasement of the beloved, whose value soon will disappear into thin air. The adoration of the feminine mediated by figures of the Virgin is a screen for the repression of the drives that Freud observes in modern culture.

Objects of Desire explores the feminine through literary and visual images of desirable objects, figures of girls and women conceived by men. Although these texts appear to take conventional gender roles as a given, their modernist renderings of madonna-like images ultimately blur gender identity and dissolve it in the text. These writings reveal a complicity with the feminine and an identification with it; their inscriptions of desire are assimilated into their portraits of the sublime.

---

[2] Sigmund Freud, *Three Essays on Sexuality*, "I. The Sexual Aberrations," I.B., footnote added 1910.

Through their innovative use of style, these Modernist works produce a discourse of subjectivity anchored in the feminine. They articulate an art of seduction and an aesthetic that transforms, suspends,
or dissolves identity—individual, social, cultural, and gender identity.
Modernism takes up the questions raised in philosophy, in theology,
and most recently, in psychoanalysis. What is at stake in the split between self-love and love of others? What are the differences between
desire and love, and between ordinary love and mystical love? How
does the self identify itself with another, and to what effects? *The
Madonnas of Modernism* traces some modernist perspectives on love
through the classical influences of Plato's *Symposium* and Sappho's
poems. In the Renaissance, the effects of their portraits of love seem
to merge with the inheritance of courtly love, Dante, and Christian
mysticism, precisely at the moment when the neo-Platonist Marsilio
Ficino rediscovers Eros the bittersweet.[3] By way of romanticism, these
elements of a Renaissance culture of love take shape in modernist
style. In a veiling of romantic self-consciousness and self-expression,
Flaubert and Baudelaire invent modernism.[4] Their new images of the
feminine include the madonna in specifically modernist allegorical
configurations. By means of Yeats and Laforgue as well as Flaubert,
Joyce reinscribes the early modernist figures of love in his texts of
high modernism. Poetics and erotics are articulated in a framework
that emphasizes the sacred and the comic, and their encounters
within literature. These encounters produce beautiful figures.

The figure of the beautiful that originates in classical philosophy
provides a backdrop for a reading of the feminine. *Objects of Desire*
shows how Socrates' concept of love in Plato's *Symposium* affects the

---

[3] See Marcilio Ficino, *Theologia platonica de animarum immortalitate*, edited by
R. Marcel (Desclée: Paris, 1955) and *De Amore*, edited by R. Marcel (Desclée: Paris,
1956). An essay by the art historian Edgar Wind that uncovers Sappho's traces in the
writings of Ficino is discussed in chapter 7.

[4] Paul de Man's writing unfolds the transformations of romanticism through the
problematics of literary modernity and especially poetry. The writing of Hans-Jost
Frey examines the poetics of modernity and modernism, beginning with Hölderlin
and Baudelaire. On Flaubert and modernism, see Jonathan Culler, *Flaubert: The Uses
of Uncertainty* (Ithaca: Cornell University Press, 1974), and by the same author,
Framing the Sign: Criticism and its Institutions (Norman: University of Oklahoma
Press, 1988). On Baudelaire, see Jean Starobinski, *La Mélancholie au miroir* (Paris: Jul-
liard, 1989). On history and modernist style, see Peter Hughes, "From Allusion to Im-
plosion: Vico. Michelet. Joyce. Beckett," in *Vico and Joyce*, edited by Donald P. Verene
(Albany: SUNY Press, 1987), 83–99.

writing of modernity. Plato's Socratic version of love combines with the influence of neo-Platonic discourse on romanticism (via the baroque theater of Don Juan, who specializes in the seduction of virgins); the rediscovery of Sappho the poet and voice of Eros the bittersweet; the revaluation of love in twentieth-century psychoanalysis; and the images of the Blessed Virgin in art. These elements shape the inscriptions of the feminine in modernism.

It is widely recognized that the philosophical ideal of Eros in Plato's *Symposium* influences a wide range of interpretations of love in modernity (including romantic and post-romantic literature, modernism, philosophy, and psychoanalysis), but most theoretical works on love and classical studies of Plato do not explore the dimensions of the Socratic Eros in modernism. Through a confrontation of texts and images, *Objects of Desire* locates Eros in relation to the question of desire in writing.[5] The accent is on modernist configurations of the feminine, beginning with Socrates' discourse in Plato's *Symposium* and Joyce's evocation of Eve and Mary, and returning to the classical Eros with the writing and erasure of Sappho's poetic texts.

Part One, "Eros the Bittersweet," focuses on classical and modernist inscriptions of Sappho's figure of Eros evoked as *glykyprikon* in fragment 131. "Platonic Love: Socrates, Diotima, and the Virgin Mary" considers love in Plato's *Symposium*, the articulation of the feminine in modernism through the figures of Diotima, the Virgin, and the Seducer, and their impact on modernism. "Love's Bitter Mystery: Edenville and Nighttown" explores Anglo-Irish returns to "Eros the Bittersweet" by way of Catholic doctrine, specifically, original sin and the virginity that Stephen Dedalus claims for himself. Through Joyce's echoes of Yeats, Stephen's impasse in love illustrates the oxymoron of Sappho's "Eros the bittersweet." A duality of love is rooted in this oxymoron: like the strange twists of mastery and passion in Platonic love, Yeats's evocation recalls Sappho's epithet.

Part Two, "The Two Loves," examines the early modernist configuration of love. In "'Che vuoi?' Desire and the Seductions of Art," the

---

[5] See Rainer Nägele, *Echoes of Translation* (Baltimore: Johns Hopkins University Press, 1997). In *Stanze: La Parola e il fantasma nella cultura occidentale* (Torino: Einaudi, 1977, 1993), Giorgio Agamben explores the knots of language and fantasy, philosophy and poetry. Part 1 of *Stanze*, "I Fantasmi di Eros," considers Eros in the contexts of melancholy developed in Walter Benjamin's *Trauerspiel* book. See also an important source consulted by Benjamin: Raymond Klibansky, Erwin Panofsky, and H. Saxl, *Saturn and Melancholy* (New York: Basic Books, 1964).

Madonna figures take shape in Flaubert's *Madame Bovary* and Joyce's *Ulysses,* with reference to "Don Giovanni." In "Encore Performances: The End of Don Giovanni," the role of Don Juan is contrasted with the feminine in some little-known works by Baudelaire and Flaubert. The bittersweetness of love enters Christian (and libertine) territory; decadence and evil contrast with passionate love, virginal virtue, and beauty. The two loves are implicated in a triangle.

Part Three, "Triangles of Desire," explores Joyce's configuration of adulterous love rooted in the prototypical text of "Giacomo Joyce," the portrait of the artist as a failed Don Juan. "Bloom in Church: Beautiful Figures and Virgin Brides" focuses on love in *Ulysses,* while "Isolde at Sea: Jealousy, Erotics, and Poetics" explores Joyce's citational poetics of love in *Finnegans Wake.* "Writing and Erasing the Feminine: Sappho's Eros, Modernist Poetics, and the Madonna" returns to the classical poetics of Eros through the fate of Sappho's texts, their traces in the lyric poetry of Yeats, and her impact on the Madonna figures of Anglo Irish modernism. The Conclusion of *Objects of Desire,* "Virgin or Madonna," considers the impact of Sappho's Eros on the portrayal of desire in modernity.

Judeo-Christian tradition invokes (or reinvents) repression to condemn the eroticism of classical antiquity as decadence and corruption. The disorderly excesses of desire lead from Eve to the rest of womankind. Because Christian culture elaborates the doctrine of original sin as the consequence of Eve's seductions in the garden of Eden and the expulsion from paradise, Biblical culture begins with the exile of the feminine. In literature, the feminine returns in the surprising constellations of courtly love, a new form of sublimation (combining erotics and poetics) that develops in the Middle Ages and the Renaissance. Eros enters modernity, in part through the concept and image of the Madonna.

In the atmospheres of rapturous intoxication, bitter irony, and melancholy disappointment that color the major writings of early modernism, there are no characters like Plato's Diotima or Socrates to articulate a philosopher's ideal discourse of love. In the writings of Baudelaire or Flaubert, moments of erotic transport that would have received little attention from the detached Socrates are ambiguously combined with images of virginal purity and beauty. Within the framework of the double form of love that pervades Flaubert's work, the madonna figure emblematizes the aesthetic consequence of un-quenchable desire ["inassouvissable"]—the mystical marriage of Eros and writing.

Flaubert's configuration of the two loves shapes romantic bliss into an early modernist form of the sublime. Flaubert's writing of rapture anticipates Freud, who theorizes the erotic origin of the sublime that permeates culture, literature, and art. Freud (and Lacan after him) investigates eroticism and the unconscious at a certain critical and philosophical distance from the raptures of Judeo-Christian religious worship and from the taboos that are its foundation. The psychoanalytic interpretations of desire in Freud and Lacan take up the Greek vision of Eros in a modernist vein.

For the poets and novelists who reshape romanticism and invent modernism, eroticism mediates between the secular and the religious. Mystical virginity, original sin, corruption, adultery, and evil are central questions for Baudelaire and Flaubert, as well as for Yeats, Joyce, and others who followed their early modernist cues. Flaubert acclaims desire as the source of love, and love as the central preoccupation of his art. Love leads him toward the sublime of Art (its "truth"), far beyond its source. He posits the superiority of Art—the work of style, sober and impersonal—above desire and above everything else. The mystical value that transforms desire into love and into the truth of art echoes Socrates. His legendary sobriety is a model for authorial principles of impersonality and nonintervention that inform Flaubert's ideal of style and the invention of modernist prose. In *The Flowers of Evil*, Baudelaire's elaboration of an anonymous lyric voice emerges as the precise poetic counterpart of Flaubert's innovation.

According to Plato's portrayal of Socrates in *Symposium* 214–220, however, Socrates is never distracted by the erotic sensibility that plays a central role in early modernist visions of love. Like Flaubert's fictional characters, the narrator of Flaubert's letters and journals vacillates among several positions concerning sexuality and the sublime, abjection and religious sanctity, abstinence and the romantic dream, bourgeois *moeurs* and the seductive excesses of eroticism. Plato opposes philosophical distance to the sublime furors of the sacred that disrupt hierarchy and its distinctions. In modernity the terms are shifted, perhaps because the sublime furors of the sacred that shaped the classical understanding of subjectivity are no longer a given. The new interiority of the modern subject competes with the established domain of the sacred: the sublime, associated with art in trans-romantic aesthetics, secularizes the transports of the sacred for its own ends.

Despite the differences between the Socratic Eros and modern formulations of sexual and spiritual love, however, the early modernist emphasis on detachment from romantic transports of feeling and expression represents a Socratic "solution" to the threatening violence of Eros. Inside and outside the explicit fictional discourse of Flaubert's novels, several strands of his vocabulary are knotted around a moment of detachment associated with a poetics of vision, memory, or poetic beauty. The evocations of "revery," "absence," "ecstasy," "ravishment," and "being carried away" lead into the famous Flaubertian silences punctuated and prolonged by an enigmatic cry detached from conventional expression and the social fabric.

Modernist detachment unfolds through an art of language. The sentimentalized interiority and the personalized self-expression that both Flaubert and Baudelaire loathed in their contemporaries are banished from their principles of style. It is the French symbolist (or trans-romantic) influence on Yeats's poetic fictions that guarantees his poetic powers in spite of some confessional moments. Joyce invokes the powers of the sacred and the comic to detach himself and his writing from Irish sentiment. His quotations from Yeats reappear in *Ulysses* with the haunting quality of involuntary memory in Baudelaire's poems where dreamed objects of desire and fragments of the past pulverize conscious thought. Masked and veiled, the Eros of modernism locates the art of love where Sappho found it, beyond the identities of speaker and author.

According to Socrates, the foreign priestess Diotima guides him through the paradoxes of desire, its pleasures and pains, with a story that is simultaneously uncanny (in its familiarity with the gods) and familiar (in its rendering of Penia's calculation and Poros' self-absorbed ignorance). In Diotima's account of the origin of love, Penia/Poverty/Want approaches the nectar-intoxicated Poros/Plenty and conceives Eros. A cross between emptiness and abundance, Eros is a daimon, since he inhabits the intermediate ground between men and gods.

Near the end of the dialogue, Alcibiades proclaims his love for Socrates and confesses the strategies of his desire. His account of his extreme passion for the philosopher concurs with the opposition between the two forms of love in Socrates' rendering of Diotima's doctrine. The sufferings that Alcibiades describes reappear in the destiny of many of Flaubert's fictional characters. His story of intoxicated desire, obsessive passion, and the pain of mourning anticipates Mâtho's lovesick pursuit of the virgin priestess in Flaubert's second great novel, *Salammbô*. The parallel between the two texts is striking in spite of the differences of literary genre, period, and culture. The detached Socrates pulls the strings that control his audience, including Alcibiades.

The Socratic connection between the sublime mastery and detachment that Alcibiades exposes in his lamentation reappears in modernism. The same connection leads Flaubert away from romantic expressivity and toward the ideal of impersonality that shapes his oeuvre. The ideal of art and the artifices of style that sustain it banish a personalized discourse of sentiment, opinion, and the heart's desires. Masked by a neutral narrative voice, Flaubert's concept of his own authorial presence disappears from the scene of the text. In the domain of the sublime, the heart with its pleasures and pains is latent, invisible, covered with a translucent veil that hides its expressivity and turns it into beautiful form.

After *Madame Bovary*, Flaubert turns his back on modernity and retreats into the writing and rewriting of antiquity. As the erased and allegorical city of the past, Carthage is the setting for an invented love story told according to the stylistic axiom of impersonality that guarantees access to the sublime.[6] Flaubert instructs Louise Colet, the recipient of his most eloquent love-letters, in the art of veiling the author's sentiments in writing. "Refoulé à l'horizon, ton coeur l'éclairera du fond, au lieu de t'éblouir sur le premier plan [Pushed back to the horizon, your heart will illuminate it from the depths instead of dazzling you from center stage]."[7] The art of veiling, for Flaubert, is a mystical act, an entry into the sublime that evokes the taking of the veil. The image recalls the representation of the Madonna throughout Western European art. In a painting by Giotto, the veil that extends from the Virgin's head to wrap the body of the Child alludes to the mystery of the Incarnation.

Flaubert's correspondence to Colet is repeatedly inscribed with the love of the sublime and its detachment from the flesh: "Aimons-nous

[6] See the letter to Louise Colet of March 27, 1853, in *Correspondance* vol. 2 (Paris: Gallimard, 1973), 284.

[7] Letter of 27 March 1852, *Correspondance*, vol. 2, 61.

1. Giotto, *Madonna and Child*, c. 1320–30, tempera on wood. Courtesy of the National Gallery of Art.

donc *en l'Art,* comme les mystiques s'aimaient *en Dieu,* et que tout pâlisse devant cet amour! [Let us love each other *in Art,* as the mystics loved each other *in God,* and may all else pale before this love!].["8] The two loves are emblematized by the mystical images of the dissolved heart (or its blood) and ink. "C'est assez de notre coeur, que nous délayons dans l'encre, sans qu'il [the public] s'en doute [It is enough that we dissolve our heart in ink, without the knowledge of the public]; Les écumes ne se répandent pas sur le papier . . . On n'y verse que de l'encre [The foam does not spread across paper . . . We pour only ink onto it]."[9]

Expression is hidden, distanced, and veiled; to the writer of prose, "toute personnalité est interdite [personality is taboo]."[10] Like Flaubert's early fascination with mysticism, his aesthetic focus on the image of the veil is confirmed by his discovery of exotic femininity in the Orient. In a letter that prefigures Flaubert's famous fictional portrayals of women, feminine form becomes an early version of the work of art.

> Elles ont sur la figure un voile transparent à travers lequel on voit le rouge de leurs lèvres peintes et l'arc de leurs sourcils noirs . . . De loin, ce voile, que l'on ne distingue pas, leur donne une paleur étrange, qui vous arrête sur les talons, saisi d'étonnement et d'admiration. Elles ont l'air de fantômes.

> [They wear on their faces un transparent veil through which one sees the red of their painted lips and the arch of their black eyebrows . . . From far away, this imperceptible veil gives them a strange pallor that stops you in your tracks and seizes you with astonishment and admiration. They look like ghosts.][11]

The artifice of the translucent veil simultaneously hides and reveals the woman behind it—it reveals her at a distance, across the nearly invisible weave of light. Since phantom, fantasy, and strangeness confront desire with the beyond of sensuality, the sublime of the Other

---

[8] Letter of 14 August 1853, *Correspondance,* vol. 2, 468.
[9] Letters of 1 September 1852 and 25 November 1853, *Correspondance,* 145, 468.
[10] Letter to Colet, 25 October 1853, *Correspondance,* vol. 2, 456.
[11] Letter to Flaubert's uncle Parrain, 24 November 1850, *Correspondance,* vol. 1, 715.

love, the viewer sees them "from far away." Flaubert's veils render the object as an image of an image—an allegory of feminine beauty, conceived as the art of being absent. Distanced from desire, the veiled woman embodies the multicultural value of virginity.

In a Second Empire context, Flaubert's description of an Oriental theater of feminine beauty recalls contemporary images of pantomime players, pierrots and acrobats, the descendants of the Italian comedy. They play an important role in the representation of aesthetics and the artist in French contexts of symbolism (or trans-romanticism) as well as in the French and Italian representations of Don Juan and Don Giovanni. In Flaubert's evocation, the heart is pushed into the background, the face is covered with a veil, the public is unaware of the heart's presence, and the viewer is unaware that the face he sees is covered by a veil. The artificial pallor over the stylized inexpressive features turns these hieratic feminine phantoms into figures of beautiful style, arabesques of form, silent masks of art. The viewer is stopped in his tracks by the aesthetic stylization that turns the erotic into the sublime.[12]

Before Flaubert's Oriental fictions, the erotic and the aesthetic objects are combined in the translucent blue veil over the fair skin of Emma, seductively costumed in inky black and blue. Emma's riding costume indicates the cultural masculinization of the "amazon" who rides into the forest and enters the dangerous world of sexual pleasure for the first time. According to Flaubert's letters, he shares in Emma's pleasure. Masked and transformed, the artist's power to illuminate form with the strange light of the sublime implies a mastery of self-expression, a distantiation of the self, and a petrification or a monumentalizing. I have explored these aspects of modernist representation through the approach to style in Baudelaire, Flaubert, and Proust. The concept of allegory leads from the author's "conversion" or turn toward writing in *The Orient of Style* to the figures of writing the feminine in *Objects of Desire*. The strange power of allegory is inseparable from the Otherness of Flaubert's conception of "mystical love"— the love of the beautiful that spreads ink on the page.

For Flaubert as for Socrates, the two loves—or the two forms of Eros—cannot be reduced to a single one. Despite the connections between the sexual and the sublime that led Freud's contemporaries in the late nineteenth century to reduce mysticism to sex, psychoanaly-

---

[12] See *Voyages* in Flaubert, *Œuvres Complètes* vol. 2 (Paris: Seuil, 1964), 611.

sis, like early modernism, owes some of its originality to the nonre-
ducibility of the sublime to the sexual.[13] The gap or distance between
the two forms of love is consummated by the figure of Don Giovanni
who refuses to repent. His erotic acts are the flowers of evil that develop into the strangely sublime fruit of mystical feminine *jouissance*, more specifically indicated in Flaubert's sketch "A Night of
Don Juan" than in the seventeenth- and eighteenth-century versions
of Don Juan/Don Giovanni. Baudelaire's feminine figures of corruption (eroticism and evil) that represented sexual transgression (*The
Lesbians*) before they became the allegorical forms of the *Flowers of
Evil* incarnate the powers of seduction attributed earlier in literary
and operatic history to El Burlador, the sexual trickster or strategist
who shrugs off promises like disguises, and is only his "true" self in
moments of mastery based on deception.

The voice singing a serenade straight to the "heart"—a lyrical presence of peerless beauty and erotic power—is the only truth of Don
Giovanni. Its sublime is the sublime of Art rather than love. In his
view, beauty keeps no promises, nor does it represent any form of the
good. The ironically used term of endearment, "mio bene," refers to
possessions or goods rather than to the good and is used repeatedly
in Mozart's opera. Outside of morality or ethics, beauty locates the
height of art in the same voice that will reject the divine and plunge,
according to its diabolical identity, to the fires of hell that end the
opera. Or almost. For the first performance, in Prague in 1787, Mozart
added a message of law and order to mask the enormously subversive
power of Don Giovanni, the figure of desire acted out on a grand scale.

It is not only the unlimited or open-ended numerical potential of
seduction that is subversive about Don Giovanni, since Freud's view
of the unconscious also leads in this direction, toward a nonethical
unlimited power of sexual desire. Don Giovanni's subversive power
lies in the effects of his desire. It occurs even beyond the achievement
of satisfied seduction, in special effects like infatuation, melancholy,
mourning, jealousy, and even conversion.

The line is endless. In a traditional lazzi, Don Giovanni's valet un-
rolls the enormous list into the audience. Don Giovanni takes his
partners and enjoys each of them once and for all time in an almost
mystical instant that ends as an eternal signature in the Book of
Names. Once Leporello (or Sganarelle, or the others who play his role

---

[13] Jacques Lacan, *Séminaire XX: Encore* (Paris: Seuil, 1980), 71.

outside Mozart and Molière) inscribes her name, the object in question holds no more interest for his master. For his objects, however, Don Giovanni's seductive effect takes the form of an excess that knows no restraint; in many French and Italian versions, he is described as "irresistible." The women loved by Don Giovanni want to possess him in the duration of earthly time. Yet the "instant"—an eternity of possession for the lover of virgins—sets into motion an eternally enduring desire for possession on the part of the beloved, who has been seduced and abandoned. Desire is played out through an art of seduction or eroticism that is not only a strategy, but also an art form.

The madonnas of modernism are particularly important in the works of Flaubert, Baudelaire, Joyce, and Yeats. In addition to their aesthetic investment in the image of the Virgin, they were fascinated by the dramatic and operatic character of the libertine Don Juan (Don Giovanni), who professes atheism but believes in virginity as an erotic value. In Mozart's opera, Leporello's aria of the Catalog reveals Don Giovanni's "dominant passion for pure young girls": "Ma sua passion predominante è la giovan principiante!" At the allusion to virginity, Mozart lowers the valet's voice to an intimate stage whisper appropriate for church or alcove. Joyce's most compelling Madonnas of modernism are presented as daughters or as ripening women who are virginal in soul and in memory. These feminine figures repeatedly recall their surrender of body and soul in a moment of experience that Joyce models on the Annunciation.

Unlike most women, the Virgin Mary says yes and remains a virgin. Her theologians go to great lengths to prevent suspicious natures from hypothesizing the rupture of the hymen, carnal intercourse, or the experience of pleasure, and remind us that the incomparable and endlessly imagined "second Eve" is alone of all her sex.[14] The mystics and the mariolaters endow the soul itself with femininity, modeled on the images of the Virgin's beauty magnified in courtly love discourse and in centuries of religious art. When the soul says "yes," it embraces

---

[14] See Leo Steinberg, *The Sexuality of Christ in Renaissance Art and in Modern Oblivion* (New York: Pantheon Books, 1983); Jaroslav Pelikan, *Mary through the Centuries* (New Haven: Yale University Press, 1996); and the richly documented book by Marina Warner, *Alone of All Her Sex: The Myth and the Cult of the Virgin Mary* (New York: Knopf, 1976). Warner quotes the "Paschalis Carminis" by Caelius Sedulius in her title. Elsewhere she writes, "She . . . had no peer either in our first mother or in all women who were to come. But alone of all her sex she pleased the Lord."[17]

passion and love. But unlike the Virgin, the modern subject who says "yes" in flesh and in spirit may be surrendering to the pleasures of concupiscence, adultery, and perversion. A Christian text like Saint Augustine's *Confessions* already illustrates the divided or split voice of modern subjectivity: (1) the soul abandons itself to desire, wallows in shame, and wonders why it cannot rise above the flesh, and (2) the soul condemns desire as sin, washed clean only by the waters of grace, and rejoices at the love of God that absolves it.

Modernism brings the two voices together for the greater ambivalence of literature concerning the status of femininity, virginity, sin, and the image of the Madonna. The powerful resonance of modernist suggestion sufficed to bring literature's ambivalence before the Law, as Baudelaire, Flaubert, Joyce, and others discovered. Baudelaire's vivid juxtapositions of the high and the low forms of feminine images are a leitmotif of his journals and published writings. In *Les Fleurs du Mal*, even the revered Andromaque does a turn as a vile animal, and the Muse appears as a penniless prostitute who sells her charms for a few coins. One of the most lurid moments in modernist literature occurs in Flaubert's novel *Salammbô*, when the monstrous Giscon accuses the mystical and virginal Salammbô of uttering raucous love-moans like a prostitute.

As early as *Dubliners*, Joyce combines the image of the Blessed Virgin Mary with perversion, the sinful unnaturalness of human sexuality. A description of Polly, the nubile daughter in "The Boarding House," evokes the portrait of the Virgin in art and in popular reproductions of her image. "Her eyes, which were grey with a shade of green through them, had a habit of glancing upwards when she spoke with anyone, which made her look like a little perverse madonna."[15] This description fits the naturalist patterns of degradation exposed in *Dubliners* without compromising the impact of the Madonna's image. Although the Irish Catholic naturalist frame of the early narrative writing is substantially transformed with each new work, the Madonna takes on increasing importance in Joyce's aesthetics.

The poetic use of the word "Madonna" is particularly resonant in literary contexts of love. When Dante addresses Beatrice and Petrarch addresses Laura as "Madonna," they are following a tradition derived

---

[15] "The Boarding House" in *Dubliners* (London: Jonathan Cape, 1964), 57. "The Annunciation" by Juan de Flandes, reproduced in chapter three, presents an example of the type that Joyce describes.

from devotional poetry, including the writings of St. Francis of Assisi and the Franciscan Jacopone da Todi, author of an Umbrian *lauda* called "Donna de Paradiso." Derived from courtly love, the role of the Lady in the poet's figuration of desire is central to European literatures through the modernist period. The literature of courtly love is shaped in part by the impact of Platonism: the results are visible in Baroque and romantic literature and beyond, in the trans-Romantic aesthetic of early modernism. Because of the rhetorical power of this tradition, as well as its lingering effects on the post-romantic conception of love that Freud explores, modernists writing about love reshape these materials in a secular framework.

In his immensely popular book, *Love in the Western World*, Denis de Rougemont blurs the identities of most of the literary, historical, and philosophical texts relevant to his subject, but he records the most symptomatic major elements of modern love in literature.[16] Rougemont quotes Ortega y Gasset's *On Love* to point out that everyone, past and present, uses Platonic concepts to think and talk about love. Although he does not mention any specific texts, and is apparently happy to remain in the dark with his readers as he navigates through history, religion, and literature in search of the myths of love, the comment is interesting for several reasons: first, because Plato's quasi-universal importance is assumed as a given in a book that focuses exclusively on love in a Christian context; second, because the importance of the madonna figure in devotional and secular literature is presented as a given in Rougemont's argument for the role played by religious heresy and mysticism in the literary tradition that develops through the troubadours and courtly love; and third, because of the devotional resonances of the Tristan material, with its courtly love motif of Isolde as a madonna figure. Rougemont's emphasis on the Tristan myth reflects the influence of Bédier's popularized and scholarly versions of the Tristan material as well as the widespread taste for Wagner's opera in early modernism. Like Joyce, who also had a taste for European popular culture of love and a familiarity with Wagner's opera, Rougemont highlights the story of Tristan and Isolde. He reads

[16] The development of Rougemont's hypothesis that religious heresy and courtly love go hand in hand remains fairly vague and lacks historical and literary development beyond the level of polemic. The author moves through the expanse of European (and primarily Romance) literary culture in order to indicate that the mystical tradition reformulates the vocabulary of courtly love.

Tristan as the central love myth of Christian ("Western") culture, and contrasts him with Don Juan.

In a book that claims to portray the modernist Madonna, Jane Silverman van Buren emphasizes the "semiotics of the maternal metaphor" and misses the feminine roles of subject and object in the historically anchored concept of the "Madonna."[17] The specificity of the Madonna is lost when it is conflated with a general portrait of motherhood. What is at stake is the madonna figures' virginal status, their relation to sin, and the roles they play and play out. The accent is on desire rather than on the evidence of motherhood. Webster's definition, quoted in the epigraph, is low-key but specific about the Madonna's connections with courtly love literature and with Catholic images of her. Through the cult of the Madonna, virginity and adultery converge for the desiring worshiping subject.

The literary vehicles that anticipate and produce the madonnas of modernism consistently locate a major source of textual authority in Plato's *Symposium*.[18] This cornerstone of philosophy and literature may be the most enigmatic, elusive, and misquoted of Plato's works to have survived the vicissitudes of time. The art of love is named in the *Symposium* (177d8, 207c), where the revelation of love's mystery (211c) locates it in relation to poetic art. Erotics and poetics are explicitly connected throughout the dialogue, and especially in the interventions of Socrates and Diotima.

[17] *The Modernist Madonna: Semiotics of the Maternal Metaphor* (Bloomington: Indiana University Press, 1989). The author treats a corpus of American artists who are women and who portray motherhood. But the term madonna as defined in Webster and as it is used in courtly love and in Catholic dogma and liturgy is outside the scope of the author's reading of maternity.

[18] *Symposium*, edited by Sir Kenneth Dover (Cambridge: Cambridge University Press, 1980). Unless otherwise noted in this book, I have quoted from the English translation of the *Symposium* by Alexander Nehamas and Paul Woodruff (Indianapolis and Cambridge: Hackett Publishing Co., 1989). Quotations from Dover refer to Sir Kenneth Dover's annotations and fragmentary translations in the edition noted above. Quotations from the translation by Shelley are indicated in the notes. I have consulted the following essays and commentaries: Stanley Rosen, *Plato's Symposium* (New Haven: Yale University Press, 1968); Sir Kenneth Dover, *Greek Homosexuality* (New York: Random House, 1978) and his *Greek Popular Morality in the Time of Plato and Aristotle* (Oxford: Blackwell, 1974); Gregory Vlastos, *Platonic Studies*, second edition (Princeton: Princeton University Press, 1981); R. A. Markus, "The Dialectic of Eros in Plato's *Symposium*" in *Downside Review* 73 (1955); Martha Nussbaum, *The Fragility of Goodness* (Cambridge: Cambridge University Press, 1986); Gerasimos Santas, *Plato and Freud: Two Theories of Love* (Oxford: Blackwell, 1988); and H. Neumann, "Diotima's Concept of Love," *American Journal of Philology* 86 (1965).

The literary path of love that moves through modernity originates in a Platonic discourse, articulated and transmitted in the inheritance of the troubadours. The path leads toward modernity via courtly love and the writings of the mystics. In this sense, the modernism that reaches from the mid-nineteenth century through the twentieth century starts with Plato and pursues an elaboration and working through of the art of love in its encounters with Dante, Tristan and Isolde, Shakespeare, Don Giovanni, Flaubert, Baudelaire, Wagner, and Yeats.

In the middle of the nineteenth century, Baudelaire observes that true civilization is not in gaslight, in steam, or in occultism, but in the diminution of the traces of original sin. In other words, there has been progress in repression, as Freud states in his reading of Hamlet in relation to Oedipus. Modernism is grounded in the consequences of trans-romanticism: Baudelaire's focus on the traces of original sin in modernity in the *Flowers of Evil* is parallel to Flaubert's focus on the excesses and banalities of love. Modernism works through the terrain of love and art, the two areas that literature has linked together since Plato's *Symposium.* The constructions of affect, memory, and subjectivity are haunted by "beauty"; the concerns of style and representation are haunted by "truth." These terms are implicated in the modernist focus on love.

Joyce locates love at the center of his writing, and like Baudelaire, he seeks the traces of sin and explicitly features them in the contexts of modernity that characterize his fiction. These contexts appear in repeated scenarios of seduction and the fall. Joyce emphasizes sin, the object of adulterous longing, and the presence of beauty; the scene of Eve's original sin in Genesis 3 is overturned by the *felix culpa* from the liturgy for Holy Saturday. Original sin is countered by the Annunciation, the aesthetic shaping and sexualizing of the Blessed Virgin that receives a special emphasis in Western art. In James Joyce's *A Portrait of the Artist as a Young Man,* the New Testament and liturgical stagings of the Virgin in the scene of the Annunciation lead Stephen Dedalus through an early religious vocation based on mariolatry. The religious vocation ends but the mariolatry remains intact, along with an admiration for beautiful writing. Dedalus plays the scene of the Virgin in his writing of the poetry of sin; outside the Church, the paradox bothers him less.

When Dedalus awakens and writes a poem, sexuality invades the scene of the Annunciation, and the poem substitutes a falling into desire for the newly erased purity of the Virgin. The poem reverses the gender roles of the Annunciation; the feminine subject has her will of the ancillary young man. The "enchantment of the heart" that shapes the scene of writing in Joyce's *Portrait* is parodied in *Ulysses* through Gerty's thoughts on poetry, menstruation, and marriage, and later, in the dark of night, Molly's monologue provides another comic version.[19] The monologue moves toward the final pages of the novel when the primal scene is replayed as a profane but mystically ecstatic Annunciation. Molly's Joycean thoughts about femininity in the context of Bloom, Stephen Dedalus, and her daughter lead imperceptibly in *Finnegans Wake* to the intertwining of Issy and Shem in similar contexts of feminine beauty and the ecstasy of desire. The Blessed Virgin (or the mother, ALP) distributes her gifts of femininity to the daughters that multiply around the central daughter figure of Issy: "She gave them ilcka madre's daughter a moonflower and a bloodvein: but the grapes that ripe before reason to them that devide the vinedress. So on Izzy, her shamemaid, love shone befond her tears" (*FW* 212.15). The mother's gift of menstruation alludes to sexual flowering and the premature fruits of obscenity, ecstasy, and the fall, in the terms of Dionysian revelry and shame/Shem, the beloved son, and the tears of passion. Dionysus is contextualized through classical discourse on love, in Plato and in other writers; in the *Symposium*, Agathon says that Dionysus will judge the speeches (175e). Prodicus defined Eros as "desire doubled" and madness as "Eros doubled," and Plato inscribes the *Symposium* with Dionysian madness in the passionate speech of Alcibiades.[20] Ambiguously virginal, Izzy the "shamemaid" anticipates the ripe fruits of enjoyment and the repeat version of Eve's tears, after the Fall. High and low, mystical and carnal, the Madonna says yes: the ravisher enters her, soul and body. This scene welds erotics and poetics together. Modernism returns to the Baroque figure of Don Giovanni in this context. *Giacomo Joyce* (the pre-Ulyssean "Don Giovanni" text that Joyce did not name or seek to publish) returns to the passionate encounter between high and low that fascinated Baudelaire and Flaubert.

I would suggest that *Giacomo Joyce* remained an unpublished manuscript precisely because the Madonna figure says no, whereas Bertha's

---

[19] The "enchantment of the heart" is discussed in the context of the writing of the villanelle in chapter 6, "Isolde at Sea."

[20] Sir Kenneth Dover, *Symposium* (Cambridge: Cambridge University Press, 1981), 2. Prodicus is mentioned at 177b.

speech at the end of "Exiles" provides a blueprint for the Madonna's ecstatic affirmations at the end of *Ulysses* and *Finnegans Wake*. Joyce's
erotics articulate desire in the context of the ascent of love on the ladder of the beautiful and the obscene. In Lacan's interpretation of Joyce,
the ladder returns as the "escabeau" of the obscene, spelled "eaub-
scène." Lacan's pointed confession of his own desire for beauty reinforces his interpretive scenario of Joyce, *jouissance*, and the symbolic.
Joyce and Lacan echo the ascent of love in Diotima's initiation of
Socrates.[21]

From the male encounters of "Greek love" to worship of virginity,
from sacred to profane, from Greek to Jew and Celt to Catholic, from
the lonely young man to the construct of the family, Joyce's Viconian
trellis of desire and the excessive qualities of love become progres-
sively more explicit as they become stylistically more challenging.
Because the obscene takes the stage of art, the obscene is encoded, ultimately, in a new language that undermines the silences of taboo and
never stops talking. Sex and talk make history: *Finnegans Wake* takes
up Molly's monologue and spreads it over the landscape of history and
memory by a "commodious vicus of recirculation." The *Wake* goes
around in the circles of waking and dreaming; seduction and fall are
arranged according to Vico's synthetic structuring of history as repetition with a difference.

The *Wake* presents a history of desire, circling through language, or
ascending and descending the ladder of love. The staging of obscenity
knows no boundaries of space and time or of linguistic geography;
therefore, in *Wake* language, the account of the obscene invades the
structure of the word. Slips of the tongue take over, despite Joyce's
limited appreciation of Freud. Joyce's Eros works on the principle revealed in a letter to Nora: the dirtiest words are the most beautiful.[22]
Lacan's "eaubscene"—obscenity as the stage for desire and beauty—
combines Joyce's dirty words with the aesthetic object to raise the
curve of an emotion into art. The letter is litter and ladder (Lacan's
"escabeau"), obscene and beautiful writing (*FW* 278). The letter at the

---

[21] See *Séminaire VIII: Le Transfert* (Paris: Seuil, 1991), 20, and "Joyce le symp-
tôme II" in *Joyce avec Lacan*, edited by Jacques Aubert (Paris: Navarin, 1987), 31–36.

[22] "Tell me the smallest things about yourself so long as they are obscene and secret and filthy. Write nothing else. Let every sentence be full of dirty immodest words
and sounds. They are all lovely to hear and to see on paper but the dirtiest are the most
beautiful. The two parts of your body which do dirty things are the loveliest to me"
(Letter of 9 December 1909, in *Selected Letters*).

Wake comes through the mail, through the dream, through divination: delivered by the post office or by magic, in an enchantment or an Annunciation. Art unfolds in "the womb of the imagination" as Joyce wrote to Nora, his almost but not quite virginal bride in exile. Not quite or "Pas encore" was Nora's mistake turned into a symptom in Joyce's French or a slip of the tongue: he wants her to be untouched for his jealousy's sake and for the sake of Don Giovanni's quiet cult of the Virgin.[23] He also wants to create her in the image of the Blessed Virgin. In Dante's dark night and as Shakespeare's Dark Lady, she will re-create him in a virgin birth, or perhaps a resurrection of the flesh. Why is it that Joyce's portraits and self-portraits of the lover almost constantly invoke weariness and the desire to sleep?

Joyce re-creates Nora's virginity body and soul so that her image may shelter him and give birth to the writer of his race: "*Everything that is noble and exalted and deep and true and moving in what I write comes, I believe, from you.* (. . .) O that I could nestle in your womb like a child born of your flesh and blood, be fed by your blood, sleep in the warm secret gloom of your body!"[24] He invokes the Madonna: "You have been to my young manhood what the idea of the Blessed Virgin was to my boyhood." And, "if you leave me I shall live for ever with your memory, holier than God to me. I shall pray to your name."[25] The Virgin Mary, Dante's Beatrice, and Bertha, whose name is a partial anagram of Beatrice, array Joyce's idea of the Madonna for the bridal celebration of purity and loss, virginity and sacrifice, from *Dubliners* through *Finnegans Wake*. The bridal preparation anticipates the Annunciation, followed by a virgin birth.

Aunt Julia in "The Dead" sings "Arrayed for the Bridal." In view of Gabriel's anticipation of her death, the song ironically figures the proper bourgeois lives of Irish spinsters and the aging singer's approaching end. Love in Joyce underscores the bridal and virginal ambivalence of Annunciation and fatality, birth and death. Jaun (another name of Shaun) delivers an obscene reprise of Aunt Julia's bridal song in *Finnegans Wake*: "You've surpassed yourself! Be introduced to yes! This is me aunt Julia Bride, your honour, dying to have you languish

---

[23] See Rabaté, *Joyce upon the Void*, 40–44.

[24] 5 September 1909, in *Selected Letters*.

[25] Letters of 31 August and 18 November 1909. The split between high and low is addressed in another letter from this period, 2 September 1909: "I wonder is there some madness in me. Or is love madness? One moment I see you like a virgin or madonna the next moment I see you shameless, insolent, half-naked and obscene!"

to scandal in her bosky old delltangle. (. . .) Come on spinister, do your stuff! Don't be shoy, husbandmanvir!" (*FW* 465.01). Most of the obscene accusations and the sarcastic comments are directed at Shem-Dave, a sensitive artist figure in the autobiographical mold. Like Stephen Dedalus in *Ulysses,* he has just returned from France. A line before the passage quoted above, Jaun says to him: "You rejoice me!" (*FW* 464.36). Joyce underscores the autobiographical reference by including a pun on his own name when Jaun combines a sarcastic allusion to happiness in a French construction ("je me réjouis [I am happy]") with a reference to echoes and doubles in the name of Joyce.

In "The Dead," Julia's nephew Gabriel recalls his wife's girlhood and the boy who died for love of her. Joyce inscribes love's bitter mystery with the paradox of virginity throughout his writing about couples. These include Gabriel and Gretta in "The Dead"; Richard and Bertha, his "bride in exile," in "Exiles"; Molly returning to Bloom at the end of her monologue in *Ulysses,* and ALP's return to HCE in *Finnegans Wake.* Love's bitter mystery inscribes the explicit combination of erotics and poetics, from Eve and Adam's in the beginning until the writer's small, weak English article, "the," marks ALP's last breath at the end of the line. Her monologue takes up where Molly left off. The *Ulysses* monologue expands from the closing of "Exiles." Bertha speaks: "Not a day passes that I do not see ourselves, you and me, as we were when we met first. Every day of my life I see that. Was I not true to you all that time? (. . .) Forget me and love me again as you did the first time. (. . .) O, my strange wild lover, come back to me again! *She closes her eyes.*"[26] Among tears, memories, jealousy, and infidelity, Joycean couples play out a Platonic encounter between love and death. Unlike the Virgin, the madonna of modernism is frequently in the wrong place at the wrong time. Desire is affirmed but its announcement misfires.

Modernism oscillates between two types of feminine objects, virginal and womanly (sensual, loving, and maternal). In Freud's psychology of love, the eroticized object inspires either love or desire. The two types are united in the idealized figure of the Blessed Virgin. Joyce observes that the Italian Church placed her at the center of Catholicism. "But it is a fact that for nearly two thousand years the women of Christendom have prayed to and kissed the naked image of one who had neither wife nor mistress nor sister and would scarcely have been

[26] James Joyce, *Exiles* (New York: Viking, 1951), 111–12.

associated with his mother had it not been that the Italian church discovered, with its infallible practical instinct, the rich possibilities of the figure of the Madonna."[27] In the Italian context but beyond it as well, throughout the tradition of Western European religious painting, her feminine (virginal and maternal) impact on the Church is inseparable from her beauty, transferred through liturgy and art in the image of the Blessed Virgin Mary. Implicitly and explicitly, she is Santa Maria Formosa, saint Mary the Beautiful. Seen in retrospect, her beauty may originate in Plato as well as in the Bible, followed by the literature of the Troubadours and the tradition of courtly love.

The writing of sin and desire frequently returns to the encounter between Eve and the serpent and to its enigmatic resolution by the Virgin. Through sacred and profane love, Joyce's circuitous Viconian route of repetition winds around the paths of early Modernists, several of their precursors, and Joyce's immediate precursor, Yeats. This route retraces the written account of Eros in Plato's *Symposium*; Joyce contextualizes his treatment of love within a modernist framework that includes Platonic Eros, mysticism, and courtly love, anchored in the idealization of the Virgin.

[27] Note to *Exiles*, 120.

PART I

Eros the Bittersweet

Vous êtes dans mon âme comme une madone sur un piédestal, à une place haute, solide et immaculée.

You are in my soul like a madonna on a pedestal, elevated, solid, and immaculate.

—Flaubert

I   Platonic Love: Socrates, Diotima, and the Virgin Mary

ELLE.—Je lui ai dit m'appeler d'un autre prénom, de celui de Diotima.

SHE.—I said to him—give me another name, the name of Diotima.
—Marguerite Duras

The major discourses on love in modernity (in literature, philosophy, and psychoanalysis) refer, implicitly or explicitly, to Plato's feast of words in the *Symposium*. Like dialectic, Socratic love is a talking art, and the priestess Diotima is the source, Socrates claims, for his mastery of the art of love. Sappho, Plato's tenth muse, raises the curtain on a concept of Eros that Plato's dialogue explores. Sappho's Eros shapes the highs and lows of love, its comedy and tragedy, the sublime extremes of idealization and the obscene and violent depths of possession. The silencing of Sappho's voice, the destruction of her writings, repeats the silencing of the feminine in the exclusive male world of Platonic dialogue. Beyond the silence, mingling with the enigmatic sources of medieval love, her voice can be heard, again, in the writings of the Italian Renaissance. The return of the feminine wears the disguise of Socrates. Neo-Platonism confronts Sappho, the poet of Eros, and Diotima, the Mantinean priestess, with the Virgin. Mary, the exceptional object, has become the Madonna—the feminine vessel who bears the bittersweetness of love.

In Plato's *Symposium*, the art of love begins with the gaze that contemplates an object of desire. Derived from Greek antiquity, the subject of love succumbs to an intimate violence that is articulated in Sappho's poetry. When Greek love surfaces in the Italian Renaissance, Sappho's image of Eros the bittersweet is translated into feminine

form. This new version of Eros shapes the scene of modernity. Literature traces the impact of Eros the bittersweet on the poetics of love.
Gestuality and the leitmotifs of desire are inscribed in scenes of operatic seduction and pantomime, the sacred and the comic, from Baudelaire and Flaubert through Yeats and Joyce. In Flaubert's *Madame
Bovary*, love brings irony and comedy into the sacred space of the
cathedral. Elements of melodrama and pantomime shape the meeting
between Emma and Leon in the first chapter of book 3: "L'église,
comme un boudoir gigantesque, se disposait autour d'elle; les voûtes
s'inclinaient pour recueillir dans l'ombre la confession de son amour
[Like a gigantic boudoir, the church was arranged around her; the
vaults bent down to gather in the shadows the confession of her love]."
In *Finnegans Wake*, Shem's riddle of love, obscene and sublime, refers
to the tradition of Eros the bittersweet: "and offering the prize of a bittersweet crab, a little present from the past" (*FW* 170.07). Eros reappears in Joyce's biblical echo of the feminine, from Eve, the first
mother, to Isolde, the Wake's incarnation of the desirable daughter:
"she sall eurn bitter bed by thirt sweet of her face!" (*FW* 291.06). Eros
turns bread into bed, and the sweat of the brow into sweetness. Hard
work, childbirth, and death await the daughters of Eve after the expulsion from paradise. Joyce's sentence recalls the mother's death in
Ulysses, her revenant, and the mystery of love.

The Extremes of Eros

In "The Individual as Object of Love in Plato," Gregory Vlastos explores some of the questions that are raised by Plato's accounts of
love.[1] In the appendix, "Sex in Platonic Love," Vlastos highlights the
modern misnomer of "platonic love" to correct the mistaken notion
that love in Plato is purely spiritual. Love in the *Symposium* is sexual
love: it is related to spiritual love through the distinction between
lover and beloved that is the foundation of Greek love between men
and boys. Desire is attributed only to the *erastes*, the lover, who wants
to possess the desired beautiful object, the *eromenos*. Greek love
implicates the lover and the beloved in an asymmetrical scenario of
desire.

[1] Gregory Vlastos, *Platonic Studies*, 2d ed. (Princeton: Princeton University Press,
1981), 3–42.

Platonic love is filled with paradox, mystery, and emptiness, for love is giving what one does not have, and engaging in a relation based on not knowing. When Socrates arrives, he lies down next to Agathon, evokes his own emptiness, and contrasts it with Agathon's plenitude (175d,e). The irony is abundant, but the images are eloquent beyond irony. Socrates describes Agathon's wisdom through images of his beauty ("shining and radiant"); Socrates contrasts light and darkness when he compares the emptiness of his own wisdom to "a shadow in a dream." Against the beauty and radiance of Agathon, Socrates posits images of darkness and interiority. Agathon objects to the ironic contrast, but defers to the authority of Dionysus, the god of wine and madness, who marks the appearance of Alcibiades.

When Agathon gives his speech, Socrates is near him and apparently ready to talk all night. The poetic plenitude of Agathon's discourse is the source of Socrates' ironic lament about being stopped in his own tracks by the beautiful tragedian's own beautiful discourse (198b,c). His punning allusion to Gorgias and the Gorgon's head seems to mock Agathon's vanity and deflate Agathon's stylistic power and beauty. Turned to stone, struck dumb, Socrates' ironic self-portrait here rejoins Agathon's flippant poetic image of Eros as an agent of secret and deadly standstill, of stillness and sleep—of erotic fiasco (197c, d). Socrates' sustained irony toward Agathon, whom he addresses once as "my beloved Agathon" (201c), allows him to mask the serious dimension of his disclaimers. Emptiness disposes Socrates to the art of love. At the beginning of his own discourse, Socrates emphasizes his parallel with Agathon as the unknowing recipient of Diotima's initiation. Socrates was to Diotima a subject for erotic initiation, as Agathon is now to Socrates (201e). Now that he claims to know about love, and only love, Socrates changes the roles of desire and dialectic (177d, e). From being the object, he shifts to being the subject of love; in the last speech, Alcibiades reveals that Socrates' effect on him echoes this development. Passion transforms Alcibiades from the object to the subject of love, from *eromenos* to *erastes*, as it transforms Socrates from lover to beloved for Alcibiades (217c, 222b).

Eros implicates beauty, accomplished form, and the tragic dimension of desire. Erotic subjectivity inevitably includes negation, defined as emptiness or lack, and the unknowing that is integral to love. Aristophanes' mythic account dramatizes the cutting and dispersing that characterize the division of the sexes (190e). Diotima's mythic account of the conception of Eros dramatizes the needy emptiness of

Penia, Poverty, and the unknowing of *Poros*, Resource (and son of *Metis*, Invention), who succumbs to intoxication and unknowingly fathers Eros. At Aphrodite's birthday celebration, the beauty of the goddess and the misery of Penia, watching from outside, mingle with intoxication and unknowing. Penia, the outsider, provokes and seduces Poros, thereby producing Eros (203b–204a).

Socrates is characterized by mastery and by ambivalence. Intoxicated by beautiful boys, he is never drunk, perhaps because of a constitutive emptiness that recalls Penia. He claims to know nothing except the art of love, and the question and answer of dialectic shape his initiation into mystery. Plato's text presents Socrates' evocation of himself in the role of the unknowing disciple, while the role that Socrates generally plays is given to Diotima. Platonic ambivalence turns on this point. Socrates says he knows only Eros, the art that he has learned from the Mantinean Stranger, a woman whose origin recalls the word for a seer. Divided and dispersed by Sparta in 384 B.C., Mantinea submitted to a fate similar to the division and dispersion of the hybristic early humans cut in half by Zeus, according to Aristophanes (190e).

Division, loss, emptiness, misery, petrification, being struck dumb, foreignness, and exile—these forms of negation inhabit the Socratic Eros. On the other side, however, the name of Diotima, the virtual woman inside Socrates, honors Zeus, invoked by Socrates in passage 202c.[2] At the end of Socrates' speech, he honors the rites of Love, and when Alcibiades claims that Socrates will not let him praise anyone, including a god, Socrates responds to his blasphemy by ordering him to be silent. Only the interpretation of Eros as daimon can contain both the negation and the affirmation of Eros—its horrors of silence and its praise–inducing virility. Socrates' strange affirmation that "now and always I praise the power and manliness of Eros as much as I am able" (212b7, 8) captures the ambivalence of Eros, its primordial misery and shining physical beauty, its emptiness and plenitude, its silence and praise.[3]

The exotic Diotima announces the shift from having to being that characterizes the sudden vision of the magically powerful and beauti-

---

[2] See Dover's commentary of 201d in his edition of the *Symposium*.

[3] "Parallel to the importance of poetry, the love of beautiful bodies is the paradigm of Eros in the *Symposium*" (Rosen, *Plato's Symposium*, 243). "How ambiguous is his remark that 'now and always I praise the power and manliness of Eros as much as I am able'," 277.

ful Eros. Socrates professes astonishment when she reveals the intimate connection between the Form of Beauty and the Good (Virtue or Wisdom) in Eros. Her occult knowledge, her reputation as priestess, and her name connect Diotima with the *agalmata*, the marvelously beautiful images of the gods, that Socrates keeps hidden inside himself, according to the Dionysian Alcibiades. He claims that the effects of drunkenness have provoked his interruption of the banquet. He brings the assembly back to earth with the realities of passion that follow Diotima's ascending path of initiation into the mysteries of Eros. He chides, criticizes, laments, and praises Socrates. Alcibiades tells the assembly that Socrates refused to satisfy his vanity, and thereby transformed his vain and beautiful object into a would-be passionate lover. In the dark night of antiquity, Alcibiades has 'fallen in love' with Socrates; he slips from the boyish, passive role of the beloved to being the lover.

Diotima locates sexual love at the beginning of the path toward the Form of Beauty. The dialogue suggests that Socrates does not reject sexual love, but rather that he withholds it from Alcibiades precisely because of the young man's intent to use Eros to gain power over Socrates. Socrates reverses the tactic, and Alcibiades falls in love with him. The evidence in Alcibiades' portrait of love resonates in terms of an interior form of beauty. Alcibiades describes Socrates as a Silenus figure and compares his discourse with the music of Marsyas. The Silenus looks like a satyr but contains beautiful images; the divine flute music of the satyr Marsyas led him to his death—either because of his hybris in competing with Apollo, or because the god was jealous of his magical music. The Silenus splits down the middle. Marsyas is skinned and dies. The interiority of Eros is physical and metaphorical, simultaneously visible as beautiful form and invisible as the object of Alcibiades' admiration for *agalmata*.[4]

The *Symposium* inscribes sexuality in philosophy as the mystery of Eros at the beginning of the ascent to the sublime vision of the Form of Beauty. Diotima begins the initiation into the art of love from the perspective of the lover of boys. In this context, Socrates' refusal of the love of Alcibiades requires some interpretation. Socrates claims knowledge about only one subject, love. He resists Alcibiades because he knows that Alcibiades is trying to possess him by forcing him to

---

[4] "This use of the Silenus enforces the insight that Socrates' interior is coincident with the interior of his speeches." Rosen, 319.

reveal a sign of his love. A glance at strangers suffices for Socrates to understand the relation of desire that identifies them as the lover (*erastes*) and the beloved (*eromenos*). Socrates knows that Alcibiades wishes to reduce him to the status of an object. Socrates' invisible power produces the passion that transforms Alcibiades from Socrates' vain beloved into his passionate lover. Alcibiades' vision of beauty *inside* Socrates points to the shift theorized in Diotima's sophistic midwifery, and Alcibiades illustrates this in the scene that he makes to express his jealousy. His desire is the effect of Socrates' discourse, his words, and the beauty inside him. This is the beauty of being, not the physical beauty that the beloved is supposed to have.

Socrates' speech presents Diotima, a messenger from the gods, as the source of his knowledge and vision of Eros. She reveals the daimonic nature of Eros, who moves between gods and men, and of Socrates. He is unknowing and knowing, sober and intoxicated with desire, empty and filled with the essential images of the gods, lover and beloved. Presented from several perspectives in the *Symposium*, the ambivalent positioning of Socrates connects the comic and tragic representations of Eros with the sublime secrets of interiority and invisibility, in the magic of love. Diotima's discourse and even her name associate her with the images of the gods that Alcibiades claims to have seen inside the Silenus-image of Socrates. Through her intervention, Socrates connects the magic of desire with a new kind of object, figured in the *agalmata* of the gods, of virtue, and of invisible beauty. Love is graded on a scale that begins with having, or the desire to possess the beloved's charms, and that reaches the heights of the highest good, the being that is revealed in the Form of Beauty. The Dionysian appearance of Alcibiades confirms the lessons of the Mantinean Stranger.

Virginwhite

Virginity is charged with a taboo. Freud's essays on the psychology of love explore the emphasis on purity in the split between desire and love, and the dangers of feminine virginity more than its value. The Virgin is possessed by God in a virtual form of the primal scene. The long-term effect of this possession is to subtract her from the debasement of the object and attribute virginity to her (reconfirmed *in extremis* by the dogma of the immaculate conception in the nineteenth century). Sacred and comic, *Finnegans Wake* swears by her cathedral and her sex, "Par the Vulnerable Virgin's Mary del Dame!" (*FW* 206.05). The washerwomen in the *Wake* find the debasement of the object even in the *Ave Maria:* "Lord help you, Maria, full of grease, the load is with me! Your prayers" (*FW* 214.18). The brother-sister triangle that runs through the text frequently alludes to love and to the Virgin. Jaun counsels Issy with a new version of the Mosaic commandments: "Twice thou shalt not love" (*FW* 433.22). In a structure dominated by original sin and the obscenity of sex, divine love must be preserved from the threat of debasement: the notion that "platonic love" is intensely romantic love without sexual intercourse owes more to the impact of the dogma of original sin on Western culture than it does to Socrates' refusal to submit to Alcibiades' desire. Plato's dialogues, including the *Symposium* and the *Phaedrus,* cite abundant evidence of Socrates' passionate interest in beautiful young men.

Virginity appeals to the jealous lover, to the courtly lover at a distance, and to the mariolater. For centuries, the virginity of the Virgin was defended in the contexts of Catholic dogma, mystical heresy, and the literature of courtly love. For Freud and Lacan, however, love is predicated on the debasement of the object as such. The emphasis on female virginity reinforces debasement, and guarantees that the lover alone possesses his beloved in soul and in body. He intimately possesses her as the object of his desire.

Linked to passionate desire, debasement remains when desire has disappeared into indifference or succumbed to the repression that Freud observed in Victorian marriages, including his own. Shakespeare's *Othello* paints a portrait of desire combined with debasement that results in abuse, jealousy, and the murder of the beloved. The blackness of jealousy frames love in a dimension of tragedy that is closer to libertine blackness than it is to the ideals of courtly love. The libertine Don Juan, who negates the ideal of courtly love in the way that Sade negates it, succumbs to jealousy if he sees a woman happy in love with someone else before he has possessed her. Once he has possessed her, however, jealousy is no longer possible for him, and the woman becomes a name in a ledger and a number in a series that will become finite only at his death. Jealous lovers portrayed in modernism have a somewhat different fate: Flaubert's Charles Bovary becomes a jealous husband after Emma's death; Joyce's Richard Rowan exalts doubt; Proust's Swann who is in love with the faithless Odette suffers without end until he ceases loving her. Bovary dies; Swann falls out of love with Odette and marries her as the former object of passion, the mother of his daughter; Joyce's husband-heroes live on.

Like Don Juan's objects, the madonnas of modernism are of particular interest to their would-be seducers if they are virgins. Although the Blessed Virgin is their model in desire, their display of maternal qualities is secondary except insofar as it connects them to the subject who desires them. In Joyce's *A Portrait of the Artist as a Young Man*, Davin tells the story of a woman who offered him milk when he asked for water and asked him to stay the night. She appears to him as an emblem of desire and a kind of *Madonna del Latte.* "I thought by her figure and by something in the look of her eyes that she must be carrying a child" (*P* 165). Half undressed, she makes her desire clear to the naive young Irishman, who is afraid to stay the night but who broods over his own refusal. Like Charles Bovary's early encounters with Emma, including the erotically charged episode when Emma serves him a glass of curaçao liqueur, Davin's story emphasizes a context of voluptuous desire, solitude, and idealization that is central to the figuration of the Madonna. Gerty MacDowell in the "Nausicaa" chapter of *Ulysses* is a parody of a Madonna-like figure of a young woman who is not maternal. Although Gerty broods about sexual difference, she is indifferent to the children and even irritated by them. She fits the Madonna category because of her obsessions, her exhibitionism, and her tenderly solicitous thoughts about Bloom as a gentleman, potential widower, and a voyeur whose attentions are meant for her alone.

At the end of the line, shortly before Vico's borrowed cycles pause for a breath (in the last word, "the"), the mother reappears. Before Joyce stops for a final signature and a last set of dates on the last page of the *Wake*, ALP as Eve and Mary, mother and daughter, clamors one last time for the first time. Like Bertha in "Exiles" and Molly in *Ulysses*, she turns back to remember the beginning: "It's something fails us. First we feel. Then we fall" (*FW* 627.11). Original sin combines the mother and daughter into a blurry figure, fading into the past. She implores the art of memory, "Bussoftlhee, mememormee!" (628.14). As beauty fades toward death, another figure will take her place. The cycles are integrated in a temporal structure based on the elaboration of memory along the Viconian trellis: the structure features original sin as the counterpart of memory. Narratives, songs, historic sentences, catchphrases, and ordinary English words succumb to the Nightworld of memory and desire, where repetition takes place, within a set of differences.

Early devotional poetry, the literature of courtly love, and the writings of the mystics provide the modern imagination with figures of the feminine. Idolized, portrayed, and preserved in beautiful images, the Blessed Virgin is prefigured by Eve, who lost her innocence in the garden of Eden. After the expulsion from Paradise, with its frontiers guarded by armed angels, all women are the daughters of Eve. All men are her sons, but Christian liturgy tends to protect them from the dangerous proximity of their mother and her desire. Women take the heat for the Fall, in modernism as well as in the book of Genesis. Mary is the second Eve. Through the adoration of her image, she neutralizes the dangers of Eve and all her daughters. Mary's femininity becomes the site of the Christian Eros: in a landscape of sexual repression and denial, she is granted exceptional status. Alone of all her sex, she is consumed by the Father and wedded to the Son in a model of successful incest. She bears fruit and remains a Virgin. In the voice of a jealous brother, *Finnegans Wake* rewrites the litany of the feminine: "Here she's, is a bell, that's wares in heaven, virginwhite, Undetrigesima, vikissy manonna. Doremon's! (. . .) Words taken in triumph, my sweet assistance, from the sufferant pen of our jocosus inkerman" (*FW* 433.03). Jaun says that the words have been written by his rival brother, the libidinous outlaw.

Plato in Modernity

Baudelaire and Flaubert use elements of Renaissance and Baroque allegory as an antidote to the literary excesses of Romantic sensibility.[5] This process of working through, or trans-romanticism, leads Baudelaire and Flaubert to the invention of modernism.[6] Within the new literary framework, Romantic heroines take the stage as the madonnas of modernism. Virginal purity is fetishized, revered, or disdained, but in any case, it locates them in a discourse of desire and brings them into the context of the fall. The higher the object in the realm of the ideal, the harder it falls, according to the paradoxical nature of love.

[5] On the road to modernism, the heroines of Shakespearean tragedy enter the early nineteenth century. Borrowed from their Renaissance context and transformed into modern shapes, Ophelia, Juliet, and Desdemona are followed by the figures of desire and loss that Romanticism shapes in the writings of Keats, Shelley, Balzac, Nerval, Gautier, Sand, Musset, and others.

[6] See Schlossman, *The Orient of Style: Modernist Allegories of Conversion* (Durham: Duke University Press, 1991).

Like religious discourse, secularization shapes the sacrifice of the feminine. The celebration of virginity coincides with its funeral rites. Purity and beauty are linked in the values of religion, art, and the commodity. Freud's mastery of Eros leads him to hypothesize the correspondences of high and low in the articulation of love. The general debasement of the object corresponds to the reverence accorded to sexual purity. Virginity is taboo—sacred and dangerous, fetishized and fatal to men. Modernist figures of virginity take their place in an ambivalent discourse of love that arranges for a confrontation between a discourse of truth and beauty, on the one hand, and a discourse of negation, destruction, and death, on the other.

For this reason, Baudelaire adds Lady Macbeth, Michelangelo's Night, and Molière's Donna Elvira to the Romantic list of tragic heroines, while Flaubert focuses on the extremes of mystical virginity (Donna Anna and Salammbô) and bourgeois banality (Emma Bovary, Madame Arnoux). Joyce's Madonna figures combine ordinary Irish girls and women with echoes of Eve, Dante's Beatrice, Isolde, and figures in Yeats. The early account of the mysteries of love in Plato's *Symposium* hovers behind many of these representations and makes them possible. Beauty and the perspective of death enter the picture of desire beginning with Plato. At the origin of the beautiful figure of the Madonna, Joyce's "Italian Church" had some help from Diotima and Socrates.

Socrates claims to know nothing except the mysteries of love. The only moment in the *Symposium* when he speaks in his own name is when he questions the beloved Agathon. Socrates deconstructs Agathon's beautiful plenitude and reveals the emptiness of his arguments, floating like Agathon's image of shining reflections on still water. Socrates' account of Diotima's discourse occurs after he questions Agathon and before the declaration of excessive and Dionysian love by Alcibiades. Agathon is absorbed in his own beauty, since he is characterized by narcissism and the innocent ignorance appropriate to the beloved. The pointed ironies of his discourse do not reveal hidden depths of meaning. In contrast, Socrates is described by Alcibiades as filled with *agalmata*, figures of virtue and the gods, that compensate for ugliness with their desirable beauty. In between these scenes, Socrates stages a virtual dialogue that draws attention away from his own knowledge and understanding of the mysteries of love by emphasizing Diotima's initiation of her moderately gifted pupil into the form of beauty.

Socrates occupies the literal and rhetorical space between Agathon and Alcibiades. From his initial self-identification as the empty one who lies next to Agathon, Socrates' emptiness has become the agalma-filled plenitude of the Silenus. He is transformed from Alcibiades' lover into the beloved, the object of Alcibiades' desire. Tragedy and comedy meet several times in the erotics of the *Symposium*, in the discourses of Aristophanes, Agathon, Alcibiades, and in Diotima's mythic account of the conception of Eros. Representation itself takes on the daimonic aspect of Socrates, who occupies an intermediary status between god and man, emptiness and plenitude, ignorance and knowledge, and ugliness and beauty. In the end, Socrates connects Eros and writing with his insistence that authors should write both tragedy and comedy.

It is the discreet and invisible Other, Diotima, who bears the mysteries of Eros. Mantinean Stranger, sophist "midwife," Priestess, and possibly an exile, Socrates' expert teacher in the mysteries of love is adept at sacrifice and other daimonic interventions in the occult. The Greek scale of erotic values explained by Prodicus leads from desire to Eros ("desire doubled"), and from Eros to madness ("Eros doubled"). Like the madness of the Maenads, the plague that menaced Athens spreads through contagion and leads to indifferentiation, chaos, and violent death. This gradation of intensity connects Socrates' initiation into the mysteries of love with Diotima's intervention in the occult when her sacrifices delayed for ten years the outbreak of deadly plague in Athens. The scale of eroticism leading in a spiral descent from desire to madness to death is implicitly contrasted with Diotima's ascending path of Eros. Although Diotima's discourse has been claimed as Plato's preferred account of Eros or "Platonic Love," recent scholarship points out that Diotima's discourse as presented by Socrates does not justify the claim.[7] The two paths of desire, Diotima's ascending scale toward the Form of Beauty and the implicit descending scale, based on the Dionysian effects of desire (with reference to the distinctions of Prodicus and the occult intervention of Diotima), originate in the same elements: the effect of beautiful bodies

---

[7] See Harry Neumann, "Diotima's Concept of Love" in *American Journal of Philology* 86 (1965), and the Introduction to the translation of the *Symposium* by Nehamas and Woodruff. The issue is complex and scholarly opinion varies widely: see Vlastos, Markus, and Friedrich Solmsen, "Parmenides and the Description of Perfect Beauty in Plato's *Symposium*" in *American Journal of Philology* 92 (1971). Markus and Solmsen emphasize the Eleatic elements of Diotima's discourse.

and the physical law of generation and corruption or life and death. These elements and the connection between the art of Eros and the verbal art of poetry are evoked in four of the discourses of the *Symposium*. In his book on the *Symposium*, Stanley Rosen comments on the implications of this connection in Plato: "The illumination of beauty which Eros generates, as derived from the body, is not false but it is incomplete. The incompleteness of beauty, which depends for its visibility upon the corporeal, both illuminates and obscures. This very incompleteness characterizes the *Symposium* and any other dialogue; they all partake by virtue of their form in poetry or *mythos*, and so are a mixture of noble lies and truth."[8]

The discourse of Alcibiades most explicitly combines the two progressions of ascent and descent. Alcibiades exposes the fatal effects of Dionysian passion by comparing Socrates to the Sirens who sing a man to death and to a poisonous snake who has bitten him. He concludes his speech with a warning to Agathon about Socrates' horrible treatment and tormenting behavior. His discourse is colored with the tragic blackness of passion: "I can't live with him and I can't live without him!" (216c). This illustration of descent remains suggestive even in late modernism. Translated as "ni avec toi ni sans toi," these words became the motto for one of François Truffaut's late films, "The Woman Next Door," in which the descent of love leads to adultery, nervous breakdown, homicide, and suicide. The motto is coined by a middle-aged character named Odile Jouve, a veteran of love who attempted suicide as a young woman because, she says, the man she loved was marrying someone else.

The *Symposium* pairs this form of descent with an ascent that takes Eros beyond the visible and into the realm of the *agalmata*, Alcibiades' repeated term for the marvelous shining and golden beauty of Socrates. His interiority is described by Alcibiades as the radiant beauty of *kalos*, the term that evokes physical beauty for the Greeks. Socrates hides his unique qualities beneath the surface of appearances, words, and skin, and Alciabiades emphasizes his comparison of Socrates with hollow statues of Silenus. Socrates is incomparable, unlike any other man. In conversation with Agathon, Socrates uses the image of "a shadow in a dream" to describe his own wisdom (175e); the image comes from Pindar's Pythian Ode 8, line 96, where it evokes man. Socrates' discourse dissolves even the invisible radiance of inte-

---

[8] Rosen, 225.

riority praised by Alcibiades. Like a shadow in a dream, Socrates' emphasis on the flimsiness of appearances anticipates Freud's understanding of the opacity of desire, a shadow that falls over the object. Socrates remains unique in his refusal of the debasement inherent in love. Words take him toward being. He eludes the strategists of having, and turns his desire elsewhere.

Claritas

Through romanticism, Eros emerges in modernity to confront the Christian account of love. The characters who are responsible for the initial tragedy of love in the west are Eve and the serpent. Before them, the first woman to produce a discourse on love, Diotima, incarnates the Other in the male world of the *Symposium*. In the dark night of antiquity, drunken revelry is suspended briefly in favor of the praise of love. Socrates invokes Diotima's initiation into the path of ascent, the mysteries of desire, and its relation to spiritual midwifery . . . and love will never again be the same.

Alcibiades' interruption confirms Diotima's sudden stark shift from "having" to "being" in the vision of love's mysteries. According to Alcibiades, Socrates refuses to enter into the labyrinth of desire and its dire consequences, but he ends his remarks with the complaint that no one else can get close to a beautiful man when Socrates is around. With this remark, the lamenting impassioned Alcibiades literally disappears. A sudden interruption of drunken disorderly guests moves in like a wave, and covers for his absence.

Socrates' contradictions remain intact. In the end, his interlocutors fall asleep. He leaves Aristophanes, the subversive writer of comedy, and Agathon, the beautiful writer of tragedy. Socrates takes with him the correspondence between tragedy and comedy in Eros. It is perhaps this Socratic mastery of different tones that Friedrich Hölderlin restages in his rewriting of the Night of antiquity in the eighteenth century. Hölderlin emphasizes the importance of sobriety in the midst of a sublime revelry that threatens to annihilate the subject with its erotic power. The poet-subject is like Semele, the mortal beloved destroyed by Zeus in a lightning flash of pleasure. She conceived Dionysus and died. Not even his reading of Plato could suspend this threat for Hölderlin. A consummate classicist, he reads the *Symposium* as a Platonic model of the experience of passion and gives the name of

Diotima to his beloved Suzette Gonthard. But Eros cannot sustain him, and Diotima could not save Hölderlin from the lightning flash. Hölderlin's vision of Christianity as an unfortunate end station for the Greek gods ineluctably submits Eros to the forces of repression.[9]

In early romanticism, Eros appears accompanied by the threat of death. Like Hölderlin, Keats emphasizes Plato's portrayal of love with Christian taboos on the horizon. His most blissful evocation of love evokes the fugitive union of Eros and Psyche, the immortal soul in Plato and Apuleius. This momentary union is inscribed in the transition from classical to Christian culture. Eros revives the beloved Psyche from an eternal sleep. They embrace for an instant in the dark; later, she unwittingly drives him away and he never returns. The embrace that revives her is captured in the "Ode to Psyche":

> And there shall be for thee all soft delight
> That shadowy thought can win,
> A bright torch, and a casement ope at night,
> To let the warm Love in!

Like Keats, Antonio Canova returns to the moment of this embrace in his marble statue of winged Amor and Psyche. Love is a suspension of death. Psyche is revived, but in the name of brotherly love, Christianity threatens Eros with extinction. The brotherhood cannot include women, the Other objects of desire; the role of Eros is partly absorbed into the feminine. In a bronze statue of the Roman period found at Amrith, Syria, Aphrodite is represented across cultures. She is naked except for some Egyptian, Greek, and Roman emblems. She is adorned with attributes of love, including the wings and arrows of Eros. Magic, fertility, and luck motivate some of her emblems. A snake is wound around her arm, and she holds a horn of plenty; the emblem of Isis and a crown of towers are on her head. Eros is absent.

Modernism lays claim to the Platonic Eros through the mediations of popular culture as well as through classical texts. The poetry of

---

[9] Paul de Man explores the temporality and poetics of Hölderlin in many of his writings on Romanticism. See *The Rhetoric of Romanticism* (New York: Columbia University Press, 1984), and *Romanticism and Contemporary Criticism*, edited by E. S. Burt, Kevin Newmark, and Andrzej Warminski (Baltimore: Johns Hopkins University Press, 1993), chaps. 3, 7, and 8. Rainer Nägele's writings on Hölderlin's poetics include a discussion of the poet's relation to Eros in *Echoes of Translation* (Baltimore: Johns Hopkins University Press, 1997).

2. Antonio Canova, *Amor and Psyche*, Rome, 1793, marble group. Copyright Louvre R.M.N.

W. B. Yeats frequently alludes to classical Greece in Platonic contexts of love. Although the autobiographical narrator of "The Tower" claims to rebel against Platonism, Yeats alludes to Italian neo-Platonism, Greek antiquity, poetry, and love on the same page:

> And memories of love,
> Memories of the words of women,
> All those things whereof
> Man makes a superhuman
> Mirror-resembling dream.[10]

In these lines, Pindar's image, evoked by Socrates, enters modernism.

"Among School Children," also published in *The Tower* (1928), first raises the topic of love in the context of an allusion to Aristophanes'

---

[10] See *The Collected Poems of W. B. Yeats, definitive edition* (New York: Macmillan, 1956), 196–97.

3. *Aphrodite panthée*, c. bronze Roman statue found at Amrith, Syria. Copyright Louvre R.M.N.

speech in the *Symposium*. The "dream of a Ledaean body" makes the speaker into a substitute for Zeus the swan who fathered Helen, hatched from a swan's egg. Their union blends them into a sphere:

> Or else, to alter Plato's parable,
> Into the yolk and white of the one shell.[11]

The dream-image borrowed from Plato also refers to the spherical humans that Zeus later cut in half as punishment for their hybris. As the swan-poet in love with feminine beauty, Yeats reshapes Aristophanes' tragicomic parable into the love that produced Helen. The poem filters the feminine body that resembles Leda through the writer's parable in Plato to articulate the enduring image of Yeatsian Eros. At the closing of "Words For Music Perhaps," Yeats invokes the Delphic Oracle, the gods of the underworld, and the philosophers, in order to end with Plato, Pythagoras, and the allegorized "choir of Love."[12] As an allegorical presence or as a poetic form, love gives music to words in lyric poetry.

Joyce's writings locate love in close proximity to aesthetics. The artist-lover character of Dedalus starts with the Platonic premise that identifies beauty as the splendor of truth (*P* 188). The historical development of love in Joyce moves rapidly from Plato, overshadowed by Aquinas, to original sin, the art of repetition on Vico's trellis, and the portrayals of love in Ibsen, Flaubert, Yeats, and other influential modernist writers. Original sin highlights a mother-daughter iconography of Eve and Mary along the road to the madonnas of modernism: Eve enters Christian iconography through the logic of the "felix culpa [happy fault],"[13] based on the beautiful image of the Blessed Virgin. Once the Madonna is on the scene, troubadours and courtly love, crowned for Joyce by Dante's creation of Beatrice, are not far away. Courtly love combines with enigmatic Celtic sources to shape the Tristan story that is central in the structuring of the *Wake*.[14]

---

[11] Ibid., 213.

[12] Ibid., 265.

[13] *Joyce's Catholic Comedy of Language* explores the "felix culpa" in *Finnegans Wake* in the context of the paschal liturgy, where it is evoked in the service for Holy Saturday.

[14] See David Hayman, *The "Wake" in Transit* (Ithaca: Cornell University Press, 1990; Jean-Michel Rabaté, "Back to Beria! Genetic Joyce and Eco's 'Ideal Readers'" in *Probes: Genetic Studies in Joyce,* edited by David Hayman and Sam Slote (Amsterdam: Rodopi, 1995), 65–83.

In the logic of modern love, Tristan's polar opposite would be Don Giovanni. Each of the two is important in the contexts of the troubadour resonances of musical performance, the magic of love and its darkness. Tristan is faithful to Isolde within a framework of courtly love and *fin'amors*; a magic philtre seals their fate in adulterous love. Tristan's faith endures in spite of all the risks, and beyond the point when the philtre wears off. He is persuaded to marry a pale echo of his beloved, but his bond to the wife of King Mark is infinitely stronger than marriage. His faith goes beyond life itself. Don Giovanni is a figure shaped by a baroque sensibility and represents the ultimate challenge to courtly love and to ethics. He is the irresistible faithless lover who asks the question of desire in the intimate form of address, *"che vuoi?"* Although Don Giovanni is a libertine who claims to believe only in material reality and in visible beauty, he values virginity. He consumes his beautiful objects one after another until heaven intervenes. His version of "marriage" functions in accordance with the pleasure principle: he takes his women one by one.

Twentieth-century popular culture has allowed the glamour of Don Juan to fade. In general, the hero of Spanish machismo has aged badly and has been degraded to farce or psychopathology. There are some exceptions, in part because of the enduring impact of Molière's play, *Don Juan et le Festin de Pierre*, and especially Mozart's opera, *Don Giovanni*. Don Giovanni's fate in Joyce's portraits is sealed in the decisive failure in seduction that we know as *Giacomo Joyce*. Richard Ellmann points out the parallel between Joyce's character of Giacomo and Stephen's remark on Shakespeare in the Library scene of *Ulysses*, "Assumed dongiovannism cannot save him." [15] Stephen's expression is a minimally anglicized form of the Italian *dongiovannismo*, named for the libertine character of Mozart's opera, *Don Giovanni*. Stephen needs the intercession of the Madonna. With the loss of his mother, the birdgirl as winged Psyche and Emma Clery, the girl in white, also vanish. He is no longer and not yet a figure of Amor. Bloom, who knows a little about love, enters the scene of Stephen's mourning. Like Bloom's love for Molly, Shakespeare's passion includes betrayal and the triangles of adultery.

In *Giacomo Joyce*, the lightness of earlier failed attempts at seduction (in *Stephen Hero* and even in *A Portrait*) has disappeared. Eros

---

[15] See the introduction to *Giacomo Joyce*, edited by Richard Ellmann (New York: Viking Press, 1968).

appears increasingly bitter, since love creates primarily suffering and solitude. The narrator of *Giacomo Joyce* casts the failure of seduction as the end of youth. His lamentations are ironic, sarcastic, disdainful, and filled with accusations. Only in dreams (or at a considerable distance from his beloved) can love soothe his melancholy and angry disposition. In the context of his attraction, he rhetorically alludes to Christ's betrayal, to the Passion, and to divine violence.

His fragmentary portrayal of the beloved shows her as rich, spoiled, and willful, while the narrator presents himself as an unrequited lover, keenly aware of his own poverty, emptiness, and desire. "Love's bitter mystery" from "Fergus' Song" will haunt the Stephen of *Ulysses*. To Don Giovanni, all women (except for Dona Anna) say yes: to Don Giacomo, his Shakespearean brother in desire, the Jewish Virgin says no. Joyce's portraits of fraternal rivals and male friendships return to this division of success in love.

Did Joyce the seducer discover the limited effects of his tragic tone, or did his reading remind him that love is irresistibly associated with comedy? The limits of Stephen Dedalus are rooted in the end of youth that Joyce celebrated in the beautiful and funereal style of *Giacomo Joyce*. His pain, Joyce reminds us in the first pages of *Ulysses*, is linked to "love's bitter mystery" and the veiled virginal figure of the dead mother, but it is not yet the pain of love. With Don Juan in the background as the vulgar Blazes Boylan, and the seduction duet from Mozart's "Don Giovanni" haunting the thoughts of both Bloom and Molly—the figure of a profane Virgin—Joyce turns again to the triangles of adultery, but this time in the form of comedy. The family configuration begins with Bloom. Through Nighttown and Molly's monologue, it leads to the young troubadour-like figure of Tristan. Molly's monologue about the mystery of love speaks from a perspective of night and interiority. The boundaries of punctuation have vanished, the outside world of characters and of Dublin represented earlier in the book has receded into darkness, and Molly speaks "inside" herself, or rather, as Joyce reception has indicated, "inside" her author. Because of the monologue, Joyce was considered an expert in matters of love, at least by Carl Jung. Like "her ladyship" in *Giacomo Joyce* and the serpent of his lost conquest, Molly appears in the author's dreams, where she makes a scene.

Through a strange coincidence, Molly resembles Diotima. She is somewhat exotic as a foreigner in Dublin, and she enjoys a form of magical and aesthetic power. Molly's most remarkable connection with

Diotima is her knowledge of the mystery of love, revealed to her at a certain specific point in the past. In spite of her ignorance and comic superstition, Joyce's twentieth-century virtual woman plays the central role in the revelation of love that Diotima played for Socrates at a point in the past as defined by the framework of the *Symposium*. Love is the word that Stephen seeks; the mystery of love leads him into the darkness of Nighttown and the confrontation of fantasy. Socrates too was young when Diotima initiated him in the mystery of love. Bloom and Molly fantasize about a potential initiation, following Stephen's disappearance into the night.

Beginning with *Giacomo* as a blueprint for the triangles of *Exiles, Ulysses,* and *Finnegans Wake,* Joyce shows the inevitable triangular configuration of desire. In the *Symposium,* Plato alludes to the triangle when Socrates denounces Alcibiades' speech as an attempt to separate him from Agathon (222d). Freud notes that "the enlarged sexuality of psychoanalysis coincides with the Eros of the divine Plato." He anchors the invention of psychoanalysis in the triangle as the structuring form of desire.[16]

Inside Joyce's fiction of night, Molly silently talks herself into an ecstatic affirmation that unveils the scene of Eros and the Fall. Following the unsuccessful attempt at the magic of "assumed dongiovannism," Joyce confirms the shape of love as a triangle and shifts his writing strategy away from the forms of Don Juan and the black tragedy of desire. He turns to Tristan and to comedy. In the *Wake,* Don Giovanni makes a farcical appearance in the guise of Jaun or Shaun the Post, jealous brother of Shem, the Stephen Dedalus/Sunny Jim figure of the mother's favorite son.

In Stephen's theory of aesthetics in the *Portrait,* the impact of the *Symposium* on Western literary culture prompts Joyce to allude to Plato: "'Plato, I believe, said that beauty is the splendor of truth. I don't think that it has a meaning but the true and the beautiful are akin" (*P* 188). Stephen Dedalus refers to Aquinas' three requirements for beauty, his poetic aspect, and his aesthetic terms of pleasure and desire. Love in Aquinas begins with the desiring appetite. Stephen's dialogue with his crude and sexually obsessive friend, Lynch, keeps love between the lines, though love becomes explicit in the later dialogue with Cranly. The dialogue with Lynch focuses on beauty in

---

[16] Sigmund Freud, Preface to the fourth edition (1920) of *Three Essays on the Theory of Sexuality* (1905), *SE* vol. 7.

women and in art, and Lynch's interest in female beauty keeps him listening, while Stephen explores the difficulties of understanding beauty as Platonic "splendor of truth," as *claritas* or radiance borrowed from Aquinas, and as Shelley's image in the imagination.

The consequences of Stephen's exposition of beauty in his aesthetic philosophy and of the Platonic connection between truth and beauty occupy the last character-oriented narrative pages of the book, before the closing sequence of journal entries rendered in the first person. The narrative pages include the final dialogue between Cranly and Stephen. Stephen's friend confronts him with the love of his mother, the love of the Blessed Virgin, and the deflowering of a virgin (*P* 215–23). Emma makes some appearances, as well, within a mother-daughter context that is underscored in *Giacomo Joyce*. The focus on unsuccessful love and on the desire for beauty connect the last chapter of the *Portrait* with *Giacomo Joyce* and *Exiles*, and with the later works. Following an early appearance in "The Dead," Joyce's Madonna figure begins to take its definitive shape in the last chapter of the *Portrait*. The suspension of meaning that Stephen pronounces on the identity of beauty and truth leads directly to the aesthetics of *Finnegans Wake*.

Throughout the *Portrait*, the emphasis on radiance or *claritas* in the aesthetic terms borrowed from Aquinas is overdetermined by the association of a flash of light, epiphany, and a vision or an apprehension of beauty. These terms associate radiance with the image of the Virgin, the image of art, and the image of mystical revelation. In the *Symposium*, Plato uses the epithet of *kalos* to evoke shining beauty in Eros. In Diotima's discourse and in the words of Alcibiades, visible beauty leads the desiring subject toward interior and invisible beauty. Daylight fades and the night of the mysteries is evoked. But the path toward the Form of Beauty is revised in the speech of Alcibiades; the figures that he glimpses inside Socrates and the music of his speech drive Alcibiades wild with passion. These figures and words shine with the magical glow of love.

Medical, spiritual, and romantic, the "enchantment of the heart" at the instant of imagination in the fifth chapter of the *Portrait* underscores the common ground between love and art. The winds are still. "He lay still, as if his soul lay amid cool waters, conscious of faint sweet music. (. . .) A spirit filled him, pure as the purest water (. . .) But how faintly it was inbreathed, how passionlessly, as if the seraphim themselves were breathing upon him! (. . .) It was the windless hour of dawn when madness wakes" (*P* 196). The artist is suspended in the image, and the lover is caught in the fatal suspension of the winds that Agathon evokes ironically as the stillness of the sea: Eros causes the erotic standstill. In bed, Stephen is fantasizing about women and preciously playing the role of the Madonna. "O! In the virgin womb of the imagination the word was made flesh. Gabriel the seraph had come to the virgin's chamber" (*P* 198). The "virgin womb of the imagination"—the feminized, sexualized space of creation—is the scene for the incense-perfumed vows of desire that shape Stephen's villanelle. Emma, the girl who says no in Stephen's waking life, becomes a poetic figure of sexual power. She reigns over the dusk and twilight that characterize Joycean darkness; epiphany comes from the realm of shadows and dreams. In fantasy as in Diotima's mysteries the visible emerges from the invisible, the sublime from the obscene. Through the shining of desire, magical as an ex-voto, the madonna of modernism connects Eros and writing, love and art.

2 Love's Bitter Mystery: Edenville and Nighttown

> When Blanchot writes: "Is man *capable* of a radical questioning, i.e. in the end, *capable* of literature?" we might say it as well, if we start with a certain thinking about life, 'incapable' half the time. Unless we admit that pure literature is non-literature, or death itself. The question about the origin of the book, the absolute questioning, the interrogation of all possible questionings, the "questioning of God" can never be possessed by any book. Unless the question forgets itself in the articulation of its memory . . .
>
> —Jacques Derrida

> —Have you the key? a voice asked.
> —Dedalus has it, Buck Mulligan said.

When Derrida rewrites Blanchot's question defining literature as a radical questioning, he shifts from the standard of judgment for the making of literature to the absolute question, the master question, or discourse, of origins.[1] Covered with the veil of the sacred or the dust of time, origins are hidden. Genetic studies lead the reader toward the work through the labyrinth of notes and scribbles, libraries and collections—the traces of literary life, the fragile clues and the invisible

---

[1] In *L'Ecriture et la différence,* Jacques Derrida writes: "Quand M. Blanchot écrit: 'L'homme est-il *capable* d'une interrogation radicale, c'est-à-dire, en fin de compte, l'homme est-il *capable* de littérature?,' on pourrait aussi bien dire, à partir d'une certaine pensée de la vie, 'incapable,' une fois sur les deux. Sauf à admettre que la littérature pure est la non-littérature, ou la mort elle-même. La question sur l'origine du livre, l'interrogation absolue, l'interrogation sur toutes les interrogations possibles, l' 'interrogation de Dieu' n'appartiendra jamais à aucun livre. A moins qu'elle ne s'oublie elle-même dans l'articulation de sa mémoire . . ." This passage is translated in my epigraph. See also *Ulysse grammophone. Deux mots pour Joyce* (Paris: Galilée, 1987).

chains that hold the secrets of "creation from nothing." A blank space comes into view at a horizon that has been identified with a moment of creation: radical differentiation encoded as a beginning, heading, or Genesis. The originary position of emptiness and absence leaves its mark on the experiences of philosophy and theology; on the writings of the mystics; on art and love.

The literary "creation" of language is always allegorical, in the widest sense, because the battleground of its otherness pins it between the rules of grammar and the play of rhetoric. The allegorical dimension that distinguishes literature is sustained by the following circumstances: (1) whether its effects are considered as consciously crafted or unconsciously produced, literature's effects are integral to it, and (2) literature is more like an agency or an instance than a substance; its status as an "object" cannot be separated from the metaphorical language that constitutes it.

Derrida points out the absolute nature of the question of origins as a kind of third-degree interrogation. The book remains silent. Blanchot's characteristic silence of literature resists questioning, and it will never give an answer. The ghost withdraws before morning light.

The Real that literature invokes exists outside of theology and science. It is the real of difference itself, of language that carves a path through the virtual deserts of silence. The "book of questions"—invoked in the formula of Edmond Jabès—talks about beginnings that unfold as literary texts, but it cannot articulate the origin of those texts. The origin appears only in allusions to the scene of writing. In *Ulysses*, this scene is encoded primarily in the terms of theology, creation, and mystical love that resonate in the literary space where extremes meet.

In Joyce, the scene of writing is shaped by coded messages, symbolic and symptomatic echoes, and by the radiant presence of other texts. These elements are pared down, trimmed of sentimental excess and precious wordiness in the fictions of *Dubliners*, and they are swallowed whole, turned inside out, or synthetically rearranged in the text of *Finnegans Wake*. *Wake* language is shaped and devoured from both ends like the alphabet of ferocious animals in the *Book of Kells*. In between Joyce's early classical restraint and his late baroque luxuriance, the tension between the rigors of parallax and the quasi-autonomy of style lead from the *Portrait of the Artist* to *Ulysses*, by way of *Exiles* and *Giacomo Joyce*. Joyce portrays the scene of writing in many forms and figures; like Proust, who also subsumes his fascination with systems to a translation of the mystery of art and love, Joyce emphasizes the fiction of beginning. At the scene of writing, theology meets eroticism. Freud and Lacan locate emptiness and plenitude, beginnings and their ever–afters, in the sphere of language. Romantic, obscene, and sublime, love's bitter mystery marks the Edenville of the literary text near the beginning of *Ulysses*. Near the altar where texts are sacrificed at the razor's edge of difference, Mulligan's parody of the Mass is dissolved in the paranoiac grandeur of Dedalus, buttressed by Shakespeare's mourning play, a portrait of the young rhetorician as an exile at home: Hamlet.

In the third chapter of *Ulysses*, Stephen's thoughts turn repeatedly and obsessively to beginnings, their visible signatures, and the Edenville of creation. The first woman enters his thoughts after observed midwives and the imagined navelcords of mystic monks. "Heva, naked Eve. She had no navel. Gaze. Belly without blemish, bulging big" (*U* 38). Stephen's Eve is pregnant and he grants her a few images borrowed from English poetry before he evokes her as "Womb of sin." Without a navel, her pure belly of fantasy marks the beginning of sin, emblematized by the signature of navelcords in the flesh and by the navel of the book. From nought to one, from emptiness to Aleph, the leap of creation is visualized through the body of Eve. As a virtual voyeur, Stephen contemplates the origin of original sin; after theology and sex are in place, he looks at bodies of fallen women. The navel of sin emblematizes the novel *Ulysses*. The wandering gypsy girl replaces Psyche on the strand, the "birdgirl" of the *Portrait*, who wore seaweed and plumage when she returned Stephen's gaze.

The navel is the center; it represents the unanalyzable, the focus of mystery.[2] Much later in the book, the locus of mystery is characterized as the meeting between "Jewgreek" and "Greekjew" (504). The

---

[2] "Each dream has at least one point where it is unfathomable, so to speak a navel, through which it is attached to the unknown." "This is the navel of the dream, the place where it sits on the unknown" (Sigmund Freud, *Die Traumdeutung* [Frankfurt am Main: S. Fischer Verlag, 1972], Band II, pp. 130, 503. My translations. See Strachey's translations of these passages in the *Standard Edition* (*SE* 4:110 and *SE* 5:525). The navel of the dream is the unfathomable spot in the dream that connects it to the unknown; it is the point of the *originating* ("anhebt") tangle of dream thoughts where the unknown takes it for a ride ("dem Unerkannten aufsitzt") or (in Samuel Weber's reading) "straddles it." Weber's reading can be found in *The Legend of Freud* (Minneapolis: University of Minnesota Press, 1982), "The Meaning of the Thallus," 65–83.

clash of the letter (and its literality) arranges for the collision between "Jew" and "Greek," monotheistic and pagan, father's captive
exile and mother's high-flown love object. Suspended in exile, motionless in flight—in the calendar slice of June 16, 1904, Stephen and
Bloom separately fit into each of these two categories. Hearing the
voices of father and mother, homeland and church, masculine and
feminine, Stephen is faced with unredeemable origins. While Bloom
listens to his libidinous God and his adulterous wife, his indelible
Otherness traces the hand of messianic script and the letters of desire. Time seems to stop, and he circles back to the song of a Mozartean Madonna.

Stephen would reflect rather than kneel down. He admires the saint
who delivered Aristotle in theological costume to Catholicism, and
his meditation on the mysteries of being articulates the metaphors
that trap him between body and soul. Signatures of the fallen world
lead him from Greek to Jew, from Mulligan and his complacent hell-
enization schemes to Bloom, another reader of signatures.

Hieroglyphs and images of exile, signatures in *Ulysses* represent the
carnal and spiritual traces of the subject. On the edge of the sea of
birth and death, Stephen invokes mystical reading in the terms of
Jakob Boehme: "Signatures of all things I am here to read, seaspawn
and seawrack, the nearing tide, that rusty boot" (*U* 37). He closes his
eyes, but when he opens them he is back at the beginning, caught in
brooding and repetition, when he glimpses a midwife (and her companion) from Bride Street. Haunted by a vision of his mother and her
final return to sacramental virginity, he recalls the morning scene in
the tower and ironizes Mulligan's comments. The scene of the mothers is repeated for Stephen. He sees the two women "coming down to
our mighty mother," and thinks again of the inescapable "creation
from nothing." Later, Bloom will sketch out a solution to endless repetition when his act of reading on the strand turns into a performance
of creation from nothing, suspended in a sacred and comic signature.

Both Stephen and Bloom combine the erotic pleasures of voyeurism
with a moment of reading and meditation, but Bloom writes the hieroglyphics of an unfinished message in the sand. With an ambiguous blurring of identity through the use of the personal pronoun, he
thinks, "Might write a message for her" (*U* 381). The shameful sweets
of sin suspend the identity of the name as the strange effect of petrification is repeated: "I . . . Am. A." (*U* 381). The watch stopped, the
hand that writes is suddenly inhibited. Reading continues, as Bloom's

"A" locates the Judaic origin in him and in the Alpha of his erotic alphabet.

From the "page of an old copybook" that he finds in the sand, Bloom's thoughts turn to love letters, to the mysterious "word" of sin that Martha claimed she did not understand, and then to the letter itself. "All these rocks with lines and scars and letters." He erases his letters of creation and prepares for the "postcreation" of the "Oxen" chapter when his thoughts mingle with those of Stephen.

Spiritual Union

Man to man, Bloom and Stephen wander, drink, talk, and mourn. It is not surprising that the Catholic perverse form of this meeting represents the Word made flesh. Father and son begin again, consubstantial . . . but that is an old story. Wide of the feminist mark, Joyce's views on women emphasize the limits of the sweets of sex and sin.[3] According to his opinion of the "short-legged sex," women are better off without brains, and the fewer blue-stockings in sight, the better. Richard Ellmann's biography provides sustained evidence of this point of view. Ideological flaws cannot explain the literary work and its history; inversely, the criteria of literature and criticism do not justify the ideology reflected in the works of Joyce or anyone else. Some feminist defenses of Joyce's ideology apologize or cover for the level of discourse of Joyce's female characters; in either case, it becomes difficult to read Joyce's portrayal of the feminine.

Like a Zen garden, the garden of reading is an allegorical space filled with lines and plowed into paths. The reader does not gaze at the splendors of organic imagery and translucence. Like Bloom on the strand in "Nausikaa," the reader traces the lines and paths of meaning from within the subjectivity of reading. The reader is always caught at the edge where the recognition of language (the only home of the speaking subject as such) encounters the unreadable exoticism of the hieroglyph (the sign that holds itself aloof from the reader by representing a strangeness of form rather than a possibility of identity, according to the widest trans-romantic understanding of what is meant

---

[3] Joyce's views on these questions are central to Christine Van Boheemen, *The Novel as Family Romance* (Ithaca: Cornell University Press, 1987), and Frances Restuccia, *Joyce and the Law of the Father* (New Haven: Yale University Press, 1989).

by the status of allegory versus the symbol). Recognition of meaning confronts the enigmatic hieroglyphic forms that resist it, a confrontation that characterizes the work of interpretation, or reading.

The reader, in this instance, does not have to like what s/he finds, but that reaction cannot change anything in the text. Like Céline's racism, Joyce's opinions on sexual identity and its roles cannot be defended or denied. In his writings, Joyce maintained that women's talk is cheap, except when it represents the secret sodomic coupling of men inside them. Joyce's notes for "Exiles" sketch Bertha's role as a body that spiritually unites two men: "The bodily possession of Bertha by Robert, repeated often, would certainly bring into almost carnal contact the two men. Do they desire this? To be united, that is carnally through the person and body of Bertha as they cannot, without dissatisfaction and degradation—be united carnally man to man as man to woman?" (*E* 123).

While the present-day reader may be amused by Joyce's claim for the play as "a rough and tumble between the Marquis de Sade and Freiherr v. Sacher Masoch" (*E* 124), the literary staging of sado-masochism is made good in *Ulysses* and *Finnegans Wake.* The constellation of two men and a common erotic object—a female guarantee against the so-called "degradation" of homosexual love or role-changing—is essential to Joyce's writing after "Exiles." Beyond its obvious importance for an understanding of the play, the "spiritual union" passage from the note quoted above gives insight into Bloom's fantasy life, his relations with Stephen and his impulse to cure the ills of his marriage and Stephen's predilection for wasting his money in whorehouses by bringing the young man home to Molly. The passage provides a sketch for the Joycean schema of desire played out in *Ulysses.*

Male masochism is the sexual focus of Joycean erotics. Stephen, Bloom, and Richard circle around the same fantasies, transformed and displaced from one object to another. After "Exiles," featuring Richard's masochism, the intervention of comedy reshapes masculine eroticism. In this sense, Richard is a station along the path that leads the Stephen of *A Portrait* to the black point in *Ulysses.* The itinerary of erotic language marks the sacramental dissolving of Stephen into Bloom, son into father. *Ulysses* builds on the Victorian frame of *Exiles* by translating its triangular structure into a Catholic comedy of language. Day and night the exile wanders among the hieroglyphics of desire; language meanders through the historical forms of literary style.

"Jocoserious" (*U* 677) implies that the theological event of transubstantiation and the consubstantiality upon which it is predicated can
occur in a comic mode. The word "jocoserious" memorializes this
event with an affirmation that will begin in the black seed at the bot-
tom of the page turned, deferred for an instant, until Molly's "Yes"
comes into view. The reader takes a breath. The feminine is doubly
inscribed in the black navel and in Molly's "Yes." "Yes because" and
"Yes because he" lead to the "yeses and yeses" of *Finnegans Wake:*
when an Egyptian god named Thoth reinvents writing at the wake of
Finnegan, affirmation marks the spot, the origin.[4]

Joyce's emphasis on male masochism rather than on a vocal performance of the feminine structures the representation of desire. The
feminine object dissolves into language as it invokes the figures of
men (father, son, husband, or lover). Only a naive reader—Jung, for
example—could fall into the Joycean simulacrum of a "femininity"
as such. The final monologue of *Ulysses* takes up where "Exiles"
ended—in consummated adultery. Sacred and comic, the Joycean
"virgin" has received the "Word." An invisible woman lying in bed
embodies the talk of her creator. The profane virgin receives the
word—the sweets of sin. Joyce's Molly-monologue is as feminist a
piece of writing as the biblical account of Eve's creation in Genesis.

In this sense, the notes to "Exiles" form a blueprint for Joyce's reading of desire in language. The categories of the obscene and the beautiful appear in Catholic and feminine terms. This reading turns into
writing, all the way to the "end" of *Ulysses,* the "beginning" of *Finnegans Wake,* and the transgressions by femininity against the Law.
In the Name of the Father, this Law marks the narrow heights of Victorian ideology. Joyce's shorthand portrayal of women has only three
alternatives: death, purity, and corruption. Mrs Dedalus in *Ulysses*
sums up all three; the whores and the sweet young things stand for a
perverse version of one or the other.

Molly is saved from this limited clinical picture only because she is
created in the image of the Madonna—the Blessed Virgin Mary, the

---

[4] See my reading of Shem the Penman and his relation to writing in *Joyce's Catholic Comedy of Language* (Madison: University of Wisconsin Press, 1985). On the question of affirmation and writing, see Jacques Derrida, *Ulysse grammophone. Deux
mots pour Joyce.* The reader of *La Dissémination* (Paris: Seuil, 1972) will recall the
inscription of the Egyptian Thoth and the Freudian/Joycean "extremes meet" in the
space of philosophy: these extremes and their meeting are disseminated in and
through Derrida's wake oeuvre.

only woman exempt from original sin.[5] The Madonna is Christ's virgin mother, celebrated in the Provençal poets, in Dante, and in the powerful tradition of courtly love. Consecrated equals desecrated, according to the lesson of the *Portrait*, where the evidence for the "cursed jesuit strain injected the wrong way" (*U* 8) is amply prefigured in the younger Dedalus. "Extremes meet" (*U* 504), especially in scenes of unsatisfied desire like the Jesuit apprenticeship of *A Portrait*, the bordello of Nighttown, and the desecrated marriage bed of Bloom and Molly, facing in different directions.

From the memory of Mrs Dedalus dying in bed and weeping at love's bitter mystery to Molly, the Joycean progression of *Ulysses* leads from the limits of the young man to Bloom. It culminates in the representation of language infinitely dissolving into the sacred and the comic. The final monologue locates Molly as a voice detached from the frames that tend to stabilize characters and narrators in the book. The voice that speaks "for" her (or in her place, i.e. from the "Other" side of the bed, in relation to Bloom) offers a disembodied image of virginity, sex, and especially vocal art. In spite of the early claims of his Mariolatry—the Catholic cult of the Blessed Virgin Mary—Joyce dismisses the Madonna as irrelevant to the scheme of language and the ideal realm of his autobiographical fantasy figure, Richard Rowan, the eloquent and irresistible Irish writer in Joyce's play. In a note, Joyce states: "Richard must not appear as a champion of women's rights" (*E* 120). Joyce also notes that Christ, distanced from all women, would never have been associated with a woman (his mother) were it not for the "infallible practical instinct" of the Italians.

But love, Catholic style, is carnal and spiritual. Brooding about virginity appears throughout Joyce's major writings. It indicates that questions of desire in language cannot be articulated without the modernist and fin de siècle crossroads between the speaking subjectivity of psychoanalysis and the figures of theology. Fiction tells the gospel truth: when the Virgin receives the Word, strange things start happening in language. The seedcake is eaten, the sweets of sin are turned into writing, and the readers of desire subscribe to the Italian point of view. In "Exiles," a writer's attempt to lead his wife into adultery, Richard Rowan does not receive any (love) letters. Brigid—the

---

[5] See Beryl Schlossman, "Ecriture joycienne: juive ou catholique?," *James Joyce* (Paris, L'Herne, 1985), 318–33.

faithful servant, the Poor Old Woman invoked by Yeats and others to personify Ireland—is asked for the mail ("RICHARD: Letters?"), but she replies, "No, sir. Only them Italian newspapers" (*E* 17). The letter has not been sent, or perhaps it hovers in the underworld, waiting for Molly to sing the "Stabat Mater." It may be hidden in the hieroglyphs of love's bitter mystery, and the undeciphered dreams that come to Stephen and Bloom in *Ulysses*.

Like *Ulysses*, designed to get inside the control room of language and the folds of rhetoric to replay the meeting between the speaking subject and the object of desire, the text of dreams includes figures that cannot be explained and enigmatic points that cannot be solved. Freud refers by analogy to the "navel of the dream," the secret, unanalyzable core of representation that leads into the unknown. Jacques Lacan alludes to the navel of the dream as the impossible point where death is represented.[6] Does Stephen's image of the navel point toward an impossible agreement between theology and psychoanalysis? The agreement might take poetic form in the allegorical dimension of Love as "mystery" or "bitter fruit." Both poetic images are effects of the Fall. According to St Paul, allegory is a consequence of the Fall, since vision takes place in allegorical form "through a glass darkly." Stephen says: "Wombed in sin darkness I was too, made not begotten" (*U* 38).

The bitter mystery takes love out of the romantic "origins" linked with innocent boyhood, the naive reading of transfiguration through the Count of Monte Cristo. The Fall bears the secrets of sex, language, and death; adultery brings the three together, in the Joycean morality play of love. Stephen emulates the brooding of Hamlet, Flaubert's characters, and Yeats's figure of the young man. Joyce pays homage to Yeats, the Irish poetic voice that functions in *Ulysses* as a code for poetic language.

The Fall implicates obscenity in its curse of bitterness. *Ulysses* includes a reflection in language of the impossible and untenable moment, the "instant" that brings the romantic and the obscene together in Shakespearean *Trauerspiel*, European modernism, and Anglo-Irish poetics. This instant is figured repeatedly in the art and life that lead up to *Ulysses* and end it by beginning *Finnegans Wake*.

---

[6] See "Le Séminaire XXII: R.S.I." in *Ornicar?* (Paris: Champ Freudien, 1974–75).

Quickening and Wombfruit

Joyce's beginner is the fictional portrait of the eternally virgin son, Stephen Dedalus. *Ulysses* spells it out repeatedly. With Bloom as a witness in the "Oxen" chapter, he claims his Christly character ("for he was the eternal son and ever virgin" [*U* 392]) and returns to the brooding of "Proteus": "In woman's womb word is made flesh but in the spirit of the maker all flesh that passes becomes the word that shall not pass away" (*U* 390). According to the memoirs of Stanislaus, Gogarty called Joyce the "virginal kipranger."[7] The young man seems to be obsessed with virginity. The influence of the Madonna and Victorianism combine in the fin de siècle idiom of eroticism to produce the particular strain of Joyce's Nighttown. The obsession with virginity points back to life, where the young man is also worried about someone else's virginal state. Joyce confides to his soundboard brother Stanislaus his chagrined discovery that Nora is something like a "demi-vierge."[8] In imperfect and Freudian French, he writes: "elle n'est pas encore vierge." "Pas encore" is "not yet," mistaken for "no longer." If Nora is no longer virgin, he will make her virgin again. Joyce plays with the Law and its objects of desire. Stephen thinks, "Am I Father?" When this possibility is taken up by Lenehan in "Oxen of the Sun," Stephen claims a Christly alibi of virginity. The voyeuristic gaze into the divine belly turns the French pigeon joke that flaps through Stephen's thoughts into an eclipse of the imagination. In Nighttown, Stephen's mind goes blank, and Joyce puts out the lights. Fantasies of innocence and guilt find their allegorical shape in the Fall. Someone else is responsible—Joyce's Bible told him so.

Within the fabric of the text and its reflective version of life, these are "reasons" for Bloom's existence. Since the "young man" has limits, Joyce wrote to Pound that Stephen's shape could not be changed.[9] Beyond a young man's portrait, *Exiles* and *Ulysses* show the other side where the romantic and the obscene of writing make it possible to return to writing about the beginning. Woman, "the ever-affirming flesh [das Fleisch, das stets bejaht]," starts talking. Or rather, since she truly has nothing to say, the affirmation, the yeses and yeses, start talking through the text.

[7] *My Brother's Keeper* (London: Faber, 1958), p. 160.

[8] Letter to Stanislaus dated 11 October 1904, in *Selected Letters*, edited by Richard Ellmann (New York: Viking, 1974).

[9] See the letter dated 19 June 1919 in *Selected Letters*.

"Beginning" is all over *Ulysses*. It is an inscription, a theme, a principle of style, and a key to mystery. Dedalus is a closed beginning. Does Bloom, a grown man like Richard and Robert in *Exiles*, have more to say? It is difficult to compare his modest and sacred-comic powers of speech with Stephen's literary virtuosity, but Bloom has entered and been exiled from more beginnings than Stephen. His talent for wandering, in urban geography and in discursive modes, offers testimony of his dealings with the "Other" of other words and worlds. It pleased Joyce to turn the Irish Jew, the father who has lost his son, into the "Other" father of the young Christ figure. Like the Messiah, Stephen Dedalus is portrayed with two fathers. This doubling is pertinent to the comic formulation of *Ulysses*, since Joyce's diagnosis of Stephen as unchangeable can be understood in view of the growing importance of comedy for Joyce. The voice of the son comes from the father. "You're your father's son. I know the voice," says Kevin Egan (*U* 43), an expert in the masked identity of exile. When Stephen thinks of the son, the voice of the father resonates in his thoughts: "Tell Pat you saw me, won't you?"

The beginning is hidden, passworded as "Edenville." Primal scenes of theology and fantasy turn to face "reality" of beginning in "Nighttown"—a "reality" that is possessed in the ups and downs of language. Joyce uses parody, irony, and indirect discourse to make a case for the symbolic. The beginning is hidden, covered up by the Catholic Mass. Parodied by Buck Mulligan, who worships the pagan sea, his "great mother," the beginning is Stephen's quandary, at the razor's edge, looking over the rocks at the sea, thinking—like Hamlet— about his mother's body and his father's voice. The song and the eternal law at the black altar of the adversary offer the bitter parable of Irish exile from the inside, or inside out: sex and religion will tear you apart, and they cannot be separated from each other.

Stephen thinks of "My consubstantial father's voice" (38). Can the poetics of sex and the erotics of art keep the pagans and the priests at bay? That is the somewhat paranoiac mode of questioning that holds Stephen and Bloom together. Before *Ulysses* it refashioned the question of beginnings that *A Portrait of the Artist* approached in the terms of symbolic apprenticeship. *Ulysses* puts away all reminiscence of naiveté and anchors the relation of the writer to the symbolic in the rigorous terms of the Catholic comedy of language.

Through Swinburne, Mulligan threatens Stephen with the great sea, the mother that Stephen cannot bear to touch. Joyce chooses to portray the son exiled from his mother, left alone to lament man's Fall into the dark womb of melancholy. Mulligan's advice to stop brooding strikes an allegorical chord of memory. Like the figure of Dürer's *Melancholy*, the Stephen who broods is a portrait of interior monologue.

Fergus's Song

The signifier of "brooding" leads back to the question of couples and beginnings, inscribed in the quoted text of Yeats's poem and in the context of Stephen's opening sequence of memory.[10] The beginning is mysteriously hidden. Stephen meditates, "Wombed in sin darkness I was too, made not begotten. By them, the man with my voice and my eyes and a ghostwoman with ashes on her breath. They clasped and sundered" (*U* 38). The mother brings death and memory, flesh and ashes, while the father gives the visible and the invisible, eyes and voice.

Where do the words come from? The scene of "Who Goes with Fergus?" bears bitter Joycean fruit in love's bitter mystery. The brooders of the first stanza, young man and maid, have disappeared into the white space that separates the two commands to suspend brooding (parodied earlier in *Ulysses* by Mulligan's injunction to "give up the moody brooding"):

> For Fergus rules the brazen cars,
> And rules the shadows of the wood,
> And the white breast of the dim sea
> And all dishevelled wandering stars.

The proclamation of Fergus's supernatural power—he rules and rules and rules—takes up the suspension of brooding. Yeats's poem of "ands" (the repeated conjunction literally holds the lines together) slips into the thoughts of the Joycean character who turns aside to think about love's bitter mystery. The "woodshadows" that follow Mulligan's quotation of Yeats arise, visible only in Stephen's thoughts. "Woodshadows floated silently by through the morning peace from the stairhead seaward where he gazed" (*U* 9). The second stanza of the

---

[10] See *The Collected Poems of W. B. Yeats* (New York: Macmillan, 1956).

Yeats poem moves rhythmically through Stephen's imagination, and recalls the Orpheus-like son: "White breast of the dim sea. The twining stresses, two by two. A hand plucking the harpstrings merging their twining chords. Wavewhite wedded words shimmering on the dim tide" (*U* 9). In the backdrop of Joyce's scene, the wandering stars of "Who Goes with Fergus?" also slip into Yeats's "The Song of Wandering Aengus," a fable of love and exile. In Joyce's writing, Irish identity and sentiment are mediated by Yeats.

The turn from eroticism to writing is hard to separate from the "turning aside" of memory; death enters writing from the "wombed in sin darkness." Like the young couple of "Who Goes with Fergus?," Beauty is at the edge of Death; Yeats's verses become a tacit argument against Mulligan's Swinburne quotation. Stephen remembers: "Fergus' song; I sang it alone in the house, holding down the long dark chords" (*U* 9). In Yeats's "To the Rose upon the Rood of Time," Fergus, the Red Branch king, is surrounded in dreams and ruin by the Druid ("Who cast round Fergus dreams, and ruin untold") like Stephen ensnared by his mother's invisible presence.

Memory gives rise to the allegorical figure that represents Death, but Death teaches the power of memory. It is a vicious cycle, like sin itself, like remorse, like the specular limits of the "retrospective arrangement." The magic mirror locates the images of past and future, but it also represents the limiting power of the image, as in the literature of courtly love. The image can stop the subject in its tracks or block the lover's access to the beloved. Beyond the "mirror stage" of early childhood and beyond its narcissistic function, the mirror leads the subject to the dead end of the Imaginary and the ultimate inaccessibility of the object. The discourse of courtly love offers an exemplary form of the Freudian Thing, Lacan's "La Chose": a knot of history, eroticism, and poetics that locates desire.[11]

"La Chose" emblematizes subjectivity. Like a prison that requires psychoanalysis as a key or a keyhole shaped-door, modeled on the Church of Saint Peter's in Rome, it presents language as the unholy combination of body and soul. Joyce writes in the labyrinth of dedalian thoughts that "darkness is in our souls." It is the only source of light, and the subject cannot transcend the "exterior intimacy"

---

[11] Lacan's seminar for 1959–60 is partly focused on "La Chose." *Le Séminaire VII: L'Ethique de la psychanalyse* (Paris: Seuil, 1986).

("extimité") that inhabits it.[12] "La Chose" marks the brief instant of mystical exaltation from which the subject Falls.

Yeatsian magic evokes the rise and fall of the subject in language as its battleground; it invokes the terms of the modernist dichotomy between the evanescent and the permanent, the image-prison and the whirling sea-change of Protean forms that occupies Stephen's attention on the strand of *Ulysses*. One Yeatsian formula of modernist magic that resonates strongly in *Ulysses* is the title of the early poem, "To The Rose Upon the Rood of Time."

Borrowed for the lyrical ending of *Ulysses* in the last pages of Molly's monologue, Yeats's invocation of the rose includes a vision of the transient ("poor foolish things that live a day") as "Eternal beauty wandering on her way." Irish exile is a state of being, from the Druids to Dedalus. It is also an aesthetic state. In "The Dedication to a Book of Stories Selected from the Irish Novelists," Yeats's romantic vision of the Irish past turns the Druids' uncanny power into "kindness" that made everyone friendly; the "now" of the poem evokes the barrenness of the once green branches of Eire. They have produced "exiles wandering over lands and seas." Stephen notes, "beauty is not here." He wanders, cloaked in the sadness of Fergus and dreams of death, to the Protean regions of the strand, with its Druid-like spells.

When Joyce adds sin to the Yeatsian profile of exile, he turns exile inward. Joyce demonstrates the interiority of modernist aesthetic strategy, its struggle to be different and to create a new beginning. Joyce's exile must begin with Yeats, in the sense that Valéry pointed to Baudelaire's need to begin with the terrain of the romantics, Lamartine and Hugo.

If theology is filtered out and the Augustinian overtones of "darkness" fall out of sight, the words reflect this change. In Yeats's verse, the dim sea is often evoked, and dim is the hair of desired women. As if a spell had been cast, beginning with Yeats's first published poems, the adjective "dim" appears forever after. When Joyce's literary darkness is Yeatsian in its erotic ambiguity, then it is "shadowed" and "dim"; style touches the landscape at the beginning: "A cloud began to cover the sun slowly, shadowing the bay in deeper green" (*U* 9). Memory overshadows the "dim" tide with the bitter mystery, the secrets, the music of "Fergus' song."

---

[12] Lacan's neologism characterizes what he calls *das Ding* or *la Chose* in *Le Séminaire VII*, 167.

Beauty goes over the edge, and terror rises in its place. Catholicism embroiders on remorse, beginnings, and endings, and the menacing image of the dead mother takes hold of memory. The repetition compulsion replays the effects of trauma on the stage of memory and the scenarios of Nighttown. Repetition within the text gives an uncanny new life to the fragments of meditative remorse (the "agenbite of inwit") that can be traced throughout the day of *Ulysses.*

Joyce repeats: "And no more turn aside and brood" (*U* 10). The couple as young man and maid does not quite fit the scene. The couple of Orpheus and Eurydice fades into the constellations of father and ghostwoman as well as son and ghost-lit mother, or the dreamer and his silent dream. "Wedded words" bring "her breath . . . with mute secret words." Who answers in "Who Goes with Fergus?" No one. The question of the title is never explained, nor is the mystery brought to light. Stephen's mother weeps; after death, her "mute secret words" escape him. He has refused to pray at her deathbed, and the prayers catch up with him now and in Nighttown. From Goethe's "Walpurgisnacht" Joyce learned again what every Catholic knows: the signifier has a life of its own.

Stephen's melancholy brooding over his mother's death revises the brooding in "Who Goes With Fergus?" in light of Catholicism, sin, and reflection. It inverts the mother-son relation of the Virgin sorrowing over Christ's death (and meditatively participating in the Passion). Stephen in mourning echoes the figure of the Virgin of Sorrow. An example of this Virgin is Germain Pilon's 1585 ceramic model for a sculpture, commissioned by Catherine de Medici and intended for Henry II's funerary chapel at Saint-Denis. The solitary figure of the Virgin of Sorrows is filled with mystical reflection. Like Shakespeare's Hamlet, Pilon's model of the Virgin in meditation illustrates the Baroque representation of brooding and introspection.

Joyce stages the confrontation between sin and the Law of its absolution, and between death and the sacrament that leads to eternal life. These terms articulate the paradox that faces Stephen. His mother's death reclaims an impossible state of virginity for her, while his view of death and the Fall makes it impossible for him to refuse the sweets of sin, but also their consequences. Translated into the stylistic terms of modernism (i.e., Yeats, Ibsen, Flaubert, and others) the death of Stephen's mother points toward the end of the Romantic virgin. Stephen's vision of Eve, the woman with no navel, unveils his brooding about sin. In Nighttown, she appears to him in

4. Germain Pilon, *Virgin of Sorrow*, 1585, polychrome ceramic. Louvre R.M.N.

the dreamform evoked earlier, first as a single signifier, when Stephen saw the midwife from "Bride Street" on the strand with her companion, and again in the recalled reminiscence of the exiled patriot, Kevin Egan: "Got up as a young bride, man, veil orangeblossoms, drove out the road to Malahide" (*U* 43). Stephen's scenario of mourning evokes the Yeatsian brooding of young man and maid, but the "wavewhite wedded words" secretly contain the white virginity of his mother, guaranteed by the Catholic sacrament for which he refused to kneel.

Stephen stands up for sin, death, and mourning, for the intimacies of Catholic exile, and the masochism of memory. "Stephen's mother, emaciated, rises stark through the floor in leper grey with a wreath of faded orange blossoms and a torn bridal veil, her face worn and nose-less, green with grave mould" (*U* 579). Although the text emphasizes Stephen's guilt and terror in its representation of the dead mother as a rotting corpse, the brief account of her bridal accessories turns back to Stephen's favorite subject of theological-erotic brooding, sin and virginity. The bride's flowers are faded and her veil is torn. Like Eve, immortal until the Fall, the mother is free from sin, and then she falls out of virginity; that is where Stephen comes from. Sin is an exile from Edenville. The mother's death is an effect of sin and replays the consequences of exile for the son. That is what Stephen learns from his pupils at school about *amor matris* and its genitives. From subject to object and back, love rules. Absence and emptiness turn love's dire mastery into the question "who goes with Fergus?" No one knows the answer. No one understands Stephen's riddle about burial or what love's bitter mystery is. And no one can decode the mute secret words that Stephen thinks his mother can tell him from the Other world.

Joyce rewrites the cathechism as questions without answers. Yeats named his riddle "A Dream of Death" and wrote the answer as a *non sequitur* of death, beauty, and horror: "She was more beautiful than thy first love, But now lies under boards." Like the Irish exiles, the stars wander, disheveled. Like the subject of the dream ("I dreamed that one had died in a strange place"), they are ruled by Fergus; but even Fergus ("king of the proud Red Branch kings") is tormented in "Fergus and the Druid," and the "little bag of dreams" that the Druid gives to him cannot suspend sorrow. There is no cure for love's bitter mystery. In a Yeatsian turn of phrase that recalls "A Dream of Death," "the mother" appears before her son in Nighttown. She tells him a thinly disguised repetition of Yeats's figure: "I was once the beautiful May Goulding. I am dead" (*U* 580).

The Joycean turn on exile includes sin, and the virgin receives the Word—perfectly Catholic. But then the virgin grows corrupt. The temporal frame is out of alignment; the prayer for the dead points toward the Freudian abyss of Joyce's slip (Nora identified as "not yet virgin"). The dead woman is protected by the virgins and confessors because she is still caught in the corruption and horror of the flesh. Like

the messages attributed to Anna Livia Plurabelle at the end of the
Wake, the evoked form of the dead woman tells Stephen that she is
turned toward the father, but she is still thinking of bridal beauty and
the Fall. Between May Goulding's apparition and Anna Livia Plurabelle's signing off, Molly provides an ecstatic version of the same
Thing, finely balanced between Yeatsian Romanticism and the obscenity of corruption. The beginning, then, will have been invoked as
the moment of a "not yet" that can only be inscribed belatedly, after
it is too late for anything but reading and writing. Remembering leads
back to the beginning, when the "not yet" of the belated set the scene
for paradise.

PART II

The Two Loves

Eros weaver of myths,
Eros sweet and bitter,
Eros bringer of pain.
    —Sappho

3   *"Che Vuoi?"* Desire and the Seductions of Art

Les trois plus belles choses que Dieu ait faites c'est la mer, l'*Hamlet* et *Don Juan* de Mozart [The three most beautiful things that God made are the sea, *Hamlet*, and Mozart's *Don Giovanni*].

—Flaubert

The seduction duet from Mozart's *Don Giovanni* hovers in the sky of Leopold Bloom's thoughts throughout Joyce's *Ulysses*.[1] The adultery of Bloom's wife, Molly, is on his mind. Joyce's explicitly profane madonna figure (or ex-champion madonna heavyweight), Molly, sings the virgin's part of the duet in her fictional 1904 concert tour. The bride Zerlina and Don Giovanni, her seducer, sing "La ci darem la mano [there we will take hands]." The aria spirals through Joyce's novel; he alludes to it between thoughts, almost between the lines. Several lines of it are taken up in Bloom's meditation on Molly's art and Boylan's interest in her. *Ulysses* echoes Flaubert's *Madame Bovary* in a different constellation; Flaubert's allusions to Don Giovanni shape his rendering of the lures and obsessions of adultery in *Madame Bovary*, the first modernist novel.[2] Joyce integrates fragments of

---

[1] "Che vuoi?" (what do you desire?) is the question that Don Giovanni asks several times in the final act of the opera. He mocks Donna Elvira with the question when she appears before him in the last act.

[2] See Peter Brooks, *Body Work: Objects of Desire in Modern Narrative* (Cambridge: Harvard University Press, 1993); Tony Tanner, *Adultery in the Novel* (Baltimore: Johns Hopkins University Press, 1979); and Roger Kempf, *Sur le corps romanesque* (Paris: Seuil, 1968), 101–130. On *Madame Bovary*, see Rosemary Lloyd, *Madame Bovary* (Boston: Unwin Hyman, 1990); Gerald Prince, "On Attributive Discourse in *Madame Bovary*" in *Pretext Text Context: Essays in Nineteenth Century French Literature* (Columbus: Ohio State University Press, 1980), 268–275, and "A Narratological Approach to *Madame Bovary*" in *Approaches to Teaching Madame Bovary* (New

Mozart-Da Ponte within his portrayal of Bloom. *Ulysses* accentuates the plight of the betrayed husband and shifts the focus away from the feminine figure as the object of desire. Like Joyce writing approximately seventy years later, Flaubert never developed his emblematic and mysterious references to *Don Giovanni*. Like Flaubert, however, Joyce's character of Bloom obsessively admires the opera. It enters the writing of Modernism as the emblematic marker for Eros the bittersweet and the Other love. Between the lines, modernism stages Don Giovanni's seductions of its Madonnas, past and present.

Flaubert wrote to Louise Colet (who may have served as a model for some of Flaubert's fictional Madonna figures) that Mozart's *Don Giovanni* was one of the three most beautiful works created by God.[3] Although Flaubert's fascination with the opera left its traces only in a few letters and in an unfinished sketch for "Une Nuit de Don Juan,"[4]

York: Modern Language Association, 1995); Yvan Leclerc, *Crimes écrits: La littérature en procès au 19e siècle* (Paris: Plon, 1991), and "Comment une petite femme devient mythique," *Emma Bovary,* edited by Alain Buisine (Paris: Editions Autrement, 1997), 8–25; Dennis Porter, "*Madame Bovary* and the Question of Pleasure" in *Flaubert and Post-Modernism,* edited by N. Schor and H. Majewski (Lincoln: University of Nebraska Press, 1984), 116–138; Dominick LaCapra, *Madame Bovary on Trial* (Ithaca: Cornell University Press, 1982); Jacques Neefs, "L'espace d'Emma," *Women in French Literature* (Stanford: Anma Libri, 1988), 169–180, and "L'Illusion du sujet" in *Voix de l'écrivain: Mélanges offerts à Guy Sagnes,* edited by Jean-Louis Cabanès (Toulouse: Presse Universitaire du Mirail, 1996), 129–37; Stirling Haig, *The Madame Bovary Blues: The Pursuit of Illusion in Nineteenth-Century French Fiction* (Baton Rouge: Lousiana State University Press, 1987); Diana Knight, *Flaubert's Characters, the Language of Illusion* (Cambridge: Cambridge University Press, 1985); the essays collected in *Madame Bovary,* translated and edited by Paul de Man (New York: Norton, 1965); *Approaches to Teaching Madame Bovary,* edited by Laurence Porter and Eugene Gray (New York: Modern Language Association, 1995).

[3] See the chapter epigraph. Letter dated 3 October 1846, in *Correspondance,* edited by Jean Bruneau, vol. 1 (Paris: Gallimard, 1973), 373. All references to Flaubert's correspondence refer to this edition unless otherwise noted.

[4] Flaubert's text was rewritten for publication by Maupassant; the original manuscript is in the form of an unfinished sketch. A historical and genetic introduction accompany the critical text in Ulrich Mölk, *Flaubert, Une Nuit de Don Juan,* Nachrichten der Akademie der Wissenschaften in Göttingen, vol. 1, no. 8 (Göttingen: Philologisch-Historische Verlag, 1984). Quotations from Flaubert's published works refer to the two volumes of the "Bibliothèque de la Pléiade" edited by Albert Thibaudet and René Dumesnil as *Œuvres.* (Paris: Gallimard, 1951). I have also consulted the Garnier edition for variants, and the edition of *Madame Bovary* annotated by Pierre-Marc de Biasi (Seuil, 1992). For the early material on *Madame Bovary,* see Claudine Gothot-Mersch, *La Genèse de Madame Bovary* (Geneva: Slatkine Reprints, 1980); Gustave Flaubert, *Carnets de travail* critical and genetic edition by Pierre-Marc de Biasi (Paris: Editions Balland, 1988); *Une Nouvelle version de Madame Bovary,*

his plans to rewrite the Da Ponte version of the story focus on love, the central preoccupation of his major texts. Like Dante's Narrator at the end of the journey leading from *Inferno* to *Paradiso*, Flaubert is "revolved" by love. But unless Saint Julien's end is interpreted as Flaubert's narrative conclusion in the way that the final vision of Dante's Narrator ends the poetic journey of the *Commedia*, the love that haunts his writing has two forms. Flaubert's subject of love is split in two.

Flaubert's attempts to construct a framework of literary composition for the view that occupies his imagination throughout his writings lead to the repeated staging of the "earthly" and "mystical" forms of love. Its double status is based on the impossibility of reducing the two loves to a single one. Through fictional and poetic representations of the encounters between the two categories of love, Flaubert and Baudelaire formulate the style and the aesthetics of transromanticism. The two-fold invention of early modernism takes up the two categories of love elaborated in theology, philosophy, art, and literature.

The two loves are as heterogeneous as the human and divine natures of Christ. The profane and mystical forms of love that are represented in early modernism are the fruit of a conception of love that leads back, via Christianity, to Plato (and forward from Plato and Christianity to psychoanalysis). The two loves can occur separately, simultaneously, or alternately. In Flaubert's *Sentimental Education*, Frédéric experiences carnal and spiritual love at the same time but with two different objects; in Joyce's *Giacomo Joyce* and other works, the two loves cannot coincide, and love varies according to the moment rather than the object. Flaubert links the two categories of love through the dimension of the *inassouvissable* (the insatiable or unquenchable quality of desire). The *inassouvissable* resembles Baudelaire's interpretation of desire in terms of the infinite and the abyss,

---

edited by Jean Pommier and Gabrielle Leleu (Paris: Corti, 1949); and especially *Plans et scénarios de Madame Bovary*, presented, transcribed, and annotated by Yvan Leclerc. Repertory and genetic bibliography by Odile de Guidis and hypertext by Daniel Ferrer (Cadeilhan: Centre National de Recherche Scientifique (CNRS) Editions, 1995). See also the *Collection Textes et Manuscrits* directed by Louis Hay, including *Flaubert à l'oeuvre*, edited by Raymonde Debray Genette (Paris: Flammarion, 1980), and the *Collection Manuscrits Modernes*, directed by Beatrice Didier and Jacques Neefs.

the insatiable and the irretrievable. These terms link erotics with poetics, through the detour of the sublime, or Art with a capital A.

Che Vuoi?

In Flaubert, the *inassouvissable* is connected to the symptoms of "estrangement." Through mystical experience, including hallucination and the visions that appear to figures like Saint Anthony, estrangement leads from the *inassouvissable* of love to Art. The aesthetic counterpart of "estrangement" is the principle of calculated distance that separates the personal voice of the author from the written work.[5] Flaubert characterizes this distance as impassibility, impersonality, dandyism, the fatality of the Orient, the calm and emptiness of the Oriental woman, and the passionless artifice of the Egyptian *almée* (dancer and courtesan).[6] Baudelaire's emphasis on dandyism, impersonality, and aesthetic artifice produces a similar construction of calculated authorial distance. It resembles the attentive reserve or detachment of the psychoanalyst, with the addition of the concept of style.

The asymmetry of Flaubert's two loves is comparable to the asymmetry of Lacan's two "others." Lacan's "small a" is the desired object as a fragment implicated within relations of identity and competition. The "other" threatens to become the "same" in a scenario of fraternal rivalry.[7] The "big A" of the Other can only be revealed as a fragment, but it encompasses the Otherness of the other sex, the Otherness of the Freudian unconscious, and the Otherness of "parlêtre" [being through, in, and inseparable from language]. Lacan glosses the "big A" as truth, God, or language—the source of knowledge (*savoir*), mastery, and *jouissance* (enjoyment, rapture, ecstasy).[8]

The asymmetry of Lacan's two "others" is related to the two forms of jouissance found in love. Lacan filters Freud's interpretation of the

---

[5] This principle is essential to the aesthetic that I have termed trans-romanticism. See *The Orient of Style* (Durham: Duke University Press, 1991).

[6] See the letter to Colet dated 27 March 1853 *Correspondance*, vol. 2, 279–89.

[7] See René Girard, *La Violence et le sacré* (Paris: Grasset, 1972).

[8] Jacques Lacan, *Ecrits* (Paris: Seuil, 1966). See also Lacan's seminars published by Seuil, especially *L'Ethique* (1985) and *Encore* (1975). Extracts from the seminar on "Le Sinthome" and Joyce, first published in *Ornicar?*, have been edited by Jacques Aubert in *Joyce avec Lacan* (Paris: Navarin, 1987).

psychology of love, based on the tension between the profane and the sacred, through the baroque split between the flesh and the spirit. Lacan's psychology of love includes two different relationships to *savoir:* he associates phallic *jouissance* with a quest for knowledge, and with a total possession of the object. This impossible possession is linked to the ego and its *méconnaissance,* i.e. its mistakes in positing identity, its ignorance of the rules of desire, and its disregard for the powers of the unconscious. The "Other" *jouissance* is linked to the dissolving of the identifications established by the ego. They melt away in a *via negativa* of mysticism.

The *inassouvissable* links Flaubert's writing of love to Don Giovanni's question, *Che vuoi?* (What do you want?). Lacan marks the structure of the inverted articulation of desire with this question.[9] He illustrates the structure of the "subversion of the subject through a dialectic of desire" in an emblematic representation of language—a graph that includes its own emblem: *Che vuoi?* The Italian words that hover in the graph like the Latin inscriptions on sails, banners, and rolls of parchment floating in the air of Renaissance and Baroque painting inscribe Lacan's essay with the question of desire that Don Giovanni asks near the end of Mozart's opera.

The question asked by the seducer literally—or rather, grammatically—turns desire around. Addressed to the Commander, the representative of the Law, Don Giovanni's question challenges death and the Other world, where Don Giovanni sent Donna Anna's father when he killed him. It is precisely the Otherness of this "Other world," the realm of the dead, that is marked by its detachment from desire. Like the figures encountered by Dante's Narrator in the *Inferno,* these shades can only allegorize desire. The Statue of the Commander reminds Don Giovanni that the dead have no use for mortal enjoyments. The Dantean writing in the margins of Otherness makes it clear that only the highest power can overturn the horrors of Hell, the end of *jouissance,* and the permanence of unsatisfied desire. But Don Giovanni does not repent. The Love perceived by Dante's pilgrim is not on the agenda of the unrepentant Seducer who kills the father in an attempt to take the daughter.

According to Flaubert's conception, the *inassouvissable* bridges the gap between the two loves. Its counterpart in the realm of vocation,

---

[9] *Ecrits,* especially "Subversion du sujet et dialectique du désir danas l'inconscient freudien."

"estrangement," also bridges the gap between flesh and spirit. Their symptoms appear in the form of spectral and supernatural images. "Estrangement" and the *inassouvissable* point beyond the here and now to visions and hallucinations, in the theaters of the infinite and the invisible.

A reading of desire as *inassouvissable* recalls Freud's emphasis on literature, the source of many insights in psychoanalysis. Symptoms provide clues that must be decoded like the rhetorical figures of "le langage des fleurs et des choses muettes [the language of flowers and silent things]."[10] The three instances of Lacan's R.S.I. (the Real, the Symbolic, and the Imaginary) are knotted together in the symptom (or "sinthome"), Lacan's fourth instance. It is significant that Lacan posits the discovery of this fourth position in the margins of Joyce's *Ulysses.*

Lacan calls the symptom a "flower of the symbolic." As an expression of suffering and sin, Lacan's symptom-flower alludes to Baudelaire's "flowers of evil" as well as to Shakespeare's "Hamlet." When the ghost of Hamlet's father tells Hamlet that his brother Claudius murdered him in his sleep, he describes himself as "Cut off even in the blossoms of my sin" (I,V: 76). Hamlet's father is murdered in his orchard, a reminder of Eden and the expulsion from paradise; he is sleeping, wrapped in the silence of dreams and desire, far from repentance and last rites. In *Les Fleurs du Mal,* Baudelaire's conception of "le Mal" locates sin and desire in the context of modern beauty and its figures of the feminine, from the mystical rose of the Virgin Mary and Dante's Beatrice to the exiles wilting in urban landscapes. The Shakespearean blossoms anticipate the flowering of desire in language.

In Flaubert's novels, the *inassouvissable* shapes the figures of the feminine and their symptoms of sin and desire. The modernist aesthetic of evil is taken up in Joyce's strategy of the *felix culpa,* the happy sin of Adam in the garden of Eden. As a strategy, the *felix culpa* combines the sacred and the comic, horror and *jouissance.*[11] Like Beckett, Proust, Céline, Genet, Woolf, and other major modernists, Joyce takes as his point of departure in modern fiction Flaubert's new

---

[10] Baudelaire, "Elévation," *Œuvres Complètes,* vol. 1 (Paris: Galllimard, 1975), p. 10. My translation.

[11] See Schlossman, *Joyce's Catholic Comedy of Language* (Madison: University of Wisconsin Press, 1985) for a reading of Joyce's use of the paschal liturgy and the *felix culpa* in *Ulysses* and *Finnegans Wake.*

writing on love. Flaubert's vision of love as abjection and ecstasy is analogous to Baudelaire's poetics of spleen and the ideal.[12] Modernism is anchored in Flaubert's writing of the "Madame Bovary blues"[13] and in its poetic counterpart, Baudelaire's writing of melancholy. Although Flaubert lacked Baudelaire's Catholic convictions, the aesthetic consequences of Catholicism shaped Flaubert's view of the sublime, from raging desire to the blue sky of stained glass.

Flaubert's *Three Stories* and especially the allegory of Saint Julien crown the representations of *Madame Bovary*, *Salammbô*, and *The Sentimental Education;* the three versions of *The Temptation of Saint Anthony* are the pre-texts of *Saint Julien The Hospitator*. Flaubert's saints yearning for love in their wilderness and desert set the scene of a fantasmatic theater of desire. Joyce reshapes it in Dublin's Nighttown, before the night theater dissolves into the serial patterns of *Finnegans Wake*.

Although the sensational horrors of love appear to dominate the innovations of Modernism, Flaubert's *inassouvissable* has a long literary history. The itinerary of love before Modernism ranges from the spells cast on Tristan and Iseut in the Middle Ages to Stendhal's exploration of passion and desire. The *inassouvissable* shapes the strange encounters between the carnal and the mystical dimensions of love, its abject depths and sublime heights. Through the ambivalence of love, through an exploration of the cathedrals and labyrinths of desire, Freud takes aim at the literary "flowers of the symbolic." Psychoanalysis constructs a new kind of love story, and a new kind of reading. Not less than the modernists, Freud read in the "book of himself" where the dark underworld offers its allegorical image in art—the fresco of the Last Judgment painted by a "Signorelli." The painter's name must be conjured out of silence, reconstructed from the traces left by the repression of a terrifying and unbearable piece of knowledge that psychoanalysis calls truth. Like Osiris, whose remnants are put back together, like Finnegan who took a fall, the name of Signorelli emerges in the flowers of the symbolic.

The encounter between the two loves at the heart of Flaubert's fiction is mentioned in a letter to Louis Bouilhet on November 14, 1850,

---

[12] In *Pouvoirs de l'horreur* (Paris: Seuil, 1981), Julia Kristeva develops the concept of abjection in literature and psychoanalysis.

[13] See Stirling Haig, *Flaubert and the Gift of Speech* (Cambridge: Cambridge University Press, 1986).

when "A Night of Don Juan" is described as "l'amour inassouvissable sous les deux formes de l'amour terrestre et de l'amour mystique [unquenchable love in the two forms of terrestrial love and mystical love]."[14] Infinite and inexhaustible, the excess of love raises the stakes of desire to the dimensions of the *inassouvissable*. Mystical experiences comes face to face with an eroticism that cannot be dismissed by the superego of humor, the subversive conspirator of irony, the harlequin of farce, or the part-time murderer of comedy.

Anchored in a trans-romantic aesthetic, Flaubert's excess of love is reflected in the writing of Joyce's contemporary, Georges Bataille. Flaubert's principle of impersonality takes his portrayal of love beyond the limits of romantic sentiment. Bataille's reading of Hegel takes his representation of pornography over the borderline of x-rated entertainment and into the arena where philosophy meets the literature of evil, beginning with the marquis de Sade. In his "Preface to *Madame Edwarda*," Bataille challenges the taboo on eroticism legislated by the authorities of religion. Decency bans the representation of death and sexuality, and consigns them to the sacred: "Laughter engages us on the path where the principle of an interdiction, of necessary and inevitable decency, turns into closed hypocrisy and incomprehension of what is at stake. Extreme licentiousness linked to joking is accompanied by a refusal to take seriously—I mean: *tragically*—the truth of eroticism."[15]

In Molière and Mozart-Da Ponte, in Joyce and Bataille, the truth of eroticism unfolds in a tragicomic representation, where the question of desire takes the stage in the silence and song of *dramma giocoso*. Figured in the exchange of masculine and feminine identities between Bataille's Madame Edwarda and her nameless lover, the dialectics of subjectivity sweeps away the tearful sentiment and the indecent laughter of repression. Bataille's preface to his account of Eros explores the discursive scene of Plato's *Symposium* in the pornographic context of eroticism in modernity. Bataille renders explicit the dramatic and tragic stature of Eros in Mozart's *Don Giovanni* and in Flaubert's fictions of unquenchable love.

[14] Flaubert, *Correspondance*, 1:708.

[15] My translation. Bataille writes: "Le rire nous engage dans cette voie où le principe d'une interdiction, de décences nécessaires, inévitables, se change en hypocrisie fermée, en incompréhension de ce qui est en jeu. L'extrême licence liée à la plaisanterie s'accompagne d'un refus de prendre au sérieux—j'entends: *au tragique*—la vérité de l'érotisme." *Œuvres Complètes*, vol. 3 (Paris: Gallimard, 1971), p. 10.

Fireworks

The *inassouvissable* stops at nothing: it mixes the highs and lows, the enchantments and the blues, purity and sin, tenderness and violence. Under its influence, the power of memory enters the imagination and subverts the limits of time. Pleasure and pain metamorphose into each other. Innocence is unmasked and altered by corruption. In *Madame Bovary*, following the disappointment of her marriage, these changes occur in Emma because of Rodolphe. Flaubert's corrosive irony in the narrative treatment of his characters does not lessen the pain of love or the lyrical power of Emma's erotic awakening. Flaubert conceived Rodolphe as Emma's one and only 'real man.' The early version of the novel underlines Rodolphe's enduring effect on Flaubert's subject: "Toute la rancune d'Emma, peu à peu, s'assoupissait sous le charme de la force et de la virilité. Elle [se] souvint de l'autre dédaigneusement [all of Emma's rancor, little by little, faded under the spell of power and virility. She remembered the other with disdain]."[16] The other is Léon, the lover who turns into a second version of Charles at the end of their affair. By contrast, Rodolphe's cavalier and even "brutal" treatment, performed in the style of a slow-moving Don Giovanni, resonates with the same effect of erotic bondage that hovers between the lines of music and text in *Don Giovanni*. The pleasures of Emma's affair with Rodolphe catalyze a second transformation. Emma's new sensuality abruptly shifts to a sentimental attachment, leading from one form of love and jouissance to the other. The Other rises into the sublime blackness of love-letters.

Emma's early perception of Rodolphe as a mere type, a lover suitable for a married woman, unexpectedly turns into obsessive suffering. Flaubert's portrait of Rodolphe as a provincial rake emphasizes the banal vulgarity that clashes with Emma's Romantic idealization and sentiment. At the end of the novel, Emma offers herself to Rodolphe once again, this time in implicit exchange for money to avoid bankruptcy. This scene confirms Rodolphe's limitations but provokes the near-mystical scene of Emma's vision. Flaubert sustains the tension between the realist and the romantic elements. Rodolphe is the only character in the novel who remains an object of feminine desire beyond the early period of seduction. In this sense, Rodolphe's counterpart as an object of desire is Emma herself, in relation to Charles.

[16] See Leclerc, and Pommier and Leleu, 593.

Loved by her inept husband beyond the grave, she is the enduring object of masculine desire.

Emma's love for Rodolphe leads her into the mystical twilight state of "estrangement," the vertiginous depersonalization marked by vivid hallucinatory fireworks ["feux de Bengale"]. This voyage into the world of memory is illuminated by the infinitely multiplied image of the beloved, frequently inscribed in Flaubert's writings:

> Il lui sembla tout à coup que des globules couleur de feu éclataient dans l'air comme des balles fulminantes en s'aplatissant, et tournaient, tournaient, pour aller se fondre sur la neige, entre les branches des arbres. Au milieu de chacun d'eux, la figure de Rodolphe apparaissait. Ils se multiplièrent, et ils se rapprochaient, la pénétraient; tout disparut.

> [It suddenly seemed that balls the color of fire were bursting in the air like flaming explosives flattening out, and whirling, whirling, to melt on the snow, among the branches of the trees. In each one, Rodolphe's face appeared. They multiplied and they came closer, penetrating her: everything disappeared].[17]

Emma's mystical fireworks seem to disappear in snow or to melt into the white page of scenery, between the lines, in a text-frame of visionary experience. The image of the beloved that enters the autonomous circles of fire like a picture in a moving frame is a single face; Rodolphe's image is named as a figure. The rhetoric of this "other" face—an image that cannot be naturalized—is dramatized in the scene of Emma's silent vision. The fiery globes of memory suddenly appear as portrait frames that reproduce the figure of desire. Their multiplication is rhetorically figured by a cascade of verbs in the imperfect. The mystical fireworks of memory end with the disappearance of the images of flames and faces. Nothing is left, after Emma's crisis of desire consumes her. The economic aspect of *Madame Bovary* concurs with the mystical quality of Emma's vision of her lover. The visit to Rodolphe that provokes Emma's hallucination is a desperate attempt to revive his desire for her and find the money to pay her debts.

The drama of fantasmagoric images and emptiness ends with the financial equivalent of "everything disappeared." Flaubert's scenario

---

[17] *Madame Bovary,* vol. II, viii, 577. My translation.

of mystical vision is mediated by a narrative frame representing bour-geois modernity. Emma's crisis is overdetermined. Her financial crisis allows Flaubert to mediate the mystical element of his portrayal of a provincial virgin through the frame of bourgeois modernity recom-mended by Maxime Du Camp. Emma's expenditure provides Flaubert with an ironic and realist motive for his account of her mystical ex-perience of love. In this double frame of modern subjectivity, Flau-bert's characterization of the merchant Lheureux blurs the distinction between the registers of earthly and spiritual love. He tempts Emma with the fantasmagoria of fashion and beautiful objects that fuel her search for pleasure. A small-time master of desire, Lheureux is Flau-bert's pedlar of the sublime.

Flaubert posits an economy of insatiable desire that produces only emptiness. It is underscored by reveries of happiness. This economy veils the mystical experience of love by motivating it within a Balza-cian portrayal of social life and Flaubert's new principle of modernist verisimilitude central to the composition of his new novel.[18] Empti-ness and absence related to "estrangement" frame Emma's loss of Rodolphe. In the tragicomic fiction of failed mystical aspirations and florid sentimentality, Flaubert inscribes the desire that takes Emma over the edge. The effect of Rodolphe's Donjuanism gives Emma's sui-cide a new taste, a mouthful of modernism. The novel draws a fine line between the low and the high, the sensual vulgarity of Rodolphe, and the virginal sublime mysticism that Flaubert imagined as the pre-textual version of Emma. Rodolphe's effect on Emma is as powerful as the singular seduction that marks Kierkegaard's writings, or as the three seductions that occur in Mozart's *Don Giovanni*.[19] The objects of seduction in Flaubert's project echo the characteristics of Don Gio-vanni's virgins: Donna Elvire, the girl seduced in a convent; Donna Anna, the aristocratic fiancée; and Zerlina, the peasant bride.

Flaubert's framework of sex and the sublime emphasizes Don Gio-vanni's seduction of Donna Anna at the beginning of the Mozart

[18] In "La Poésie du mal chez Balzac," *L'Année balzacienne* (1963), 321–35, Max Milner discusses the connections between Flaubert's study of *moeurs* and Balzac's fiction.

[19] Søren Kierkegaard, "Journal of a Seducer" in *Either/Or* (Princeton: Princeton University Press, 1970). Kierkegaard devotes many pages of *Either/Or* to exploring the effects of Don Giovanni. The opera focuses on the seduction of Donna Anna and Donna Elvira, followed by the ongoing attempt to seduce Zerlina. Both of the aristo-cratic women react with a range of effects that include the sublime of mysticism.

opera. In "A Night of Don Juan," the virginal object of desire appears as "la soeur Thérèse [the nun Theresa]" and then "Anna Maria." Named for the mystical saint or for the Blessed Virgin and her mother, she foreshadows Emma in *Madame Bovary*, described on the first page of the first scenario as "Marie (. . .) élevée au couvent à Rouen [Marie raised in a convent in Rouen]."[20] Donna Elvire is briefly mentioned and then dismissed. While Flaubert's emphasis on the figure of Donna Anna is typical of Romantic portrayals,[21] his sketch also includes many features of Don Juan according to Molière and Da Ponte; the romantics repressed the darker sides of the libertine in favor of a more idealized and heroic image. "A Night of Don Juan" evokes an original reformulation of the baroque Don Juan. Flaubert integrates a transromantic spirituality of meditation, melancholy, and memory within the inherited framework of Don Juan or Don Giovanni. Flaubert's Don Juan sketch preserves the scandal attached to Don Giovanni—his sublime aesthetic of artifice in the service of unethical, desentimentalized carnal love. Based on the amoral imperative of desire, Don Giovanni's strategic constructions lead him toward the *inassouvissable* of violence and the sublime, the carnal and the mystical.

The Don Juan of Molière and Mozart-Da Ponte demonstrates that the seductions of art—beautiful representations and bel canto—attain the heights of sublimation without surrendering the drives to the law of repression. Art cannot be interpreted as a sexual act, but sublimation implies that the seductive powers of art originate in Eros. Don Giovanni elaborates both forms of seduction when he sings his nocturnal serenade in Act II of the opera. "Deh vieni alla finestra" employs sublime singing in the service of desire. The familiar images of the bitter-sweetness of love borrowed from rhetorical tradition are sustained by the lyrical power of the melody and its mandoline accompaniment.

Don Juan's power of seduction originates in Tirso de Molina's sadistic Burlador. His practice of seduction inverts the cultural hierarchy that posits the value of the sublime as superior to sexuality. Don Juan uses the sublime to attain sexual satisfaction. The violence implicated in this reversal is cultural as well as social. Don Juan's social status adds to his authority and his freedom to commit violence, but does not explain or motivate the erotic spell that he casts. However,

---

[20] See Leclerc.
[21] See Jean Rousset, *Le Mythe de Don Juan* (Paris: Colin, 1974).

when the moments of magic and pure music come to an end too soon, he resorts to rape.

Act I of Mozart's opera begins with a double denunciation of Don Juan's violence. The valet Leporello sings a comic refusal to serve his master.[22] Donna Anna chases Don Giovanni and denounces his attempted seduction. Leporello accuses his master of raping Donna Anna, but her angry scene with Don Giovanni as well as her later account of the incident contradict Leporello's conclusion. She probably remains a virgin, and her father dies at the hand of the irate intruder.

Leporello's self-interest undercuts his moral critique of his master; he rebels against the Seducer's hybris and his infinite "aspirations." Don Giovanni's dark presence in Donna Anna's bedroom forms the primary scene of the opera. From her perspective, Eros the bittersweet is overpowering, with a suggestion of *jouissance* inseparable from suffering, rapture inseparable from rape, and love connected with the murder of the father. The violence of love is exposed in the horror of the father's brutal death (a consequence of the Seducer's forced intrusion) and the ambiguous attraction that Don Giovanni will hold for Donna Anna. Her beloved father is murdered while defending her honor, and her devoted fiancé attempts heroism on her behalf. She alternates despairing melancholy and a thirst for revenge, but it is Don Giovanni's magical attraction that keeps her running after him. The mysterious initial darkness in Anna's bedroom forms the primal scene that continues to agitate audiences. The Overture shapes a musical dialogue between erotic attraction and dark terror that expresses the invisible scene. The music shapes the two strands of love (lyric tenderness and violent, tumultuous, or raging desire) that alternate throughout the Master's seductions. The division of love into two (or the alternation between love's two strands) is sustained in the feminine registers. Donna Elvira's shrill anger gives way to the tenderness of Christian charity following her conversion, and Donna Anna's oscillation between tender mourning and a desperate pursuit of vengeance resonates according to the two feminine voices of Donna Elvira's love for Don Giovanni. Mozart's music reveals the power of desire that the character of Donna Anna (and her benighted fiancé, the hopelessly weak but lyrically expressive Don Ottavio) cannot recognize: Donna Anna's unspeakable and unavowed fascination for the

---

[22] The *Non serviam* of Stephen Dedalus in *Ulysses* recalls Leporello ("non voglio più servir") via Lucifer.

intruder who murders her father after trying to make love to her. Donna Anna has no choice but to mistake this desire for something else—an obsessive desire for revenge and an all-consuming love for the Commander, her father. From the alternation of lyrical melody and suspenseful dramatic tension in the overture until Don Giovanni's unrepentant end, the magic of desire and the abyss of death polarize the two loves.

Through its split formulation of love, the opera represents the extremes of the erotic sublime. The supernatural is evoked to represent the Law of the Father through the Commander who conquers Don Giovanni from beyond the grave and consigns him to the flames of Hell, but the rest of the story does not need the literary conventions of the fantastic. Its depiction of desire is fantastic enough—its verisimilitude or "realism" underlines the subversive power of Eros according to Don Giovanni. For Flaubert, this power is rendered as corruption.

In the Don Juan sketch, Flaubert's term of "corruption" is repeated each time aesthetic artifice is suggestive of eroticism. French definitions of *corrompre* include "decompose," "alter," "denature," "pervert," and "deprave." Baudelaire's poem entitled "Une Charogne" also explores corruption from the erotic-aesthetic perspective of modernism. The illusions of love have vanished. The corpse is scandalously and frighteningly real, but the poem transforms it into an allegorical object of meditation. In this sense, early modernism maintains the baroque vision of Molière, Mozart, and Da Ponte. Baudelaire and Flaubert locate the common ground between eroticism and aesthetics within the frame of modernist allegory. In contrast to the romantic revisionist readings of Don Giovanni, they do not provide him with a monogamous love story, a new reverence for the fair sex, or a happy ending.

In addition to its focus on corruption, the mystical emphasis of Flaubert's sketch reflects the early modernist emphasis on an aesthetic of excess. Mysticism appears in a passage that blends realism and the fantastic: "le moins heurté possible—sans qu'on puisse distinguer le fantastique du réel [with the fewest possible shifts of movement, so that the fantastic cannot be distinguished from the real]."[23] Flaubert's story shifts the emphasis from Don Juan to Anna Maria (or

---

[23] Mölk, *Flaubert, Une Nuit de Don Juan,* 19.

Theresa), the mystical heroine, in an exploration of feminine *jouissance* (Lacan's "Other enjoyment"). Her name probably alludes to the mystic writer, Saint Teresa of Avila. Flaubert's feminine figure is temporarily resurrected from her deathbed by Don Juan; she is suspended in a night of love and mysterious revelations, a supernatural wake that artificially revives her until dawn. The sketch begins with her death and Don Juan's flight: "La soeur Thérèse allait mourir [Sister Teresa was going to die] (. . .) Deux hommes descendent de cheval [Two men get off their horses]."[24] The symmetry of departures and separations brings into relief the moment of unity. "L'objet principal c'est l'union, l'égalité, la dualité, dont chaque terme a été jusqu'ici incomplet, se fusionnant [the primary object is union, equality, duality of terms, each one incomplete until now, when they combine in fusion]."[25] Otherwise impossible, the combined carnal and mystical love between Don Juan and the virginal nun has lasting effects. "Ce qu'elle avait donné à Don Juan ne périt pas quand la statue du Commandeur l'engouffra [What she gave to Don Juan did not perish when the Commander's statue swallowed him into the abyss]."[26] Flaubert's virginal feminine sublime is indestructible, and resists hell itself. The magical love of Anna Maria shapes her into a figure of the Madonna.

The mystical communion includes the pleasure of the flesh ("volupté") that obsesses the pure Anna Maria. Flaubert accounts for her perspective in Don Juan's reaction to it. "Comment se fait-il que je désire et qu'elle désire ce qu'elle ne sait pas? [how can it be that I desire and that she desires something that she does not know?]."[27] She does not recognize her own desire, disguised in the sinless variations of eroticism. "Désirs fréquents qu'elle a de la communion—avoir Jésus dans le corps—Dieu en soi [Her frequent desires for communion—to have Jesus in your body—God inside you]."[28] In anticipation of Emma, she is unsatisfied. She wonders why Christ does not answer her love; she enters the abyss of eroticism that Flaubert names the *inassouvissable*, the sensual and mystical point of no return for Flaubert's Don Juan and his madonnas of modernism.

[24] Ibid., 19.
[25] Ibid., 25.
[26] Ibid., 19.
[27] Ibid., 21.
[28] Ibid., 25.

In a letter written in Patras to his friend Bouilhet, Flaubert says
that he has been thinking a lot about his Night of Don Juan while trav-
eling on horseback.[29] The paths of sensual and mystical love cross:
Flaubert anticipates the flights of his Seducer, riding away on horseback after each new conquest. The identities of Don Juan, the rake
who seeks the carnal love of all women, and Anna Maria, the pure
mystical nun who has died a virgin, will be transformed in the physical and mystical communion that unites them. This passage of Flaubert's sketch takes the rhetorical form of a chiasmus. Anna Maria has
"aspirations toward the flesh and true love (as a complement to mystical love) parallel to the voluptuous aspirations of Don Juan, who
had, in his other loves, especially at the moment of lassitude, mystical needs."[30] Don Juan's desires veer toward mysticism, while Anna
Maria's passion includes the desire for the happiness of women who
sin. Don Juan's carnal appetite mysteriously pales—love suddenly
disgusts him, while Anna Maria's mortifications unexpectedly turn
the effect of "disgusting things" into pleasure ("volupté").[31]

Flaubert's account of their "perfect communion" posits the sacrament as a metaphor for love. He reverses the religious hierarchy of values by perfecting Anna Maria's cult of desire through a supernatural
consummation of love. According to the erotic sensibility that influences Flaubert's major characters, jouissance and suffering (or "bitterness," a favored Flaubertian term for suffering) are inseparable. For
this reason, Flaubert attributes Don Juan's superiority to his sensibility and his desire itself. Virtue and vice melt together in perfect communion. The early version of *Madame Bovary* reveals that Rodolphe's
brutal treatment of Emma elevates her into a superior being, devoured
by love. Emma develops the combination of sensuality and sublime
love ("haut amour") that characterizes the aesthetic-erotic sensibility
marked by the *inassouvissable*. The Eros of Flaubert's madonnas of
modernism is sweet and bitter. Like the beauty and terror that inhabit
the realm of the sublime, the two cannot be separated. In two of Flaubert's early scenarios, Madame Bovary incarnates the double nature of
Eros. Flaubert translates the aesthetic-erotic code of the dandy into a
feminine figure who reflects his own sensibility. "Elle jouit et souffre
de tout parfums, fleurs, nourriture, vin—elle fait longuement sa toi-

[29] 10 February 1851, *Correspondance*, vol. 1, 750.
[30] Mölk, *Flaubert, Une Nuit de Don Juan*, 24.
[31] Ibid., 25.

lette—elle frémit de volupté en sentant lorsqu'elle se peigne ses cheveux tomber sur ses épaules—elle ne porte plus que de la baptiste [sic]
[everything gives her enjoyment and suffering: perfumes, flowers,
food, wine—she grooms herself slowly—she shivers with voluptuous
pleasure in combing her hair when she feels it fall on her shoulders—
she wears only cotton batiste]."[32]

Fictions of Love

Flaubert shapes the project of "A Night of Don Juan" as an encounter
between the two forms of love. Don Juan represents the *inassouvissable* that originates in Flaubert's figure of the feminine. As Lacan observes in *Encore* the erotically ambitious libertine embarks on the
conquest of an infinite series of women, taken one by one.[33] The emphasis on the One is supported by Don Juan's tendency to take each
partner only once. While the master's valet (Sganarelle or Leporello)
thinks that all women are the same, the libertine distinguishes one
object from another. In Molière's play as well as in Flaubert's sketch,
Don Juan describes his jealousy in love.[34] Unlike Casanova, whose
fantasies lead toward undifferentiation and sexual disguise, Don Juan
or Don Giovanni is engaged in a series of one to one encounters, inscribed in the Catalog, the list of names. These singular identities are
the source of Don Juan's seductions in Molière's play, in the Mozart
opera, and in Flaubert's sketch.

The portrayals of Don Juan and his objects seem to blend together
in Flaubert's pre-texts. The three projects evoked in his letter anticipate his exploration of love in the three major novels of early Modernism. He complains that the three projects may be a single work:
the novel of the Flemish girl who dies a mystical virgin ("mon roman
flamand de la jeune fille qui meurt vierge et mystique"); the story
of Anubis, the woman who desires a god ("l'histoire d'*Anubis*, la
femme qui veut se faire baiser par le Dieu"); and the "Night of Don
Juan."[35] Flaubert's idea of a Flemish virgin is suggestive of certain
typecast images of the Virgin in Flemish painting. One type is the
pale simple figure with upturned eyes, evoked by Joyce in *Dubliners*;

---

[32] Leclerc, 10. Flaubert crossed out the words "et souffre."
[33] See chapter 4, "Encore Performances: The End of Don Giovanni." Lacan, 15, 116.
[34] "Dom Juan ou le festin de pierre," Act 1, Scene 2.
[35] *Correspondance*, vol. 1, 708.

5. Juan de Flandes, *The Annunciation*, c. 1508–19, oil and tempera on wood.
Courtesy of the National Gallery of Art.

an example of this type is visible in *The Annunciation* by Juan de Flandes (1508–19).

Another type that Flaubert may have had in mind corresponds to the dark-haired figures that haunted him in paintings by Murillo. Although Flaubert associates the Murillo Virgin with the exotic passion of Spain and the Orient, the same type can be seen in the Flemish paintings of Anthony van Dyke. With its erect figure of the Virgin Mary in white, its roses and putti, small angelic versions of Eros, *The Assumption* is a very different portrayal of the mystical Flemish virgin (1628–29). The three projects elaborate a concept of sexual and spiritual love. Flaubert's sketch marks a shift in the dominant poetics of his writing. Joyce's pre-Ulyssean text of *Giacomo Joyce* makes a similar shift, with strikingly similar preoccupations—seduction, Don Juan, and the two loves. Through the relation between the claims of the flesh and the heights of the sublime, these shifts in writing lead to the madonnas of modernism.

The relation between earthly and mystical love dominates Flaubert's examination (or dissection) of the heart, the focus of his writing. The pivotal articulation of the *inassouvissable* that connects the two loves brings the heart into Flaubert's "marinade" of desire, a workshop of revery and rewriting. The *inassouvissable* draws the subject into the Other world, where desire goes beyond Freud's pleasure principle, based on the repetition of a limited satisfaction.[36]

Beyond the pleasure principle, the seemingly opposed dimensions of earthly and mystical are reconciled within the frame of eroticism and the sublime that originates in Plato's *Symposium*. Freud makes an explicit connection between Plato and psychoanalysis in his discussion of Eros. Lacan follows Freud's lead, and locates the beginnings of a psycho-analytic theory of love in the *Symposium*. The romantic "heart" is the fantasmatic organ of the subject's passion; the encounter between the two loves unfolds in the heart through writing.

The passionate subject suffers pain and pleasure. Desire and ideal love meet in the suffering of passion, from the Latin *passio*. "Platonic love," an epithet that would have amused Socrates, is the name of a relationship that dances on the edge of the volcano while remaining

---

[36] Sigmund Freud, *Drei Abhandlungen zur Sexualtheorie, Gesammelte Werke* (Frankfurt am Main: S. Fischer Verlag, 1960–), vol. 5; *Three Essays on Sexuality, Standard Edition of the Complete Psychological Works*, edited by James Strachey, vol. 7 (London: Hogarth Press and the Institute of Psychoanalysis, 1953–1974).

6. Anthony van Dyke, *The Assumption*, c. 1628–29, oil on canvas. Courtesy of the National Gallery of Art.

faithful to the ideal. If the narrator of *Giacomo Joyce* had been less conscious of the sexual elements of his passion for the idealized figure of the bourgeois Jewish virgin, then he might have pursued in relative silence the pleasures and renunciations of Platonic love. In this case, the pre-text of *Ulysses* might not have been written.

The development of a narrative poetics of love is partially obscured by the claims of biography, emphasized in the context of Joyce's pre-text. The discourse of psychoanalysis challenges biography's claims to tell the truth about a life. Given Joyce's modernist taste for veiled self-inscription, the claims of biography blur the borderlines between life and writing. Freud problematizes the biographical claim to authenticity in these terms.

> Whoever becomes a biographer sets himself up for lying, hushing things up, hypocrisy, whitewashing, and even for hiding his own lack of understanding, because biographical truth cannot be had, and if one had it, it could not be used. Truth has no accessible path, men don't deserve it, and besides, isn't Prince Hamlet right, when he asks whether anyone would escape whipping if he were treated according to his just deserts?[37]

Freud's interpretation of the impossibility of biography in itself is equally valid for the application of biographical insights to a work of literature. The textual economy of *Giacomo Joyce* speaks for itself, without the necessity of defending biographical authenticity.

The split between desire and love haunts the territory of the speaking subject from Plato to Freud and Lacan. In the *Symposium*, the split is developed through a layered succession of narratives in indirect discourse. At the greatest remove from the outer narrative frame, in the dialogue's most indirect discourse, the brilliant, unrepeated lightning flash of the exotic one speaks for the feminine. The prophetic stranger, as she is called, the Exotic one bears the mysterious femininity that speaks in Socrates' discourse. She is Diotima, the erotic Other. Hölderlin will celebrate her in the nineteenth century but without the sexual and prophetic power that indirectly takes her into the masculine world of the *Symposium*.

The *Symposium* posits a relation between the forms of love; it places them in a continuous hierarchy. This connection between desire and love seems to have been dissolved by the Father—the Libidinous God named in *Giacomo Joyce*, the terrifying God of Abraham, Isaac, and Jacob—who banished the idols of polytheism. Unlike classical antiquity, the stage for the gods and the range of their passions, modernity blocks the relation between desire and love. Exemplified by the sensational violence of conversion hysteria, the effects of Victorian morality confronted Freud with this blockage. Historically, psychoanalysis originates in the need to develop a cure for the victims of modernity.

---

[37] Sigmund Freud, Letter to Arnold Zweig dated 31 May 1936 in *Briefe 1973–1939* (Frankfurt am Main: S. Fischer Verlag, 1980), p. 445. My translation.

The distance between Socrates and Freud can be measured in religious terms, but the subject of Modernism combines a Christian perspective with secularization. Christianity enthrones the God of the Old Testament, but the rage is gone. He no longer sacrifices his own people. A discourse of love and death arises around the Son who has been sacrificed on their behalf. Psychoanalysis and literature raise the question of how to bridge the gap between Socratic midwifery and the discontentedness of modernity. The successful incest between the Son and the Virgin resonates in the framework of love posited by Socrates and the virtual priestess, Diotima, who speaks with his tongue. The Christian mediation allows the body of the mother to return to the surface.

A compromise between Judaism and paganism, the Virgin Mary is sanctified by dogmas and liturgical forms that appear in the Middle Ages. She incarnates the Otherness of the sacred and the uncanny articulation of eroticism that Socrates located in Diotima. But sexual mastery is not on the Virgin's agenda. The attribution of sexuality to Christ's mother sounds blasphemous. Artistic and theological evidence, however, seems to overturn the condemnation of Marian eroticism as scandalous. In *The Sexuality of Christ in Renaissance Art and in Modern Oblivion*, Leo Steinberg explores the medieval and Renaissance iconography of Christ and Mary as "a couple embraced in reclining position in the marital act" evoked in Canticles 2:6:

> The words were understood to refer to the consummation of physical love as a figure for the spiritual. Origen, (. . .) setting the course for all subsequent Christian interpretations of Canticles, weaves back and forth between the literal sense and the mystic: 'His left hand is under my head, and his right hand shall embrace me.' The picture before us in this drama of love is that of the Bride hastening to consummate her union with the Bridegroom.[38]

Steinberg suggests that the symbol of amorous union is used in the visual arts to convey both literal and mystical connotations. Affirmed through liturgical, patristic, and apocryphal texts, Mary's mystical virginity allows desire and the flesh to enter the territory of the sublime. Under cover of the sublime, the tradition of religious painting illustrates mysticism through sensual images. The loving tenderness

---

[38] (New York: Pantheon/October Books, 1983), 113.

that unites Mary with the handsome resurrected Christ in Agnolo Gaddi's "Coronation of the Virgin" (1370) is a consequence of the twelfth-century cult of Mary. In Vittore Carpaccio's *Flight into Egypt* (1500), the Madonna and Child ride under the watchful gaze of Joseph, in the pose of amorous union that Steinberg attributes to Origen; a beautifully veiled Virgin is shown in a physical and mystical embrace with the child Christ.

Mary submits to an "overshadowing" will, although, strangely enough, she appears to be ignorant of its identity. Her submission— and her ignorance, or mystical unknowing—are unreserved. The ignorance that Flaubert's Don Juan discovered in his figure of the Virgin echoes the scene of the Annunciation. Mary's gesture shapes the Christian sublime. Christianity takes its distance from Diotima's occult mastery and erotic teachings, but the Modernist aesthetic of the two loves includes both figures of the feminine. In the virtual space of the pivotal *inassouvissable* that connects the two loves, fiction and psychoanalysis shape the figures of Don Juan and his feminine objects.

The opposition between the two loves has been stated frequently in other terms, including Eros and Agapé, and the Christian poles of sin and grace. Early modernism undresses the traditional dichotomy of body and soul, or carnal desire and spiritualized love, to reveal the complicity that inhabits it. The heart (Baudelaire's naked heart, "Mon Coeur mis a nu") is the site for the modernist articulation of the link between the two: the complicity of the two loves, the complicity of erotics and poetics, lead back to their point of origin in Plato's text.

In the *Symposium,* the opposition is reflected in the division between the two Venuses, between men and women, between the lover and the beloved. Fictional frames, blurred identities, and divisions of jealous passion multiply at a dizzying rate around them. In addition to the splitting and doubling, however, the Dionysian ecstasy that marks the text subverts fixed identity and sweeps away clear oppositions. As the dialogue unfolds, allusions to banquet revelry introduce the irreducible Otherness that marks Socrates' intervention. He conjures up the Dionysian sea of desire, and he alone does not dissolve in its spell. The *mise en abyme* of the dialogue within a dialogue projects the figure of Socrates into a virtual space of desire and emptiness, comedy and tragedy. Eros the bittersweet takes form in the night of intoxication.

Socrates invokes Diotima, the "feminine stranger" who is his double. Her position of mastery is transferred later to Socrates himself

7. Agnolo Gaddi, *Coronation of the Virgin*, 1370, tempera on panel. Courtesy of the National Gallery of Art.

8. Vittore Carpaccio, *The Flight into Egypt,* 1500, detail, oil on panel. Courtesy of the National Gallery of Art.

in the discourse of Alcibiades. She reveals the identity of Eros as fundamentally divided—between Beauty and Poverty, acquisitive scheming and philosophy, mortality and immortality, wealth and poverty, and ignorance and wisdom.[39] Diotima is the only feminine speaker quoted in the discussion; Socrates submitted to her teaching—or her talking cure—to remedy his declared ignorance about love. Socrates claims that Diotima unveiled to him alone the origins of the divided figure of Eros, represented as the child of the allegorical figures of Poverty and Plenty.

When Socrates takes the floor, Plato ends the ironic presentation of the easy rhetorical flourishes that occur in several of the early speeches in the dialogue. At the projected source of love, the closer the text gets to something like truth, the more disquieting—and mysteriously dissseminating—appear the signs of Eros. These signs

[39] Quotations refer to Shelley's translation, in *Shelley on Love,* edited by Richard Holmes (Berkeley: University of California Press, 1980). Diotima's revelation of Eros occurs in passage 203.

transgress boundaries. They overflow onto the pages of literature, starting with Socrates' fictions and a prophetess whose secret knowledge originates in her ability to obtain the favor of the gods. Her mastery of love is anchored in the Other, and anticipates the unconscious. Diotima knows how to get answers to the question of desire (*Che vuoi?*) addressed to the gods. The love talk of sacrifice finds favor with them. She saves the Athenians from the plague for ten years.[40]

Diotima's discourse is relayed and estranged in a tragi-comic mode by Alcibiades, who claims to be in love with Socrates. His narrative describes the philosopher as sublime, asexual, lacking in external beauty, and yet passionately loved. Socrates is the Silenus who contains images of divine virtue beneath (or inside) a grotesque exterior form. Alcibiades confirms the connection between Diotima and Socrates. Socrates contains the invisible secrets of love. Eros turns the tables on Alcibiades, the beloved object who turns into the subject of passion, the lover. In his confessional account of the effects of love, Alcibiades recognizes the misery of the lover that afflicts him.

From the ancients to the moderns, enjoyment mingles with suffering. The words of the beloved enchant the lover: "I have suffered from his words, and suffer still. When I hear him speak, my heart leaps up (. . .) my tears are poured out."[41] The power of music has turned into language. This declaration of love could be applied to an infinite number of love objects. The beloved "surely ought to be obeyed, even like the voice of a god." The speaker is neither Saint Teresa of Avila nor a serenaded conquest of Don Giovanni, although the lament and praise of the effects of Eros pay homage to the most superior and the most beautiful of all objects. With these words, Alcibiades offers himself to Socrates, the ultimate master of love.

[40] Ibid., p. 147.
[41] Ibid., p. 163.

4 Encore Performances: The End of Don Giovanni

Par vous, Marie, je serai fort et grand. Comme Pétrarque, j'immortaliserai ma Laure. Soyez mon ange gardien, ma Muse et ma Madone, et conduisez-moi dans la route du Beau.

Through you, Mary, I will be strong and great. Like Petrarch, I will immortalize my Laura. Be my guardian angel, my Muse, and my Madonna, and lead me down the road of the Beautiful.

—Baudelaire

In the play by Tirso de Molina, "El Burlador de Sevilla, y convidado de piedra [The Trickster of Seville]" (1630), the master subject of desire takes the form of Don Juan Tenorio, an insatiable trickster-lover.[1] The figure of Don Juan occupies dozens of literary works in many languages (Spanish, French, Italian, English, German, Danish, and Russian) and in several genres: tragicomedy, opera (including *commedia* and *dramma giocoso*), narrative, pantomime, essay, and verse.[2] From

---

[1] Tirso de Molina, *Obras*, edited by Américo Castro, vol. 1 (Madrid: Espasa-Calpe, 1932). For an English translation, see Oscar Mandel, *The Theater of Don Juan: A Collection of Plays and Views, 1630–1963* (Lincoln: University of Nebraska Press, 1963).

[2] My reading of a Modernist Don Juan focuses on the specifically literary quality of Don Juan, within a constellation of love subjects and objects. Following the first edition of the important book by Giovanni Macchia, *Vita, avventure et morte di Don Giovanni*, 2d ed. (Torino: Giulio Einaudi editore, 1978), Jean Rousset's structuralist study interprets Don Juan as a myth rather than a specifically literary figure, and recent works on Don Juan tend to accept the definition of Don Juan as myth. See Jean Rousset, *Le Mythe de Don Juan* (Paris: Librairie Armand Colin, 1968). Rousset's study includes an extensive bibliography of primary and secondary literature. Other useful bibliographies can be found in Armand Edwards Singer, *A Bibliography of the Don Juan Theme* published by the *West Virginia University Bulletin* (1954), with supplements appearing periodically beginning in 1956; Leo Weinstein, *The Metamorphoses*

the perspective of modernism, the most important elements of the Don Juan tradition include (1) Molière's "Dom Juan ou le festin de pierre" (1665); (2) Mozart's *Don Giovanni* (Prague, 1787), with a libretto by Lorenzo da Ponte;[3] and (3) E. T. A. Hoffmann's novella *Don Juan* (1813), translated into French by H. Egmont in 1836. Lord Byron's *Don Juan* is of undeniable importance, especially for Romanticism, but its emphasis on a single character and its light, satirical tone do not fit the baroque dramatic framework of Molière or Mozart. The modernist return to baroque tradition shapes Don Juan's objects of desire, the feminine figures who appear as Madonnas of Modernism.

In French Romanticism, Don Juan (or Don Giovanni, the Italian form of his name associated with Mozart's operatic version) is evoked in the writings of Musset, Mérimée, Gautier, and Sand. Modernism puts aside the Romantic autobiographical and Byronic Don Juan; instead, it accentuates the feminine in its account of baroque Eros. Don Giovanni's objects of desire appear as subjects of love, outside religious and secular institutions (the convent and marriage). Early modernism approaches Don Juan or Don Giovanni from the margins of its new subjectivity, characterized by a focus on the artifices of style, a taboo on the unmediated representation of the author as subject, and an emphasis on the feminine.

In the writings of Flaubert (who revered Mozart's *Don Giovanni*) and Baudelaire (who admired the opera and especially the Molière play), Don Juan makes brief appearances.[4] Except for one of *Les Fleurs du Mal* entitled "Don Juan aux Enfers [Don Juan in the Underworld]," the privileged figure of Baroque imagination and speculation remains behind the scenes of early French Modernism. Although Don Juan is absent from the catalogue of major works by Flaubert and Baudelaire that establish their shared invention of Modernism, he led each of them toward an encounter with opera. While their predecessors contributed to the variations on the Don Juan "legend" with a series of

---

of *Don Juan* (Stanford: Stanford University Press, 1959); *Don Juan: Darstellung und Deutung*, edited by Brigitte Wittmann (Darmstadt: Wissenschaftliche Buchgesellschaft, 1976); and the special issues of *Obliques* devoted to Don Juan, no. 4 (1974) and no. 5 (1975).

[3] Da Ponte borrowed extensively from Giovanni Bertati's libretto for Giuseppe Gazzaniga's opera, "Don Giovanni o sia Il convitato di pietra," first performed at the Venetian carnival in 1787. For an interesting discussion of models and innovations, see Macchia.

[4] See chapter 3.

"corrected versions" that attempted to rehabilitate Don Juan along romantic lines, Baudelaire and Flaubert intended to rewrite "Don Giovanni" without sacrificing the dimensions of scandal, corruption, and impenitence staged in Mozart's opera. Both writers make their interpretation clear in a sketch about desire and seduction. Flaubert's "A Night of Don Juan" takes up Mozart's framework in a précis for a prose work; Baudelaire's "The End of Don Juan" outlines an opera libretto. A reading of these sketches indicates how the deferred "Don Juan" enters their oeuvres according to the demands of style that set Baudelaire and Flaubert apart from their contemporaries.

Don Giovanni's return, his encore performance, is not yet written, and forever unwritten. The sketches by Baudelaire and Flaubert provide the skeleton of an "encore," indirectly fleshed out by Lacan's seminar entitled *Encore* and its approach to love. "En corps"—Lacan's pun for his own encore performance as a reader of desire—points toward a reading of Don Juan that diverges from the notion of Don Juan as myth. This perspective shapes Jean Rousset's study, *The Myth of Don Juan*, in several ways.

Rousset's focus on myth seems to emphasize Death at the expense of eroticism. The sketches by Baudelaire and Flaubert formulate the role of Don Giovanni in erotic terms that cannot be reduced to a showdown with Death. Rousset's framework of myth sacrifices the specific qualities of literary texts; it also reduces the impact of Eros, the element of the Don Juan tradition that the Modernist imagination borrowed from the Baroque. Rousset's emphasis on the major variants of myth and model cannot include Flaubert and Baudelaire, who differ from their Romantic contemporaries precisely because they maintain the troubling aspects of Mozart's *Don Giovanni* that are overwritten by the Romantics.

The Myth of Don Juan

Don Giovanni's anticipated performance is both suspended (caught without movement and denied) and suspenseful (indicative of an event that is about to take place). A reading of Don Giovanni as this double suspense locates his performance in the "pas encore" of negation, of something that has not yet happened. The denial is subjected to denegation: "not yet" allows for the possibility of an encore performance. Through the motif of the encore, the anticipations of theater in the sketches by Baudelaire and Flaubert cast the Don Juan story in a fictional temporality. Rousset uses a Lévi-Straussian perspective to justify the view that Don Juan's death, rather than his seductions, controls the dramatic scene of his appearance. Despite the importance of Don Juan's death and the "legendary" fascination of his fate, the fictional elaboration in the sketches by Flaubert and Baudelaire resists the structural homogeneity formulated by Rousset. Their modernist return to Molière and Mozart challenges the view of Don Juan as myth.

Unlike some of his earlier writings, Rousset's study leads the role of myth away from the baroque Don Juan. As an application of structuralist anthropology, Rousset's study analyses an extraordinary range of literary materials, but leaves the reader wondering what is at stake in his enterprise. Within the framework of interpretation, it is difficult to question the theoretical modesty of *Stoffgeschichte*—thematic source studies of "legendary" figures like Faust and the Wandering Jew, who find unlikely companionship in the library section where studies on Don Giovanni are shelved. Structuralist works often come under attack in the name of more contemporary thought, labeled post-structuralism, but the question here is of a different order. With Giovanni Macchia, Rousset sweeps aside the assumptions that colored many of the earlier studies on Don Juan. What is at stake is the potential intersection between myth and literature, and the application of mythical structure to a literary traditon. What is the status of myth in Rousset's book, and how does it affect its literary object of study? An essay by Lévi-Strauss entitled "The Structural Study of Myth" gives insight into Rousset's interpretation of the Don Juan literature according to a mythical framework.[5]

In his attempt to modernize the anthropological study of religion, Lévi-Strauss uses language as an object of scientific study to defend his claim for the analogy between primitive and scientific thought. He refers to Benveniste and especially to Saussure; he concludes that "The same logical processes operate in myth as in science."[6] The structuralist inspiration at the source of many forms of modern thought—linguistics, literary studies, psychoanalysis, and anthropol-

---

[5] This essay was first published in the *Journal of American Folklore* (October–December 1955). It reappeared with slight changes in *L'Anthropologie structurale* (Paris: Plon, 1958), chapter 11. Quotations are taken from *Structural Anthropology*, translated by Claire Jacobson and Brooke Grundfest Shoepf (New York: Basic Books, 1963).

[6] Ibid., 230.

ogy—focuses on the concept of logic. Language, system, and structure, implicated in Lévi-Strauss's account of "logical processes," are discovered within the Other: previously inexplicable and uncanny, the alterity of the Other now can be scientifically codified. The supernatural can be explained, its terrors interpreted, and its magic kept at bay. Rousset's application of the discourse of myth dissolves Don Giovanni's "mythical" powers. His emphasis on the Death of Don Juan confirms the victory of structure.

Within the context of his argument in favor of a structural study of myth, Lévi-Strauss formulates two principles that have consequences for the question of reading Don Giovanni and for the application of the category of myth to literature. In his discussion of language, Lévi-Strauss distinguishes myth from other "linguistic phenomena": "Myth is the part of language where the formula *traduttore, traditore* reaches its lowest truth value. From that point of view it should be placed in the gamut of linguistic expressions at the end opposite to that of poetry." He adds, "Its substance [the substance of myth] does not lie in its style, its original music, or its syntax, but in the *story* it tells."[7] While this commentary hints at the relevance of myth for a narratological perspective, it excludes all other elements of literary discourse. On the contrary, the absorption of literary material into myth gives rise to the second principle. In his study of the Oedipus myth, Lévi-Strauss states that the versions of Sophocles and Freud should be included "on a par with . . . seemingly more 'authentic' versions." "We define the myth as consisting of all its versions." He says, "If a myth is made up of all its variants, structural analysis should take all of them into account."[8]

First, Lévi-Strauss's structural study locates myth in opposition to poetry: mythical narrative erases the formal and aesthetic qualities of literary language. Second, the blending of variants important for an anthropological study of myth threatens the concepts of difference and singularity that are inherent in the notion of what constitutes a text. For literary interpretation, difference and singularity provide meaning, value, and pleasure. The mythical reading moves toward an ultimate identity. Rousset sees it in the form of Death, his structural common denominator. From one text, genre, and language to another, literary tradition has reinvested the energy of Don Giovanni in the articulation of desire.

[7] Ibid., 210.
[8] Ibid., 217.

In its application to Don Juan, the term of "myth" is a way of saying that after all, eroticism is really only about the death of the seducer. In literature and opera, however, Don Giovanni's poetics of the
erotic challenges Death. Myth is undermined by a valorization of differences that appropriate meaning in a literary aesthetic framework.
Like the names of Don Giovanni's women, these differences can be
written down; they include the figures of rhetoric, and they unfold in
a poetics of the figural (or what Paul de Man calls "allegory").

Rousset's emphasis on Death uses the function of myth to sacrifice
the erotics of Don Giovanni in the interests of ethics and brotherly
love.[9] Death appears in the monumentalized mask of divine justice,
the ultimate authority for the defeat and punishment of Don Giovanni. Within the theoretical frame of myth, the erotic power of Don
Giovanni is defeated and destroyed. Myth confirms the social and
moral framework that erases Don Giovanni's art.

Libertine Encores

The alternative to a mythical reading of Don Giovanni is literary and
rhetorical. He seduces his objects once and forever with beautiful
figures. Forever and never again—the "not yet" of attraction, the feminine fragrance, ceases abruptly. After consummation, the object fades
out of sight to become a name on the list. When Don Giovanni is approached for an encore by women who desire him in marriage, he van-
ishes into new adventures. He has no form of remembrance of past
loves, and does not seek to retrieve any particular object. Time is neither lost nor regained. For Don Giovanni, there is only the first time.
The performance is over, and there will not be an encore.

Don Giovanni personifies the baroque figure of inconstancy (or constant change) and libertine desire. The combination produces the
serial encores of "love" or erotic conquest. His artifices of love turn
seduction into an aesthetic form—the pure eroticism of music, according to Kierkegaard. His most appealing victims are virgins who
belong to the father, the church, and God. Blank of the traces of another's desire, with nothing, as Hamlet says to Ophelia, between
maid's legs, they are suspended in Don Giovanni's consummation of

[9] Rousset, pp. 21–22.

them. These madonna-like figures anticipate the madonnas of modernism. Like Kierkegaard, who preferred to hear the opera in the dark, they close their eyes in enjoyment. Later they will recognize Don Giovanni as the author of their loss and their punishment, the consequences of libertine pleasure.

The women in Don Giovanni texts are deprived of social or legal identity outside of marriage. History suspends them in the reproductive function, and Don Giovanni suspends them in an erotic episode never to be repeated. The evaporating image of pleasure turns into a petrified figure uttering black threats and imprecations. These women (and the men who defend them) seek punishment for Don Giovanni in the name of the social order, the domestication of desire, the value of virginity.

Rejected, Don Giovanni's female objects become his adversaries. They overturn his challenge and temporary victory over the Father figures who attempt to reclaim a mastery that Don Giovanni does not concede. Don Giovanni's refusal to confess and repent is a sign of an erotic mastery that he will not relinquish, even at death. It is his own will, his law of *jouissance,* the gratuitous flowering of evil. While Leporello would like to make a Luciferian refusal of service to his master, Don Giovanni's refusal of repentance locates the battle of service and mastery on the ethical ground, where *jouissance* turns pleasure into corruption, and where the erotic ambiguities of Anna's mourning for a lost seducer and a murdered father seem to coincide. This blackness is masked by the shrill tone of victory over Don Giovanni, and his defeat in the name of law and order. Rousset's emphasis on Death within his analysis of myth articulates a strange repetition of the controversial last scene in Mozart's opera.

The anticlimactic affirmation of heavenly vengeance appears as an afterthought: "tutti . . . vendicati siam dal cielo [we are all avenged by heaven]." This anticlimax unites the other characters and ties up the threads of fiction: their destinies are safe now that Don Giovanni is out of the picture. The end of Mozart's "Prague version" affirms the death of the evildoer as the deserved end of evil in life. The libertine's troubling effects are denied and masked. The hasty proclamation of victory, highly ambiguous in the Mozartean context, appears as a strategic move on the part of the composer and librettist. It brackets the scandalous, infinite, and unlimited effects of Don Giovanni's corruption with a moral sentence of closure, and yet its abruptness and brevity ironize the gesture of morality.

The victory song acts out the repression of Eros represented in Don Giovanni. Repression occurs as dismissal, denial, and denegation; the flames of hell that swallow him are inseparable from the flames of desire. The moment when the other characters celebrate Don Giovanni's death to affirm the predictable course of their lives highlights his story as the true drama. Their narratives sound like an afterthought. When Don Giovanni is out of the picture, the picture dissolves. The dramatic threads that held them together as characters fall away. Only Donna Anna suspends the normal (non-libertine) course of life that eventually takes the other characters offstage. Donna Anna hovers in the vaporous ambiguity of mourning.

Dark Nights

Mozart cut the moralizing epilogue in the Vienna performance of 1788. Until the early twentieth century, the curtain usually came down after Don Giovanni's death. The majority of the modern versions of the opera take up the moralizing impulse that appears in many Don Juan texts; Mozart, on the other hand, threw away the thin disguise of moral righteousness as soon as the opera became popular.

The undisguised thirst for revenge against Don Giovanni is absorbed into the tragic and comic modes of the opera, and it counterpoints the lyrical mode of seduction. Although Mozart's characters and types of discourse are different from the configuration in *Dom Juan*, a similar counterpoint of modes and identifiable genres occurs in Molière's play. In both works, the desire for revenge is personalized in the libertine's female victims. The libertine consumes the virginity of his objects and disappears. The abandoned women are devastated and furious.

Images of feminine vengeance hover in the background of Flaubert's scenes of Don Juan's flight, and they escalate in Baudelaire's poem, "Don Juan aux Enfers." Social history and the study of gender roles cannot explain the violence of these images.

> Montrant leurs seins pendants et leurs robes ouvertes,
> Des femmes se tordaient sous le noir firmament,
> Et, comme un grand troupeau de victimes offertes,
> Derrière lui traînaient un long mugissement.

> Showing their hanging breasts and open dresses,
> Women writhed under the black sky,
> And like a great herd of offered victims,
> Dragged a long bellowing behind him.[10]

The wild mourning of this scene and the unflattering image of a crowd transformed into a "herd" are the Dionysian effects of Don Juan. The violence of this scene cannot be attributed to the explicitly porno- graphic element found in the writings of Sade or Casanova, and asso- ciated with Don Giovanni. Like the accounts of desire and seduction in Mozart and Molière, the brief texts by Flaubert and Baudelaire re- main decorous.

The libertine's broken promise does not explain the insistent pur- suit of Don Juan by hordes of women. The feminine lamentation of Baudelaire's poem and other texts in the Don Giovanni tradition evoke the performative act and the breach of promise because the promise is the only act associated with single dark nights and unfa- miliar boudoirs that can be discussed in the open.[11] Between daughter and father, sister and brother, the incest taboo allows these discus- sions to pass beyond the limit of censorship. The structural and Lévi- Straussian element of the drama is only the beginning; it alone can elude the censor. As Hamlet says, the rest is silence.

Mozart's *dramma giocoso* [comic drama] is not a mourning play, however, and the grief of disappointed women is covered by shrill anger more appropriate to the mode of exteriority associated with Don Giovanni. The rest, then, might be song rather than silence. Some- thing that cannot be said in so many words takes aesthetic cover, in music. In a highly modernist turn appropriate to Baudelaire and Flaubert, the obscene wears a veil of beautiful style. The Romantic alternative to libertine pornography presents the shadowy alcove of aesthetics:

> Les soirs illuminés par l'ardeur du charbon,
> Et les soirs au balcon, voilés de vapeurs roses,

[10] Charles Baudelaire, *Œuvres complètes*, edited by Claude Pichois, vol. 1 (Paris: Gallimard, Bibliothèque de la Pléiade, 1975), p. 20.

[11] See Shoshana Felman, *Le Scandale du corps parlant* (Paris: Seuil, 1979). This study focuses on the performative aspect of *Dom Juan* as the crossroads of psycho- analysis, literature, and linguistics.

Que ton sein m'était doux! que ton coeur m'était bon!
Nous avons dit souvent d'impérissables choses
Les soirs illuminés par l'ardeur du charbon.

Evenings illuminated with the ardor of coal,
And the evenings at the balcony veiled in pink mists,
How your breast was sweet! how your heart was good!
We often said deathless things
On evenings illuminated with the ardor of coal.[12]

Unlike many of the normative literary attempts to bend Don Giovanni's knee in repentance and celebrate the punishment of erotic evil, or to rehabilitate him and neutralize his powers, the variations on Don Juan by Flaubert and Baudelaire remain faithful to Molière and Mozart. Don Giovanni is less a character than a text, an allegorical figure who represents the baroque Eros. Don Giovanni is the imaginary body or incarnation of the text, *en corps/encore*. His art of seduction appears to go on forever; it is limited only by the morality that leads to Don Giovanni's end. The moral of the story is inseparable from the mortality of the author of evil. Leporello describes his master's condemnation. "Giusto là il diavolo / Se'l trangugió! [On the spot the devil dragged him down!]" With Zerlina and Masetto, he repeats himself: "Resti dunque quel birbon / Con Proserpina e Pluton [Let that good-for-nothing stay with Proserpine and Pluto]." At the end of the scene, all affirm the symmetry of evil in life and death: "Questo è il fin di chi fa mal; E di perfidi la morte / Alla vita e sempre ugual [This is the end of the evil-doer; and for scoundrels death is not different from life]."

Don Giovanni's love objects cannot quite get their hands on him, in flesh or spirit; he eludes their silent desire and their loud requests for marriage. His denial of the Commander's request for repentance figures his refusal to surrender to God. The Virgin Mary, however, is Don Giovanni's ultimate object in Flaubert's sketch; according to Joyce's *Portrait of the Artist as a Young Man*, she is the favored confessor of Catholic sinners. The end of the opera finalizes Don Giovanni's refusal to renounce desire. The horrors of hell open up, as unquenchable as his corruption.

---

[12] Charles Baudelaire, "Le Balcon," in *Œuvres complètes*, p. 37.

At the last minute, morality imposes order on the "inassouvis-sable," the infinite, the incommensurable. Christian ethics breaks Plato's link between Eros and the good (between Beauty and Truth); Don Giovanni emblematizes that break, and his end awakens us from dreams of Eros. In the name of the fathers, Eros is condemned as evil, and relegated to the hell that swallows Don Giovanni at the end of the opera. Mozart's erasure of the final scene allowed a flashing image of Don Giovanni's limitless and immeasurable end—his descent into Hell—to "end" the opera. The conclusions to be drawn by the viewer are more subtle than those proclaimed by Leporello and his compan-ions in the scene that Mozart cut, because the easy balance of vice and virtue has disappeared. In its place, a final image remains. This encore cannot be erased—the body of Don Giovanni, the flash of fireworks, the horror of corruption, and the image of the abyss. The curtain falls on this scene, the Other side of seduction. Its violence and horror translate the infinite art of Don Giovanni's poetics.

In this context, the inventive detours taken by Flaubert and Baude-laire in the Don Juan sketches remain faithful to the textual conse-quences of Molière and Mozart. The figure of Don Giovanni breathes new life into French Romanticism. Flaubert wrote to Baudelaire after reading the recently published *Flowers of Evil:* "You found the way to rejuvenate Romanticism. You do not resemble anyone else (this is the most important quality of all)." [13] Flaubert's remark could be applied to their trans-romantic sketches of Don Giovanni and his virginal objects.

The mysterious rejuvenation of literature that Flaubert's letter de-scribes consists of style. [14] In the context of Don Giovanni, the seduc-tions of art appear in the allegorical forms of the Seducer and the Ma-donna. The allegory appears with the literal violence of a figure who interrupts the imaginary constructions of the organic, the natural, and the human. Don Giovanni's allegorical identity lies in the beds of all women, in the dreamlike fantasies of all men. To call him a myth is to see him as a source of culture, an organizing principle, and an an-swer to nature. He cannot incarnate this answer, however, because his desire is incandescent, destructive, and all-consuming. He is too close

[13] Letter from Flaubert to Baudelaire, dated 13 June 1857, in Gustave Flaubert, *Cor-respondance,* edited by Jean Bruneau, vol. 2 (Paris: Bibliothèque de la Pléiade, 1980), p. 745.

[14] See *The Orient of Style: Modernist Allegories of Conversion* (Durham: Duke University Press, 1991).

to the Freudian-Lacanian category of the Other. His contours are too dark: he eludes order and morality. He evades religious worship, ethics and sentiment. Trickster and seducer, he moves from one erotic encounter to the next. As a figure of Eros, he represents *jouissance*— pleasure transformed by the sublime delights of transgression—and bel canto, the beautiful vocal art of seduction. In his wake, he leaves lost illusions, consumed virginity, and broken promises of marriage. The trickster or "burlador" produces ruined illusions, "desengaño" or the Italian "disinganno." Don Giovanni tears the veil of illusion. In the end, these remains of erotic destruction impose silence on the sexual partners and victims of Don Giovanni's erotic acts, endless beautiful love songs, and flights in all directions.

The Stone Guest

In light of moral and mythical logic, it is strange that only one act of seduction brings Don Giovanni into the cemetery. It sets up the three encores of Catholicism: (1) decay, corruption, and death; (2) the monuments that represent those who have succumbed to them; and (3) the anticipated resurrection that transcends them. The Last Things of Catholicism inform the artistic production of allegory as a baroque mode of erotic (and Other) representation. This encounter between the theologically shaped encore/en corps and the artful (or artificial) representation of it in allegory shape Don Giovanni's encounter with the father and the Other world—the Stone Guest. Molière, Mozart, and many of their predecessors, including Tirso de Molina, establish the role of Don Giovanni through the murder of the Commander.[15] Transfigured into a monument of allegory called the Stone Guest, he confronts Don Giovanni with the consequences of unlimited desire.

As a sexual strategist accused of transgression and as a secret immoral ideal of masculine erotic power, Don Giovanni can be compared with the representation of Eros in Giacomo Casanova's *Mémoires*. The a-sentimental and stratagem-absorbed lover relies on artifice and dissimulation in the pursuit of his objects of desire. Un-

---

[15] In Tirso de Molina's play, the Commander is Don Gonzalo de Ulloa. In 3.8, the final scene, Catalinon, the servant of Don Juan Tenorio, retells the story of the encounter between his master and the Statue; all present rejoice at Don Juan's death.

like Casanova, however, Don Giovanni uses his cunning and artistry to disappear after the first encounter has taken place; his powers of seduction are inseparable from his powers of invisibility. All of these first times add up. In many versions of the Don Giovanni story, they are written down by the master's valet. The long list of his conquests that Casanova reportedly took from one café to another in Venice had venerable literary models.[16]

Although the famous List or Catalog could be reformulated as an impressive chronology, it strangely eludes the question of time. The names of women are inscribed on a quasi-endless roll of paper, but the pre-romantic Don Giovanni does not seem to age. Permanently youthful, Don Giovanni emblematizes the "rejuvenated romanticism" that Flaubert shares with Baudelaire. In their romantic reshaping of a baroque topos, both writers look toward Don Giovanni when they recast a Catholic frame of eroticism in the gothic blackness of modernity.

This blackness includes suffering and transgression, passion and corruption. Between flights of violent desire, fleeting moments of mastery, the secret "communion" between subject and object unfolds as the ultimate secret, described only in Leporello's generalized vulgarizations. The monument of absence, of Eros in flight, is revealed in the blackness of baroque allegory, and in its modernist resonance.

The two opponents of the opening scene, Don Giovanni and the Commander, posit two figures of allegory, Eros and Death, that sustain the text. Don Giovanni's Eros is associated with movement, flight, displacement, intoxication, musical representation, song, and rhetoric, while the Commander as the figure of Death is associated with disappearance, permanence, mourning, terror, petrification, sculpture, and paternal authority. When the two meet again as Don Giovanni and the Statue, they represent the Seducer and the Father, or the agent of desire and the representative of divine will.

Their final meeting repeats the battle of act 1, scene 1, in different terms. At the beginning, the battle over Donna Anna's ambivalent erotic-sublime figure ended with the Commander's death. The dark

---

[16] The idea that Mozart–Da Ponte got the idea for the Aria dell Catalogo from Casanova is logical within the somewhat apocryphal frame for Don Giovanni–Casanova connections, but it is more likely that Casanova took his cue from the same sources known to the librettist and composer. For the apocryphal version, see April Fitzlyon, *The Libertine Librettist* (London: John Calder, 1955), 146. The importance of the Catalogo theme is indicated in the texts presented by Mandel, Rousset, and especially Macchia.

night of this first scene at the Commander's address and its potential double crime of seduction (or rape?) and murder are turned inside out in the second battle. The bright banquet and the invitation leading from the graveyard to Don Giovanni's dinner table include an ironic repetition of the Seducer's invitation. This repetition is reappropriated by the strange figure of the Statue, the Stone Guest, when he condemns Don Giovanni after reciprocating the invitation.

In beginning his seduction of Zerlina, Don Giovanni describes her as "in man d'un Cavalier [in the hands of a Knight]" (I.8). She will take his hand and say yes to him: "Là ci darem la mano, / Là mi dirai di si" (1.9). In act 1, scene 20, Don Giovanni invites all the peasants to "una gran festa di ballo [a great festive ball]" and continues his attempted seduction of her. In the penultimate scene of the opera (2.14), the Statue invites Don Giovanni to a banquet and asks for his hand as a pledge. "Dammi la mano in pegno!" Don Giovanni offers his hand in an enigmatic assent to the forces that punish him. This vendetta is disguised as divine punishment. The object of desire has been displaced, elided, or dissolved. Beyond marriage or justice, the submission of Don Giovanni is the Commander's object of desire.

Mozart quickly erased the final scene, a structural addition designed to appease its royal audience with an unequivocal moral message. If Mozart and Da Ponte wished to linger over Don Giovanni's subversion, then the concluding image of the Don caught in the fires of Hell could no longer fade into the scene of restored order that mimed a happy ending. Don Giovanni's grandeur is preserved as "rejuvenated Romanticism" in the formulations of modernism. Beyond eroticism and inseparable from it, challenging the finality of death and refusing the Catholic ultimatum that allows for a symbolic antidote to it, Don Giovanni dies. Through the ambitions of his corruption itself, however, he becomes a strange figure for the transcendence of death.

In the second and final battle between Don Giovanni and the Commander, the question of desire that has become an emblem of Lacanian analysis is asked for the last time in the opera: "Che vuoi?" (2.15).[17] In an impossible configuration, the character who speaks with the voice of Eros dies while saying no to Death. He refuses the Catholic assent that turns death into virginal felicity through the last rites and their articulation of virtue, redemption, and a prefiguration of resurrection.

---

[17] Don Giovanni asks Donna Elvira this question in the preceding scene, "con affettatta tenerezza": "Che vuoi, mio bene?" (2.14).

Within the framework of libertinism, eroticism turns into the cornerstone of a "new" series of modernist principles. The encounter that leads Don Giovanni to ask the question of desire ("Che vuoi?") before he is thrown into the flames of Hell marks his end with a refusal to abdicate erotic mastery. His experience of the inexhaustible can be understood only within the context of the terrible knowledge of desire that is highlighted in Molière and Mozart.

Baudelaire and Flaubert formulate this knowledge in the theory of love attributed to the Don Juan of their sketches: "Ce qu'elle avait donné à don Juan ne périt pas quand la statue du Commandeur l'engouffra [What she gave to Don Juan did not perish when the Commander's statue swallowed him into the abyss]."[18] Flaubert's sketch ends with a mysterious link between the two forms of love that takes Don Giovanni beyond his own death. In two contexts that appear very different from Flaubert's sketch, Baudelaire makes the same point. "Don Juan aux Enfers" seems untouched by the menacing theater of hell that surrounds him. The last lines of the poem clarify his indifference:

> Mais le calme héros, courbé sur sa rapière,
> Regardait le sillage et ne daignait rien voir.

> But the calm hero, bent over his rapier,
> gazed into the wake and refused to see them.[19]

In the fragmentary "La Fin de Don Juan [Don Juan's End]," Baudelaire's character eludes death in a different way; he exercises a strangely permanent attraction for his "jeune danseuse," despite their difference in age, and the Romantic "mal de siècle" that afflicts him: "UNE JEUNE DANSEUSE DE RACE BOHEME, SOLEDAD OU TRINIDAD, enlevée, élevée et protégée par Don Juan, et malgré la différence d'âge, ne trouvant rien de plus beau, de plus aimable et dont elle ait le droit d'être plus fière, que son amant [A YOUNG DANCER OF BOHEMIAN RACE, FROM SOLEDAD OR TRINIDAD, kidnapped, raised, and protected by Don Juan, and who, despite their age difference, finds nothing more handsome, attractive, and inspiring of pride than her lover]."[20]

In this description, Baudelaire preserves an aspect of the Don Giovanni tradition that disappears in many other romantic and post-

---

[18] Gustave Flaubert, "Une Nuit de Don Juan." See chapter 3, note 4.
[19] Baudelaire, 1:20.
[20] Charles Baudelaire, 627.

romantic versions. Don Juan's aesthetic and erotic charms are countersigned by the adoration of his ingénue who is described as an idealized romantic feminine type. A young dancer uprooted from her
home in the islands, she resembles some of the exotic objects of desire
in the *Flowers of Evil*. Without the seductiveness that is essential to
the renderings of Molière and Mozart, Baudelaire's Don Juan would
lose the connections with Eros and beauty that are essential to his
role. The threefold danger is amply documented throughout the literature on Don Giovanni. As an object of disgust or scorn, as a brutal
rapist, or as an idealist in the tradition of Faust, Don Juan would have
been of little interest to Flaubert or Baudelaire.

Baudelaire's Don Juan searches for the charm of the unknown and
he orders his servant to accompany him in his attempt to examine
what he calls "éléments de bonheur que je ne connais pas [elements
of happiness that I do not know]."[21] Like Sganarelle or Leporello, the
fearful servant protests against the master's command "de risquer
sa vie pour sauver des filous [to risk his life to save criminals]." The
subjects of Don Juan's analysis of happiness are gypsies and thieves
hunted by the police. In Baudelaire's configuration, independent of
Molière or Mozart, Don Juan's excesses are based on the seduction ex-
ercised by the unknown.

Happiness brings him to the feminine and the aesthetic; he attains
an almost divine form of permanence. His erotic thirst and his analytic detachment combine in a god-like figure of the Seducer. His servant, a mixture of Sganarelle, Leporello, and Benjamin Franklin, obeys
him: "Que votre volonté soit faite [Thy will be done]." Like the Virgin at the Annunciation, the servant bows before Don Giovanni.

The Flowers of Evil

Without transgression there would be no flowers of evil, artistry of seduction, or erotic mastery. Without death, the allegory of the Statue—
the only opponent that Don Giovanni cannot outwit or elude—would
be meaningless. The ambivalent Donna Anna, the figure on all borderlines, is a mere pretext for the Commander. She is a figure of the
object, a player of the primal scene that sets the opera in motion.
Donna Anna provides imaginary consistency for the feminine image

---

[21] Ibid., 628.

of the inner dialogue between the power of eroticism and the anticipation of death. Flaubert develops this dialogue of the en-corps and a
mystical Beyond throughout his writings, including his novels and
personal correspondence.

The final image of Don Giovanni captures the paradoxes of the
meeting between death and eroticism, between divine mastery and
unlimited desire. *Che vuoi?* is the emblem of this encounter, when seduction's shifts of desire are riveted by the flash of the will that distributes hell and heaven, vice and virtue. Riveted but unmastered,
Don Giovanni refuses to repent. The final dazzling scene of the opera
offers the audience a vision of Don Giovanni as an image of paradox—
a visual flash that represents neither the surrender nor the victory
of Eros.

This scene anticipates the dialectical image that Walter Benjamin's
Zentralpark shapes within a reading of Baudelairean allegory.[22] Don
Giovanni brings together the two nocturnal scenes (or stages) in a
third one—the lightning flash of the "Other" scene of death, provoked
by the supernatural return of the father. His apparition as the Statue
sets the stage for the supernatual punishment of Don Giovanni: its
image is rendered in an instant, and he disappears. Don Giovanni's
"No!" denies obedience and refuses the transfiguration of death into
an eternity. His exclamation becomes a brief cry of horror; the love
songs are over. Like Meryon's engravings of Paris streets, his banquet
room turns into an abyss under a sky that is implied but not seen.[23]
Hell suddenly opens up in a baroque response to an excess that cannot
be limited to libertinage.

The faithfulness of Flaubert and Baudelaire to the meaning of Don
Giovanni takes creative form in new versions of the story. These
sketches can be interpreted only within the complex frame of "Don
Giovanni" as the scandalous text of eroticism and mastery. The detours imposed by "rejuvenated Romanticism" on Don Giovanni's
course seem to locate the corruption that both Flaubert and Baudelaire
found seductive within a complex aesthetic, textual, and theoretical
framework. Their refusal to rehabilitate Don Juan and turn him into a

---

[22] Walter Benjamin, *Zentralpark* in *Gesammelte Schriften,* edited by Rolf Tiede-
mann and Hermann Schweppenhäuser, vol. 1.2 (Frankfurt am Main: Suhrkamp Verlag, 1980), 655–90.

[23] "Meryons pariser Straßen: Abgründe, über denen hoch oben die Wolken da-
hinziehen. ["Meryon's Parisian streets: abysses. High above them the clouds drift]."
Zentralpark, 33, 681.

repentant libertine, a responsible citizen, or at least a good husband implies that the questions raised by the Molière and Da Ponte texts are as valid for modernism as they are for seventeenth- and eighteenth-century Baroque presentations.

Caught between comedy and tragedy, the *dramma giocoso* of Don Giovanni locates the origin of corruption in the abyss separating subject and object. The quasi-virtual Don Juans of Flaubert and Baudelaire would agree on this point with Molière and Mozart that eroticism breaks the body's illusory integrity into pieces. The divided body of corruption enters the texts of Flaubert and Baudelaire with the exquisite sensibility—voluptuous, painful, demanding, and melancholic—of Emma Bovary or the speaker in Baudelaire's "Le Balcon [The Balcony]."[24] Corruption hovers in the shadowy abyss between lover and beloved, at the site of absence where love mingles with mourning.

In this sense, the modernist Don Giovanni originates in a portrayal of one of the least seductive characters in French literature. The abyss opens when Charles Bovary discovers Rodolphe's letter to Emma. He says to himself, "Ils se sont peut-être aimés platoniquement [Perhaps they loved each other platonically]."[25] This denegation is confirmed by the narrator, "il recula devant les preuves [he retreated before the evidence]." The message of betrayal anticipated in Charles's hypothesis of Platonic love is confirmed when he finds Emma's collection of love letters in the secret compartment of her desk. "On s'étonna de son découragement . . . on prétendit qu'il *s'enfermait pour boire* [People were astonished at his discouragement . . . they claimed that he *locked himself up to drink*]."[26] Instead of ending his desire and love for Emma, the discovery of her betrayals confirms Charles's loss. Mourning assails him, and his heart is broken in true Flaubertian style. "Charles suffoquait comme un adolescent sous les vagues effluves amoureux qui lui gonflaient son coeur chagrin . . . Il avait la tête renversée contre le mur, les yeux clos, la bouche ouverte, et tenait dans ses mains une longue mèche de cheveux noirs . . . Il était mort . . . Il [M. Canivet] l'ouvrit et ne trouva rien [Charles was suffocating like

---

[24] To the fragments of the *membra disjecta*, frequently evoked in baroque allegory, correspond Freud's theory of the drives and Lacan's continuation of it with the "corps morcellé [body in pieces]" and the "objet petite a (object little o)."

[25] Gustave Flaubert, *Madame Bovary* in *Œuvres*, edited by Albert Thibaudet and René Dumesnil (Paris: Bibliothèque de la Pléiade, 1951), 1:604.

[26] Ibid., 609.

an adolescent under the vague flow of love that swelled his afflicted heart . . . He had leaned his head against the wall, face up, eyes closed, mouth open, and in his hands a long lock of black hair . . . He was dead . . . [Dr. Canivet] opened him up and found nothing]." Charles dies of his love for Emma. The doctor who looks inside his corpse finds nothing organic, nothing at all—the figure of virginal desire.

Once the virginal sublime is affirmed, the comic aspect of Flaubert's portrait of Charles wears thin. Although Flaubert consistently uses the character of Bovary to represent bourgeois mediocrity, there is nothing funny about Charles in the last pages of *Madame Bovary*. The day before his death, Charles makes his second tragicomic statement. It contains the last words he pronounces in his fictional life and in the text of the novel. Except for his daughter's call to him ("'Papa, come on!'"), Bovary's words also mark the last instance of direct discourse in a novel that began with his awkward silence, his pathetic comical cap, and his inarticulate "stammering voice."[27] Charles meets Rodolphe and declares that he no longer resents him. "Il ajouta même un grand mot, le seul qu'il ait jamais dit: 'C'est la faute de la fatalité!' [He even added a great statement, the only one that he ever pronounced: 'Destiny is to blame!']"[28]

Charles unconsciously echoes Rodolphe's letter: "'Pourquoi étiez-vous si belle? Est-ce ma faute? O mon Dieu! non, non, n'en accusez que la fatalité!' 'Voilà un mot qui fait toujours de l'effet,' se dit-il ["'Why were you so beautiful? Was it my fault? O my God! no, no, accuse only fate!' 'There's a word that is always effective,' he thought]."[29] Flaubert uses this passage—letter and commentary—as evidence of Rodolphe's vulgarity, indifference, and strategic use of Romantic cliché. In his own *Dictionary of clichés*, Flaubert writes: "FATALITE.— Mot exclusivement romantique. Homme fatal se dit de celui qui a le mauvais oeil [FATE.—Exclusively romantic word. A man doomed by fate (destiny) is one who has the evil eye]." Flaubert's narrative effects contradict Rodolphe's interpretation of Charles as "bien débonnaire pour un homme dans sa situation, comique même, et un peu vil [rather cavalier for a man in his situation, even comic, and a little abject]."[30]

[27] Ibid., 294.
[28] Ibid., 610.
[29] Ibid., 476.
[30] Ibid., 610.

Published manuscripts of the novel confirm the textual evidence of Flaubert's portrait of Rodolphe as an insensitive "lurron [*sic*] dans toutes les extensions du terme" whose effect on Emma does not alter his essential vulgarity. Emma's attraction to him contrasts with the repulsion produced by Charles's "intimate vulgarity."[31] The difference between their two forms of mediocrity is taken up at the end of the novel, when Flaubert indicates that Charles's love for Emma elevates him. The scenario describing Bovary's vulgarity includes the following comment: "ADORE sa femme et des trois hommes qui couchent avec elle, est certainement celui qui l'aime le plus. [—c'est ce qu'il faut bien faire voir] [ADORES his wife and of the three men who sleep with her, is certainly the one who loves her the most [—this must be made clear]." Flaubert's acute observation of stupidity does not flinch before this trans-romantic paradox: the most unattractive character is the only lover capable of depth of feeling or "true love." The Madame Bovary blues include the passion of the most inept lover in modernism.

The ironic resonance of Bovary's invocation of fate as romantic cliché, or as an echo of Rodolphe's calculated use of the term in his letter to Emma, is undercut by the fascination that Charles feels in Rodolphe's presence.

> Charles se perdait en rêveries devant cette figure qu'elle avait aimée. Il lui semblait revoir quelque chose d'elle. (. . .) il y eut même un instant où Charles, plein d'une fureur sombre, fixa ses yeux contre Rodolphe . . . Mais bientôt la même lassitude funèbre réapparut sur son visage. (. . .) Et Charles, la tête dans ses deux mains, reprit d'une voix éteinte et avec l'accent résigné des douleurs infinies: "Non, je ne vous en veux plus!"

> [Charles lost himself in revery looking at this face that she had loved. It seemed to him that he saw once more something that was a part of her. (. . .) there was even a moment when Charles, filled with a dark fury, fixed his eyes on Rodolphe . . . But soon the same funereal lassitude reappeared on his face. (. . .) And Charles, his head in his two hands, spoke again with a lifeless voice and the resigned tone of infinite pain: "No, I no longer hold it against you!"][32]

---

[31] See the genetic edition by Yvan Leclerc of Flaubert's Bovary manuscripts (and the scenarios published by Jean Pommier and Gabrielle Leleu in *Madame Bovary: nouvelle version* (Paris: José Corti, 1949), 9, 17, 95, and 21.

[32] Ibid., 610.

The melancholy gravity of Bovary's mourning puts his statement about fatality into a new light; Rodolphe, the small-time Don Juan seen by Bovary as a rival for his wife's affections, misses the point.

Emma, says the narrator, corrupts Charles beyond the grave.[33] The fatality of love links eroticism to death: the question of jouissance weaves a net between them. The abyss that separates the subject from the object of desire only allows them to meet in a constellation of mourning, memory, and what Flaubert sometimes describes as exquisite and unbearable sensibility. In this sense, Charles resembles the bored and melancholic Don Juan of the two sketches.[34] Baudelaire states that pleasure is to be found in evil (or suffering).[35] This remark, a cornerstone of modernist aesthetics, is illustrated by the corruption that closes in on Charles Bovary.

In the twentieth century, the encore performance of Modernism continues to challenge easy ethical solutions of a revisionist reading of Don Juan. On the blackened stage of the mid-1930s, at the edge of an abyss of political and social violence, a novel by Georges Bataille that is generally left on the pornography shelf returns to the scandals of Don Juan without disavowing the contemporary context. This novel gives an account of corruption as necrophilia—an explicit reinscription of the death drive within eroticism—and its monstrous counterpart in political ideology. As he moves between "bonheur" and "malheur," the narrator invokes both comedy and tragedy. At strategic moments in the text, he echoes the following remark:

> Il y a quelques jours, je suis arrivé—réellement, et non dans un cauchemar—dans une ville qui ressemblait au décor d'une tragédie. (. . .) Au milieu de la nuit le Commandeur entra dans ma chambre: pendant l'après-midi, je passais devant son tombeau, l'orgueil m'avait poussé à l'inviter ironiquement. Son arrivée inattendue m'épouvanta.
> Devant lui, je tremblais. Devant lui, j'étais une épave. (. . .) Mais je n'aurais qu'un cri pour répéter l'invitation (. . .) Le bonheur à l'instant m'enivre, il me saoule.

> [A few days ago, I arrived—in reality, not in a nightmare—in a city resembling a stage set for a tragedy. (. . .) In the middle of the night the

---

[33] "Elle le corrompait par delà le tombeau [She was corrupting him from beyond the tomb]," ibid., 604.

[34] Baudelaire, 627.

[35] Baudelaire writes, "dans le mal se trouve toute volupté." *Fusées, Œuvres complètes*, vol. 1, 652.

Commander entered my room: during the afternoon, I was walking past his tomb, pride impelled me to invite him, ironically. His unexpected arrival horrified me. Before him, I trembled. Before him, I was a wreck. (. . .) But it would take only one cry to repeat the invitation. (. . .) At this moment happiness intoxicates me, it makes me drunk].[36]

Like James Joyce's *Ulysses* or *Giacomo Joyce*, this text does not fit into anthologies or thematic studies of Don Giovanni. What is the identity of this speaker who refuses to repent? Although he is not anonymous, he speaks anonymously in the name of Don Juan. He seems to use the same voice as the character in Georges Bataille's *Madame Edwarda* who says: "Le plaisir, à la fin, nous chavira [Pleasure, in the end, capsized us]."[37] In the preface to *Madame Edwarda*, the author points out that laughter is an inappropriate response to sexuality; it is a way of dismissing the potential implications of sexual "apotheosis." He speaks through a pseudonym: he does not speak in the name of Georges Bataille, or Dionysos, or Don Giovanni, although the text bears their implicit and invisible signature. In the same way, the character in Bataille's *Le Bleu du ciel* who describes his arrival in a town that looks like a tragic stage set for his victims, his solitude, and the encounter he arranges with the "Commander" is a pseudonym or a mask for Don Juan. His name anagrammatizes the message of Bataille's preface to *Madame Edwarda; on en rit trop*, Henri Troppmann. The name tells us that too much laughter about sex is human, too human, and indicates tragedy in the background.[38] This name, however, is merely an emblem. The message hidden in it keeps raising the stakes of eroticism to the heights of a baroque-modernist Don Giovanni, whenever Bataille's figures of the philosopher hover on the threshold of the boudoir.

When the fragmentary text of *Le Bleu du ciel* was first published in 1945, it began with an epigraph from Hegel. The writer who sometimes signed his name as "Pierre Angélique" evokes Hegel in the context of vertiginous pleasures and Dionysian delirium (sexual "apotheosis") when the tragic seriousness of eroticism brings writing face to

---

[36] Georges Bataille, *Le Bleu du ciel*, in *Œuvres complètes*, vol. 3 (Paris: Gallimard, 1971), 395–96.

[37] *Madame Edwarda* in *Œuvres complètes*, vol. 3, 22.

[38] After Bataille's evocation of the city-stage of tragedy, Troppmann evokes his own unhappy laughter as he remembers his erotic intoxication while watching two old men dancing.

face with Madame Edwarda's delirium and the *via negativa* that moves her creator through philosophy to nonsense and unknowing:

M. Non-Sens écrit, il comprend qu'il est fou: c'est affreux. Mais sa folie, ce non-sens—comme il est, tout à coup, devenu 'sérieux:'—serait-ce là justement 'le sens?' (non, Hegel n'a rien à voir avec 'l'apothéose' d'une folle . . .)

[Mr. Nonsense writes, he knows that he is mad: it is awful. But his madness, this nonsense—suddenly it has become 'serious:'—would that be, precisely, 'meaning?' (no, Hegel has nothing in common with the 'apotheosis' of a madwoman . . .)][39]

[39] *Madame Edwarda*, 30.

PART III

Triangles of Desire

I am Aphródita of the shifting eyes.
My servants are Eros and you, my Sappho.
—Sappho

5 Bloom in Church: Beautiful Figures and Virgin Brides

> The veil, the curtain in front of something, still provides the most accessible image of the fundamental situation of love. (. . .) Absence is painted on the veil. (. . .) In the veil as an idol, man incarnates his sentiment of the nothingness that is beyond the love object.
>
> —Lacan

In the name of philosophy, the marquis de Sade denounces the Virgin Mary and implies that her virginity is a lie. "The reign of philosophy finally annihilates the reign of imposters . . . Reason replaces Mary in our temples, and the incense that burned at the knees of an adulteress will be lit from now on only at the feet of the goddess who broke our chains."[1] When Sade replaces her as an object of worship with the goddess of reason, he returns the feminine to the sphere of divinity, as an allegorical figure or a goddess. Sade's public denunciation of Christianity is the other side of his relation to the feminine. He vilifies Mary as an adulteress and takes her off the pedestal where she is adored in church. In her place, reason will be worshiped as "the divinity closest to his heart." The libertine Sade, who speaks here in the name of the French people, echoes Molière's Dom Juan in his rejection of religion but preserves the value of virginity and the adoration of the feminine.

Sade takes the figure of Mary out of church, and Don Juan abducts Donna Elvira from the convent. Joyce, however, returns Stephen to

[1] "Le règne de la philosophie vient anéantir enfin celui de l'imposture . . . La raison remplace Marie dans nos temples, et l'encens qui brûlait aux genoux d'une femme adultère ne s'allumera plus qu'aux pieds de la déesse qui brisa nos liens" (Pétition de la section des piques aux représentants du peuple français." Signed: "Sade, rédacteur." Approved, printed, and presented on 15 November 1793. Marquis de Sade, *Œuvres complètes* vol. 6 (Paris: Pauvert, 1986).

Mary, the second Eve, through Molly, his profane figure of the Virgin. Like Sade's Blessed Virgin, Molly Bloom is an adulteress (and a Jew, on her mother's side). Molly sings the part of the virginal bride, Zerlina, in Mozart's *Don Giovanni*. She unconsciously pities Bloom, the victim of her adultery, as Zerlina feels sorry for her jealous bridegroom, Masetto. Molly takes Zerlina's role as she plans her strategy, but she is not frightened like Zerlina when her Don Juan approaches her. She remains in the mood of seduction that is reflected in the aria "Là ci darem": "Singing a bit now and then mi fa pietà Masetto then Ill start dressing myself to go out presto non son più forte" (*U* 641).

Flaubert refines the libertine strategy when he tentatively proposes the Virgin as Don Juan's ultimate object. After the early modernists Baudelaire and Flaubert, Joyce turns to the libertine Don Juan and his consumption of beautiful figures and virgin brides. In a self-styled exile, Stephen Dedalus broods about his mother, and the Virgin who carried Christ, the other virgin son. Wandering through Dublin, Bloom cannot keep from thinking about sex and love, or about Molly and her betrayal. Through some madonnas of modernism, Joyce explores the poetics of the object of desire.

In the first scene of Molière's *Dom Juan*, Sganarelle informs his horrified interlocutor that not only has Dom Juan had his will of Done Elvire, but that he has used a promise of marriage to the same effect on infinite numbers of other women. He adds: "If I told you the names of all the women that he has married in different places, it would take all day."[2] Although it would not take as long to recite the names of the women interested in Ulysses, they lend their sex and their names to several of Joyce's chapters. The effects of these feminine roles, however, are quite different from the results achieved by Dom Juan or Giacomo Casanova. "It will never be," laments the narrator of the pretext of *Ulysses* that Richard Ellmann published in 1968 as *Giacomo Joyce*.

Sganarelle writes down the names after the fact in the evanescence of a desire that can be satisfied only once. Joyce writes them to preserve the ineluctably fleeting moment—the fugitive encounter between the woman passing by and the voyeur with eyes like coals—in the resurrections of art that transform the cristallized moments of

---

[2] "Dame, demoiselle, bourgeoise, paysanne, il ne trouve rien de trop chaud ni de trop froid pour lui; et si je te disais le nom de toutes celles qu'il a épousées en divers lieux, ce serait un chapitre à durer jusques au soir" (act 1, scene 1).

"bio-graphical" confrontation with Eros into writing. Its modes of representation include the comic and the sacred, realism and idealization, the satiric and the lyrical, and understatement and hyperbole. In *Ulysses*, the contrast between the highs and lows of these modes of representation reflects the confrontation with the Other. This contrast can be understood as the tension between romanticism and obscenity. The early modernism of Flaubert and Baudelaire constructs its aesthetic around this tension. The evanescent encounters between erotics and poetics that are central to Joyce's fiction turn into a modernist rhetoric of desire. The temporality of desire is fractured, fragmented, allegorical: it is based on the Fall.

In the wake of sin, at the scene of writing, the scandals and corruptions that Christianity associates with the feminine render desire permanent, sublime, and obscene. The effects that filter through the discourses of theology, philosophy, and psychoanalysis are formulated in the symptoms of neurosis and the letters of desire, or literature. The effects of desire produce certain questions, including Freud's most famous one, "What does a woman want?" Freud shifts Don Giovanni's question of desire ("Che vuoi?") from Donna Elvira, the consumed object, to the woman as woman, "Was will das Weib?" Lacan moves from "Was will . . . ?" and "Che vuoi?" to an articulation of the infinite returns of desire in writing by positing a feminine Other in the context of mystical writing. Joyce's view of desire reflects his refusal of asceticism and, especially, his Catholic affinity for an aesthetics of the feminine. He answers the question of feminine desire with the "language of flow"—the language of water, flowers, and roses of all descriptions. The discourses of modernity shatter the silence of submission and taboo—the silence of the virgin.

The presence of desire in literature confronts the reader with the unconscious, with sexual difference, and with the seductive powers of language. The symptom (Lacan's *sinthome,* with a play on the name of Aquinas) leaves its traces on the subject. A psychoanalytic reading of desire in literature leads to the question of how the symptom of sexuality is transfigured in the erotics of writing. Socrates and Plato offer an answer, in the voice of Diotima. Another answer comes from Christianity, in the portrait of the most mysterious act of procreation for the past two thousand years, and the most famous love triangle since Oedipus.

Filtered through religious and secular art, the appearances and apparitions of women in the chapters of *Ulysses* derive from the

Christian model, based on the triangle. Within its form and economy, the Other role is a feminine one. Cultural stage directions shape her into a seductive and yet unattainable figure, central to the Irish Catholic imagination. This erotic and poetic feminine figure is the Madonna.

Ulysses formulates and fantasizes her among the living and the dead. The end of the line is the triangle, borrowed from Dante, for Stephen's demonstration in "Oxen in the Sun": "Vergine Madre, figlia del tuo figlio."[3] The bittersweetness of this love is depicted in representations of the life of Christ from the Annunciation and the Passion to the Resurrection and beyond, in Mary's Assumption and Coronation. The tenderness that connects Christ and the Virgin is reflected in medieval and Renaissance iconography. Mary's mimesis of the Passion is visually linked to the seductive beauty of Mary Magdalen and the tenderness of John. When they appear with Christ, these secondary figures echo the amorous relation of Mary and Christ in their combined repentance and desire.

Renaissance tradition includes the ambivalent power of Eros the bittersweet. Emblems of the crucifixion (red coral, goldfinches, and fruit) and anticipatory signs of mourning (pallor, eye-circles, and solemn expressions) appear in scenes that celebrate maternal-filial love and Christ's carnal and sexual form. Signs of Mary's passionate emotion embellish the portrayals of the violent scenes of Christ's suffering and triumph.

As discussed in the context of the love between the Virgin and the Son in chapter 3, Carpaccio's *Flight into Egypt* also illustrates the impact of Eros the bittersweet on the Christian love triangle. On the left side of the painting, Christ the Son (consubstantial with the Father) amorously holds his mother; on the right, separated from them by a stretch of landscape, Joseph turns around to observe them. His vigorous movement contrasts with the hieratic pose of Mary and Christ and although his gaze is directed at them, they are not looking at him. He is moving in human time, while they appear in an erotic and mystical stillness.

As in Carpaccio's contrast of moving exile or flight and motionless

---

[3] I have discussed Joyce's use of Dante in *Joyce's Catholic Comedy of Language* (Madison: University of Wisconsin Press, 1985). For a commentary on the "Vergine Madre" passage, see especially chapter 3, "Modus Peregrinus."

9. Carpaccio, *The Flight into Egypt*, 1500, oil on panel. Courtesy of the National Gallery of Art.

mystical depth, Bloom and Stephen Dedalus circle homeless in Dublin, while Molly's appearances in the novel confine her to bed, to a sexual flow, and to a mystical non-progression of time. Joyce's return to the Oedipal model of adultery begins and ends the book of exile and return. At the end, the accessible profane Madonna figure of Molly Bloom restages the Fall in her seduction of Bloom, recalled in an ecstatic mode. Back at the beginning, Mulligan's travesty of the opening of Mass provides a liturgical frame for the painfully remembered obsessive prayer for the Dead. Lying in bed, Molly remembers the first time that she had sex "with all the talk of the world about it people make its only the first time after that its just the ordinary" (*U* 610). Molly's emphasis on the "first time" underscores her connection to Don Juan, and her link with Eve, original sin, the seedcake. Earlier the same day, Stephen is standing in the doorway and remembering that he stood at his mother's bed: he refused to kneel for the prayer that consecrated his mother's death by restoring her lost virginity.

The time is out of joint in Dublin on June 16, 1904. The Fall comes at the end, instead of in the beginning. The text of Molly's free association projects her thoughts inside out. In the end, an ecstatic

repetition of the Fall confirms her role as a profane Madonna figure.
Eve and Mary are intentionally blurred in the carnal poetics of Molly
Bloom, the rose of the mountain. Her jubilation of flower and seed,
of red and white, spirals through time and dissolves its markers. Possessed by Father and Son, Stephen's private Madonna-figure since the
Portrait—his own mother—weeps. Before the beginning of the book
that belatedly recalls her memory, on the morning of June sixteenth,
she laments love's bitter mystery. Then she dies.

She will reappear to her son in the baroque form of a rotting corpse
wearing her wedding gown, and he will ask her for the Word. It is not
clear whether this counter-Annunciation is (or can be) consummated
(*U* 473–74). It is not clear, or rather, it is no longer visible; Stephen
puts out the light. Love remains a mystery, and the model of creation
is double-distanced;[4] from the margins, maternity re-enters center
stage. The Catholic erotic model of the Annunciation to the Virgin
Mary is rejected by the fallen Stephen, but it insistently pursues him
through his mother's death and the prayer for which he refused to
kneel. The figure of Molly and her figures of speech provide a reconciliation of the two, from the doubly-distanced extremes of her identity as a profane Madonna in the final pages of *Ulysses*.

Love's bitter mystery lingers on the scene of *Ulysses* until the end.
Molly's sensualized Annunciation and Joyce's fictional discourse of
her desire project that mystery over the edges of masculine silence,
sleep, and communion. Molly's blurry flow of language gathers together the sacred and profane figures of the Virgin, the artful brides
figured in various states of seduction and Fall in the feminine fictions
of *Ulysses*. At the threshold of the dissolved codings of *Finnegans
Wake*, the figure chosen to weave her self-portrait in Penelope's tapestry is the Bride: "vergina madre" and daughter of the new Bloomusalem, bride of Christ and bride of Bloom. Her verbal tapestry portrays
Eros through scenes of the sacred and the profane, the comic and the
tragic. Lyrical and obscene, she gathers together the figures that Joyce
found in Flaubert, Yeats, and others—objects of desire, Madonnas of
modernism.

---

[4] See David Hayman, *Re-forming the Narrative: Toward a Mechanics of Modernist
Fiction* (Ithaca: Cornell University Press, 1987), 19–42. Near the conclusion of the
chapter, Hayman writes: "Born of the tradition of marginality (Sade, Flaubert, Lau-
tréamont), double-distancing seems to bring into being an aesthetic or aestheticizing
urge that simultaneously centers the margin and destabilizes the center," 42.

The Fruit of Thy Womb

The midwives come flapping down from Bride Street to the sea, Mulligan's (and Swinburne's) "great Mother" (*U* 5, 31). Stephen sees them in "Proteus" on the strand-scene of his erotic and poetic performance. This encore occurs without the birdgirl of the *Portrait*. She has been replaced by spectral and specular bridal visions of the bride of Adam, the bride of Christ, and the bride of Stephen's father (*U* 32). Later in the novel, at the scene of a birth, Stephen quotes Saint Bernard and Augustine to remind his listeners of Mary's power—but in the same breath, he recalls original sin: the Virgin is the second Eve. The profane Madonna figure of Molly Bloom completes a series of sublime bridal figures of art and corruption in *Ulysses*. Gerty's bridal aspirations are an indispensable prelude to Molly's monologue and an essential connection in *Ulysses* between the falsehood and trivial chatter of woman, "the flesh that says yes," and a Joycean eroticism of castration, countersigned by the social orders that Stephen Dedalus rejects.[5]

Women are accused of using their power against men, and Bloom's fate in Nighttown takes up the consequences of the terms of "humiliation," "weakness," and "dark shame" that shape the vocabulary of castration in the *Portrait*. Stephen's scenario at his mother's deathbed repeats the same persecution fantasy, and Molly's plotting against Bloom in the final pages confirms it. Attempts to read Joyce as a feminist writer are misleading, since there is no common ground for Joyce's often-quoted occasional statements on the desirable social advancement of women (or his double-edged critique of marriage) and the constant affirmation within his writings of a fantasmatic scenario based on the identification of the feminine with the agent of castration. Joyce's terms are perfectly Catholic; his discourse of castration includes the disguises of sacrifice, martyrdom, and victimization.

In Gerty's intermittent monologue, Joyce's accomplished performance of style includes elements of stereotyped preciosity, narcissism, a keenly self-deluding awareness of the opposite sex, and its Joycean counterpart, a strong sense of a Catholic sublime. These elements

[5] The important connection between Gerty's discourse and Molly's monologue has been made by Jean-Michel Rabaté in *Joyce: Portrait de l'auteur en autre lecteur* (Petit-Roeulx: Cistre, 1984), 79–91.

move through Gerty's memories and anticipations and converge on her obsession with the eventual possibility of being "arrayed for the bridal" on one of two altars. In Gerty's text Joyce represents the perverse feminine Irish Catholic virgin, arrayed for the future. From the advertising clichés and homilies of domesticity to the lyrical evocations of clean underwear, Gerty's discourse "translates" the language of the other into something that might have arrived just now from the laundry.

The negative qualities that emerge in her discourse will be attributed to the feminine element that she represents. Molly's self-portrait confirms Gerty's flaws designated within the projected feminine discourse of "Nausikaa." Both characters are obsessive, false, self-serving, vain, ignorant, trivial, wanton, and calculating. Gerty's adolescent characteristics lead away from Molly, however, into another terrain of Joycean aesthetics, erotics, and poetics.

Gerty's variations on the stereotypes of the feminine that are thematized in Molly's monologue include saccharine sentimentality, a denial of sexuality, and an extreme form of idealization. Symptoms of castration in feminine discourse lead Joyce back to the rather precious moments of the earlier Stephen Dedalus in *A Portrait*. Gerty's sentimentality and Stephen's idealizations meet retroactively in Stephen's bad faith and falsification during his brief period of reform. In Joyce's writing, the perils of castration lead back to the repression of sexuality, accompanied by self-delusion. Gerty sees herself as a nun or a self-styled "gentlewoman": "From everything in the least indelicate her finebred nature instinctively recoiled" (*U* 298). Ladylike Gerty and Stephen the sinless priest are briefly united in an inner display of Irish sentimentality. "The old love was waiting, waiting with little white hands stretched out, with blue appealing eyes. Heart of mine! She would follow her dream of love, the dictates of her heart that told her he was her all in all, the only man in all the world for her for love was the master guide" (*U* 299). These lines parody several moments in the *Portrait*, especially the motifs of the fourth chapter ("On! On! his heart seemed to cry" [*U* 179]) and the "unrest" passages of the second chapter: "He did not want to play. He wanted to meet in the real world the unsubstantial image which his soul so constantly beheld . . . a premonition which led him on told him that this image would, without any overt act of his, encounter him" (*P* 68). Restless, passive, dreamy, convinced that she too is "different from others," Gerty's portrait parodies the Stephen who is inspired by Mercedes in *The Count of Monte Cristo.*

Joyce underscores Gerty's connection with Stephen: "Nothing else mattered. Come what might she would be wild, untrammeled, free" (*U* 299). In the fourth chapter of the *Portrait,* Stephen experiences an ecstacy of erotic and poetic fantasy, couched in the lyrical terms that will sound somewhat double-edged in the following chapter, when they return to Stephen's "dewy wet soul." On the strand, Stephen decides, "He would create proudly out of the freedom and power of his soul" and "He was unheeded, happy, and near to the wild heart of life. He was alone and young and wilful and wildhearted, alone amid a waste of wild air and brackish waters" (*P* 179, 180). When Gerty preens for Bloom, her underwear is not plumage; the birdgirl on the beach in the *Portrait* has vanished.

The suprising parallel between the beached Gerty and Stephen on the strand in the *Portrait* is somewhat duplicitous. Stephen's self-proclaimed new freedom is the effect of his celebrated return to Life (namely, the repeated fall into Sin), and his decision to fly past the social nets of Ireland, while Joyce's witty parody of it in Gerty's thoughts has a darker side. In addition to her "typically feminine" (narcissistic and self-serving) illusions, Gerty's notion of freedom is all that women get. According to most of Joyce's portraits, it is all that women deserve: the freedom to follow a master, "the only man in the world." Joyce's use of "Nausikaa" to portray feminine castration is ultimately confirmed by an additional Oedipal defect. Bloom discovers it when Gerty leaves the scene, "She's lame! O!" He adds: "A defect is ten times worse in a woman. But makes them polite" (*U* 301).

Blessed Art Thou among Women

In *Ulysses,* the sublime brides of art and corruption discreetly locate their origin in the figure of the Madonna, and the liturgical framework of Catholicism that highlights her in *A Portrait of the Artist.* The Madonna is disseminated throughout *Ulysses;* the literary forms of her emergence are tuned to Joyce's principle of parallax. Her fantasmatic appearances occur according to the perspectives of individual characters, Dublin sites, and Irish popular culture. The connection between erotics and poetics that shapes the Madonna's portrait through the sensual images and literary pleasures of her cult is articulated in the third chapter of the *Portrait*, immediately following Stephen's discovery of sin and sex. The exquisite and ideal seductions of the Madonna in Joyce's later writings are based on this text.

Who are these figures of the Madonna, the sublime brides of art and corruption highlighted in *Ulysses*? The Blessed Virgin Mary frequently enters the text but she remains virtual. Like Diotima in the *Symposium*, she is quoted, invoked, and evoked, but she does not appear. Her images and liturgical emblems are inscribed in the thoughts of several characters and in intertextual narration, while her appearance is covered with the veils of absence and the sublime. The *Magnificat* is a subtle balancing act; it combines sublime exaltation and the erotics of the flesh, including Mary's maternity as the assimilation of paganism within Christianity.

This paradoxical vision—the Catholic figuration of desire and purity in the Madonna—can occur in Joyce's novel only in the profane mode of Molly Bloom, whereas the Christ figures in Nighttown are more boldly sketched in parodic and symbolic terms. The impossibility of a parodic representation of the Madonna marks another parallel with the Socratic love scene in the *Symposium*. The volatile Diotima threatens the exclusively masculine circle of the banquet with her feminine otherness, her occult mastery, and her version of the sublime. This explosive combination can be kept under control only if Diotima is rendered virtual. Her existence for the audience of the *Symposium* derives solely from Socrates' evocation of her in his speech. He implies that she is the author of the doctrine that he offers in her name. In any case, her appearance in the dialogue is an invisible one.

Diotima's virtual existence in the *Symposium* is confirmed by Socrates alone within a double narrative frame that quotes him. Unlike the Blessed Virgin, Diotima is not inscribed in a scriptural authority at the end of the line, beyond Plato's text. An acrobat of the sublime, Diotima might be a fiction of the feminine created by Socrates: the erotics of the other, or a midwife in Bride Street.

In *Ulysses*, the Madonna inspires images of brides in flower and fruit, and in ruin. They are the vectors of allegorical renderings of pleasure and evanescence, love and art, hell, paradise, and invisibility. The female characters who figure these bridal fantasies take the Joycean curves of emotion that turn the text in the direction of the Madonna. From the beginning and its retrospective arrangements,

from Martello tower and Edenville, the perverse turns of Annunciation are articulated all the way through Nighttown to the other Night.
In its darkness, Molly's adulterous bed of silent free association is
the Annunciation's end point. Perverse and *Père-verse,* writes Lacan:
turned toward the Father, in the model of successful incest that
Joyce's Catholic shorthand sowed in Edenville to reap in *Finnegans
Wake,* the never-never land of *felix culpa.* Lacan's vision of the perverse is tailor-made for Joycean erotics. Mariolatry and patriarchy fit
together perfectly, at least according to the Christian model of the triangle. Somewhat less perfect, however, is the human model that
filters down to Freud from antiquity. Oedipus is its filial protagonist
caught in an unhappy love story that Freud views as the ultimate
source, beyond Edenville, of the key to the riddle of desire that is our
point of origin. In other words, Freud's working through transforms
the story of Oedipus into an allegory of modernity.

In *Ulysses,* Oedipus is seconded by Odysseus. Their two modern
counterparts take on a series of common problems, starting and ending with the womanly flesh that says Yes, as Joyce would have it, in the
inversion of Faust's negation.[6] Unlike Oedipus or Odysseus, Joyce's
models of modernity are obsessively interested in virginity, in brides,
and in figures of the Madonna. These figures appear in the novel within
a series of triangular formations: the most important ones reinforce
the connections between Stephen Dedalus and Leopold Bloom.[7]

Joyce's sublime brides of art and corruption end the novel, mark its
opening scene, and structure a crucial mid-point, in "Nausikaa." This
chapter recalls the important strand scene of the *Portrait* and echoes
the "Proteus" chapter, when the brooding Stephen lingers among the
images and questions associated with the Blessed Virgin Mary, inscribed in "Telemachus." "Nausikaa" marks the peak of Bloom's desire and ends with Bloom writing in the sand, in a Judeo-Christian resonance of the Laws of Moses and Christ; its characterization of Gerty
and the simultaneous accompaniment of the Roman candles and the
Blessed Sacrament parody Stephen's erotic visions in the fourth and
fifth chapters of the *Portrait.*

Among women in *Ulysses,* the last one has sex, commits adultery,
is unfaithful, and talks non-stop to herself. Her ambivalent discourse

---

[6] In Goethe's *Faust I,* Mephistopheles first introduces himself to Faust with these
words: "Ich bin der Geist der stets verneint [I am the spirit that always says No]."

[7] See Rabaté, *Joyce: Portrait,* chapter 4.

weaves and unweaves a flow of monologue. "Penelope" is Marion-Molly, the profane Blessed Virgin who bears a strange resemblance to Sade's provocatively paranoiac epithets of the "adulterous woman" and the "Jewish whore." She is the singing "Siren" who seduces Odysseus with her voice, heard by Bloom alone, in memory, on June 16. Molly is a source of unlimited triangular formations for Bloom. They lead to her anticipated encounter with Stephen Dedalus.

The first woman is dead. She reappears in "Telemachus," in "Proteus," and in "Circe." May Goulding Dedalus is or was the late wife of Simon Dedalus and the mother of Stephen and a cluster of bedraggled daughters. After her death, she remains suspended between the heavenly Father, the less than heavenly father of Stephen, and the Luciferian son who feels her breath and hears her whisper "mute secret words," as he remembers hearing her weep for love's bitter mystery.

In between the beginning and the end, Joyce inserts the truly virginal Gerty MacDowell, the disfigured and aspiring figure of the bride. In her reveries, she pictures herself as the bride of either Reggy or Christ. She poses on the strand in full view of Bloom and during the church service of the Blessed Sacrament. "The fragrant names of her who was conceived without original sin" (U 292). Her Oedipal foot causes her to brood, like Stephen on the strand, about what happens in Eden; like him, she rehearses the Annunciation. She makes her confession to Father Conroy, who reassures her "that that was no sin because that came from the nature of woman instituted by God, he said, and that the Blessed Lady Herself said to the archangel Gabriel be it done unto me according to Thy Word" (U 294).

Gerty's carnal and spiritual triangles of erotics and poetics connect her with other virginal figures in the novel. They include Molly, Don Giovanni's Zerlina, Mrs Dedalus, who is purified in death, and Stephen Dedalus, the self-proclaimed son forever virgin: "But he said very entirely it was clean contrary to their suppose for he was the eternal son and ever virgin" (U 321). When Gerty watches Bloom and imagines his "wounds that wanted healing with heartbalm" (U 293) as she sits daydreaming among her bridal fantasies, the link between her and Molly is mediated by the "balsamo [balm]" that the still virginal Zerlina offers to Masetto in Mozart's *Don Giovanni*. Gerty's connections to Stephen are underscored by Joyce's parodic reference to her love of poetry in a context of sacrifice, weeping, and mourning (U 298).

Vergine Madre

Joyce's erotics of Catholicism is marked by the turn toward the Virgin. Gogarty's real-life epithet of the "virginal kipranger" is an oxymoron that marks Joyce's connection with the erotics of Baudelaire and Flaubert. The portrait of an artist is painted in the rutilant lily-white of Virtue at the site of feminine Vice—in the licentious atmosphere of the bordello in Nighttown. There he meets the sexual Other of femininity—the Other to whom knowledge is attributed, Lacan's "L'Autre supposé savoir [Other who should know]." One of Modernism's favored locations for her is Shakespeare's "nunnery," the whorehouse evoked by Hamlet in the raging Oedipal crisis that ends the possibility of happy sexual union. The Other is out there like the bird-like girl in the water. The paranoiac reciprocity of love implies that he is going to "get" her; she will "get" him; he will meet her in bed, but first, he turns her inside out. Her avatars include figures of virgins, mothers, and letter writers like Martha Clifford, Bloom's correspondent. "The Other who should know" is a constellation of women including Stephen's mother, Bloom's adulterous Virgin, and Molly as a fantasmatic body of language, the flesh that says yes. The tapestry of desire weaves affirmation and negation, memory and forgetting, into sentences without punctuation.

Figured by the black seed or navel that ends "Ithaca," the voice of masculine communion and navigation disappears inside the object of desire, the speaking feminine flesh of Molly, who begins with the "Yes" that once was her answer to Bloom's desire. The paranoiac ending celebrates the feminine element—earth, sea, memory, and death—into which the masculine appears to disappear. Joyce uses Molly to challenge or counter the masculine powers of Don Giovanni, the master of virginal beginnings. Molly points out that Boylan is no match for Bloom; she observes that Bloom is more attuned to women, and to love. His fantasies, and the knowledge that he ascribes to the feminine Other, place him inside her monologue, her one-woman Symposium.

The Socrates of Plato's *Symposium* represents an inversion of the closed masculine universe of contemplation. "Darkinbad the Brightdayler" disappears into the verbal body of the Other, whereas Socrates contains the Other inside his sentences. One of the fantasmatic anchoring-points of the *Symposium* is that Diotima is "inside" Socrates the philosopher. He possesses her; she has become part of him. She represents the paradox of being and having: these mutually exclusive alternatives have become one. Diotima will never appear, except in the virtual form projected by the voice of Socrates.

It is not by chance that the only other moment of the *Symposium* that reaches the dramatic height of Diotima's erotics is the closing discourse of Alcibiades' passionate love for Socrates. The feminine Other has been absorbed into the masculine space of Greek philosophy. Diotima's wisdom and the Eros of Socrates locate the question of love in the context of the sublime. As Benjamin points out in the preface to the *Trauerspiel* book, the *Symposium* takes up the relation between truth and beauty only insofar as truth is an object of desire.

The triangular discourse on love in Plato's representation of Diotima, Alcibiades, and Socrates remains central in philosophy, psychoanalysis, and literature. Kierkegaard, Freud and Lacan explicitly name Plato's *Symposium* in their considerations of love. Socrates' fiction returns to illuminate the love rhetoric that shapes modernist literature. The Socratic Eros provides a blueprint for the Modernist emphasis on the sublime, on love, and on the feminine. Some of the most influential Modernist writers—including Baudelaire, Flaubert, Mallarmé, Joyce, Yeats, Woolf, and Proust—have focused on the trans-romantic sublime of love, its erotics and poetics, its post-romantic excesses, and its complex reckoning with desire.

Modernism articulates the doubleness (and duplicity) of love as the confrontation between desire and love, earthly love and spiritual love, and idolatry and art. Modernism reinvests the detachment, virtue, knowledge, and sublime mastery of the philosopher in the *Symposium* in the figure of the artist-lover. This figure is the narrator, the ambitious future artist, the poet, and the priest. When the duplicitous lover and artist of love enters the scene in the figure of Don Juan, he combines the strategy of seduction and enjoyment with the art of rhetoric.

A Portrait of the Artist

Although Plato's portrayal of love in the *Symposium* is not addressed directly in Stephen Dedalus' conception of the "indifferent" artist, it seems to take effect, belatedly, on the modernist principle of detachment. Names are not pronounced by chance in Joyce's fiction, and the name of Plato appears only a few paragraphs before Joyce's protagonist articulates a "portrait of the artist" in the name of Aristotle and Aquinas (*P* 188). Like the Socrates described by Alcibiades, this artist speaks like a god and reveals divine images that have nothing in common with his own individual appearance. His exterior, personal, and visible form covers the images that emerge in his discourse.

Joyce applies Aquinas to the "divine images" associated with Socratic discourse in Plato's *Symposium*. The emphasis shifts away from philosophy and toward art. *Integritas, consonantias,* and *claritas* describe the created "object" (the work of art) with the same disinterested calculation that is reflected in the authorial subjectivity claimed by Stephen Dedalus: silence, exile, and cunning construct the "subject." Stephen's idealized creator is detached from the "nets" of spoken language, homeland, and submissive belief.

The figure of the artist, according to Joyce, plays the role of Don Juan. In *Ulysses,* Don Juan emerges in Bloom's fantasies and Molly's singing, in erotic forms, the winged language of the beautiful voice, and in its art. Don Juan is present at the rendez-vous between Joycean erotics and poetics; his presence guarantees the principle of detachment. Like the "cunning" verbal artist, he disappears into silence following the moment of his lyrical and erotic performance. He flies past the nets of the social order. The act of marriage that he repeatedly promises never takes place; he never stops moving. Artist and lover, he plays himself against the rules.

In *A Portrait of the Artist as a Young Man,* the principle of the artist's detachment has no visible origin. Stephen Dedalus' image of the creator as an invisible God is offered as "applied Aquinas" with philosophy hovering in the background. The original signature of Joyce's modernism, however, is missing. Stephen's claim that "the artist, like the God of creation, remains within or beyond or above his handiwork, invisible, refined out of existence, indifferent, paring his fingernails" (*P* 194–95) echoes Flaubert's aesthetic of authorial invisibility: "L'auteur, dans son oeuvre, doit être comme Dieu dans l'univers, présent partout, et visible nulle part [The author, in his work, must be like God in the universe, present everywhere, and invisible]."[8]

---

[8] Letter to Colet, 9 December 1852, in *Correspondance II* (Paris: Gallimard, Bibliothèque de la Pléiade, 1975), 204. See the letter to Mlle. Leroyer de Chantepie dated 18 March 1857. For the relation between Joyce and Flaubert, see David Hayman's essays in *PMLA* and *Orbis Litterarum,* as well as his recent book on modernism. The Flaubertian influence on Joyce via French modernism leaves its traces in another important work by Hayman, *Joyce et Mallarmé* (Paris: Lettres Modernes, 1956). Joyce's

Joyce takes up Flaubert's view of the necessary separation between art and the artist's self-identification: "Il faut . . . faire de l'art impersonnel. . . ." "L'impersonnalité est le signe de la force [One must . . . produce impersonal art. Impersonality is the sign of power]."[9] Distanced from the claims of autobiography, "impersonality" safeguards the autonomy of art; its effects and its truth are paradoxically guaranteed as fiction. The ideal art is "impersonal" because the relationship between writer and oeuvre is an invisible one. In this sense, the "personality" of the writer can be compared to the imperfect exterior of Alcibiades' Silenus figure in the *Symposium*, and the created work of art evokes the "divine images" that are hidden inside the Silenus. Alcibiades uses the opposition between exterior and interior to mark a contrast between the images of visible perception and the divine images of Socrates' discourse.

Joyce makes a Jesuitical show of using theology to reformulate Flaubert's trans-romantic principle of impersonality. This principle preserves writing from authorial displays of opinion and personalized emotion that might corrupt the work of art.[10] While Joyce develops the corrosive power of comedy and parody into an antidote for sentimentality, Flaubert uses irony as an extension of the principle of impersonality. His break with French Romantic self-portrayal is a model for the Joycean antidote to sentiment. Flaubert's non-comic fictional

---

connection to Flaubert was the subject of a colloquium at the Sorbonne and the Ecole Normale Supérieure sponsored by the *Institut des Textes et Manuscrits* (C.N.R.S.). The collected papers appear in *James Joyce 2, Scribble 2*, edited by Claude Jacquet and André Topia (Paris: Minard, 1990). At the *Institut des Textes et Manuscrits* colloquium of May 1997, André Topia gave a talk on style in Joyce's *Dubliners* and Flaubert that pursued some of the questions raised in his essay in *Scribble 2*. Topia's work on Joyce and Flaubert reflects an understanding of modernism as a trans-national European phenomenon.

[9] Letter of 18 April 1854, to Colet, *Correspondance II*, p. 555, and Letter of 6 November 1853, in *Correspondance II*, p. 463. See also the letter to Colet dated 25 October 1853: "prosateurs, à qui toute personnalité est interdite (et à moi surtout) [prosewriters, for whom all personality is taboo (and especially for me)]." In *A Portrait of the Artist as a Young Man*, Joyce writes: "The personality of the artist impersonalized itself" (P 194). Joyce's comment in the voice of Stephen seems to borrow French syntactic forms—especially the Flaubertian term of impersonality, integrated in the form of a reflexive verb—to mark its French modernist derivation.

[10] See Schlossman, *The Orient of Style: Modernist Allegories of Conversion* (Durham: Duke University Press, 1991) for an account of this principle and its effects in Proust, Flaubert, and Baudelaire.

elaboration of love and the sublime cuts close to the bone of the sensibility that unfolds in his private correspondence and journals. Sentiment haunts Flaubert's writing of fiction; it is a primary motive for his slow process of crossing-out and rewriting in the interests of style.

Flaubert considers any display of authorial sentiment within the work as a transgression of the Modernist principle of "impersonal art." Flaubert conceptualizes his art through metaphors of desire. These images take effect in his writing, especially from *Madame Bovary* to the *Three Stories*. The mystical image of the heart (or its blood) dissolved in ink—rendered invisible to the reader—presents Flaubert's "Other" love, the sublime alternative that he uses to challenge Louise Colet's "earthly" or carnal confusion between life and art.

Although Flaubert often describes art in feminine terms, he occasionally uses images of "muscular" or "virile" masculinity to counter Colet's sentimentality. In Flaubert's words, the "milk products" of sentiment compromise the ideality of art. He proposes instead the models of the dervishes and the flow of ink. Like the whirling skirts of the dervishes and their strange mediation between the flesh and the spirit, the mystical sea of ink takes love to the highest power. Feminine artifice turns into art. The inky taste in the mouth of the dying Emma Bovary hides the dissolved heart of her creator. He will be resurrected in the sea of ink that will turn the suffering and blood lust of Julian's "ferocious heart" into sainthood. Desire is memorialized in the beautiful line, color, and light of stained glass that Flaubert translates into an inscription, a legend, or a text.[11]

Art dissimulates the personal and sentimental identity of the heart, its suffering and enjoyment. The "Other" love, the spirituality essential to art, masks personality. The *Portrait* and *Ulysses* echo Flaubert's figure of a covering-up. Saint Julien in his monk's cowl, Salammbô and Mme Arnoux in their cloaks, and the goddess Tanit wear modernist versions of the veil—the artifice that Flaubert admired on women in the Orient. Through the effects of distancing, the veil of form transforms earthly elements into radiant and beautiful figures.

While Joyce's "theory" of the impersonal artist is rooted unmistakeably in Flaubert, the importance of the veil in Christian allegory and revelation is an overdetermined influence. It leads Joyce to the

---

[11] See *The Orient of Style: Modernist Allegories of Conversion* for a reading of style in "The Legend of Saint Julian the Hospitator" and its relation to *Madame Bovary*, *Salammbô*, and *The Sentimental Education*.

inscription of the veil image in *Ulysses* through the bride-like figures of the Virgin. Mrs Dedalus is surrounded by the white radiance of lily-white confessors in the Prayer for the Dead before she reappears in a decaying bridal apparition in Nighttown; the daydreaming Gerty struggles with her dwindling hopes of being a bride. She contemplates the Catholic alternative, "if ever she became a Dominican nun with their white habit" (*U* 294). At the men's temperance retreat, among candles and flowers, "the litany of Our Lady of Loreto" is recited to the "mystical rose" (*U* 290, 292) and the "benediction of the Most Blessed Sacrament" is enacted: "Canon O'Hanlon was up on the altar with the veil that Father Conroy put round his shoulders giving the benediction with the Blessed Sacrament in his hands" (*U* 298). The humoral veil is put on at the moment of Benediction when the priest's hands do not directly touch the monstrance.

Liturgical, aesthetic, dramatic, and erotic, the veils that hover in the air of *Ulysses* point toward the "wondrous revealment" of the mystical rose (*U* 300). The veil worn by Father Conroy connects the strand scene with *The Dead* and its converging figures of bridal loss, virginity, mourning, passion, and death; Gerty's poetics of veiled twilight echo the Virginal poetics of Stephen Dedalus. Meanwhile, Gerty's virginal revelation takes Bloom to the imaginative heights of pleasure. Fireworks are followed by his cool observations, in contrast to Gerty's high-flown histrionics of sentiment. "Why that highclass whore in Jammet's wore her veil only to her nose." The veil over sensuous form conceals and reveals, like Gerty's "transparent stockings, stretched to breaking point" (*U* 304). Bloom passes judgment on the overworked feminine erotic imagination and the twilight poetics of religion in the service of the Virgin Mary, who "is too a haven of refuge for the afflicted because of the seven dolours which transpierced her own heart" (*U* 294). Bloom thinks, "Virgins go mad in the end I suppose" (*U* 301). Joyce locates Flaubert's veil of artifice within a Catholic framework.

Associated with "divine images" in Flaubert and Joyce, the veil is a metaphor for the art object that is fabricated in modernist style. Since the "object" is aloof from life and the viewer, it is detached from inner and outer "reality." It is calculated, distanced, and beautiful. The metaphoric resonances of the veil bear witness to the mystical and spiritual dimensions of love, the Romantic double or counterpart of the sexual dimension of Eros. The "Other" love does not deny the passions and the flesh of the "earthly love," evoked by Flaubert; the

"Other" love veils them with beautiful figures. Flaubert's Oriental women appear within a constellation of the sublime. Joyce pays indirect homage to them in his strategic use of the "morning star"—the veiled Virgin Mary, who seductively and sublimely opens her arms to Dedalus the young sinner. In *Ulysses*, the bridal veils of Mrs Dedalus, Gerty, and Molly-Zerlina blend these figures of the Madonna into the modernist cityscape.

Bloom's Gossamer: The Most Beautiful Ones

The sublime is the meeting point of Eros and writing. Desire is articulated as sin, fall, flight, and the lyrical seductions of the voice; the theme of sublimation is central to Flaubert's modernism and to Joyce's Irish Catholic version of it. In the process that Freud calls sublimation, desire enters the sublime realm of art according to the enigmatic process of displacing the end-points of the drives without repressing them. Sublimation is paradoxical, because the sublime maintains its difference from carnal desire, even though it cannot rely on repression to hold it aloof from the drives and insure its existence in spite of their primary powers. For Flaubert, the violence of desire is taken up into writing as "the rage of sentences" and "the love of art." Their power establishes the principle of impersonality and the ideal of style that prevent the sublime from collapsing into the sentimental.

Like Flaubert's Don Juan, Joyce's figures of masculine desire seem to transcend the usual limits of eroticism. Following the writing and rewriting of sex, the endless repetitions of a seduction that always requires a new imaginary object (and if possible a "pure" one, untouched by other men), Don Juan suddenly comes face to face with the Other. From Saint Anthony to Don Juan and the romantic young men, Flaubert's focus on estrangement opens the language of fiction to the poetics of Eros. Flaubert's staging of fantasy is a blueprint for Nighttown. The whores, professional experts in sin, abjection, and sexual difference, take the stage for the interior theaters of Stephen and Bloom. In Nighttown, Stephen meets his dead mother, and Bloom is taken for a long ride by the Other that he most ardently desires in Molly.

Flaubert's Don Juan scenario is a variation on the essential moment of mystical experience described by Augustine, Theresa of Avila, John of the Cross, and others. This experience leaves traces in Lacan's account of feminine *jouissance,* a mysterious enjoyment that is veiled in the language and silence of mystical unknowing. Flaubert's Don Juan hears the seductive voice of the feminine Other speaking to him from beyond the margins of death, and his erotic domain suddenly expands to include the sublime. Flaubert introduces a mystical perspective into his scenario without denying Don Juan's corruption. In his sketch, the ideal and the scandalously sexual elements are woven together. Joyce follows Flaubert in this decisive modernist combination and its Baroque effects. The shining lilies of the Prayer for the Dead in Catholic liturgy and the rotting bridal corpse of Mrs Dedalus are inseparable in the underworld of *Ulysses.*

The double discourse of mystical purity and carnal corruption that literally haunts some of the key texts of modernism is not far from the twofold nature of Freud's sublime. Freud's modernist representation interlaces the artistic heights and the driven depths. Lacan's exploration of the fabricated products of sublimation adds a figure of shining and mystical femininity to its repertoire; he serves her up in gold and shiny paper marked *Encore.* Lacan's gift to his readers (and retrospectively, in hommage, to Freud) is the purloined figure of Bernini's Saint Theresa.

The writings of Flaubert and Joyce (as well as Freud and Lacan) stage a vision face to face, and no longer "through a glass darkly" of the sexual and sublime versions of love. Like Flaubert's evocation of the heart and the ink, Joyce's re-writing of the "sweets of sin" also focuses on the meeting of eroticism and style. When the lights go out in the Nighttown of *Ulysses,* a voyeur's theater of desire unfolds in styles ranging from the "pardon my French" monologue of Stephen's "parleyvoo" to Bloom's sadomasochistic dialogues.

The Nighttalk of *Ulysses* anticipates *Finnegans Wake,* a sustained exploration of language as an event that goes beyond the limits of the speaker's consciousness. This language introduces opacity into what it is supposed to be saying. The complexity of the code produces meaning through new patterns, and through repetition. Eroticism and poetics take the stage and turn out the lights on language itself. The strategy of the "unreadable" reshapes the literature of high modernism. In Nighttown, sexuality challenges the limits drawn by propriety, and dreaming unravels the borderlines of identity. Stephen scandalizes the bordello population with some allusions to classical and biblical antiquity (including the "first confessionbox") that Bella can understand only as an allusion to homosexuality: "None of that here. Come to the wrong shop." Lynch defends Stephen: "Let him alone. He's back from Paris." Immediately following this exchange, Zoe asks for "some parleyvoo" (P 464).

Stephen amuses them with his French marionette speech of religious and sexual drama. Horror and rapture combine in his "heaven and hell show" (U 465). "Parleyvoo" takes the scandals out of the confessional and into a virtual theater. The whores call for more: "Encore! Encore!" (U 466). Hamlet suddenly arrives, in word if not in form, as Stephen stops the show: "Mark me." He continues, "I dreamt of a watermelon." Freud also appears, in the unlikely form of Florry, "Dreams go by contraries." From parleyvoo to the dance of hours, the French language makes an autonymous appearance in the commands of Maginni the dancing master, and Stephen's solo dance or "pas seul" (U 472). The dance of the hours turns into the dance of death. The bridal object of desire appears as the dead mother, surrounded by the "choir of virgins and confessors" and the shining of white lilies ("Liliata rutilantium . . .").

Joyce's French connections among sexuality, the Church, and theatrical performance are increasingly visible from his early writings through *Ulysses* and *Finnegans Wake*. Joyce's "French" aesthetic is retrospectively illuminated by Flaubert's accounts of erotic fantasy in churches and the sublime vision of theater. After a visit to La Scala, Flaubert writes,

> J'ai marché sur la scène . . . en pensant vaguement à toutes les pièces et à tous les ballets; je suis entré dans deux loges, et j'ai songé à tout ce qui pouvait s'y dire. Un théâtre est un lieu tout aussi saint qu'une église, j'y entre avec une émotion religieuse, parce que, là aussi, la pensée humaine, rassasiée d'elle-même, cherche à sortir du réel.

> [I walked on the stage . . . thinking vaguely about all plays and ballets; I went into two boxes, and I thought about everything that might have been said there. A theater is as holy a place as a church, I enter it with religious emotion, because there too, human thought, weary of itself, seeks release from the real].[12]

---

[12] "Notes de Voyage", in *Œuvres complètes*, vol. 2 (Paris: Seuil, "L'Intégrale," 1964), 467.

At the scene of holy communion, personal and singular sweets of sin dissolve in the fantasmatic flesh and blood of the Word. Joyce reverses Flaubert's terms and compares the church to the theater. When Bloom goes to church, he thinks about Christian narrative as a drama of the "adulterous woman" with a discreet reminiscence of Sade. Sade writes in a political document that "La raison remplace Marie dans nos temples, et l'encens qui brûlait aux genoux d'une femme adultère ne s'allumera plus qu'aux pieds de la déesse qui brisa nos liens [Reason replaces Mary in our temples, and the incense that burned at the knees of an adulterous woman will only be lit at the feet of the goddess who broke our chains]." In *Philosophy in the Boudoir*, his staging of desire places the birth of Christ in a fantasmatic theater of abjection. Sade's character Dolmancé rejects Christian morality with a verbal violence that anticipates the anti-semitic delirium of Céline as well as the sado-masochistic whirlwind of Nighttown: "C'est dans le sein d'une putain juive, c'est au milieu d'une étable de cochons, que s'annonce le Dieu qui vient sauver la terre! [In the womb of a Jewish whore, in the middle of a pigsty, the God who is coming to save the earth announces his arrival]."[13]

Bloom's remarks in church remain decorous, or at least allusive. Sade and Flaubert, Freud and Lacan, are hidden in the confessional when Bloom imagines the possibility of "telling all":

> How long since your last mass? Gloria and immaculate virgin. Joseph her spouse . . . Confession. Everyone wants to. Then I will tell you all. Penance. Punish me, please. (. . .) Woman dying to. And I schschschschschsch. And did you chachachachacha? (. . .) Husband learn to his surprise. God's little joke. Then out she comes. Repentance skindeep. Lovely shame. Pray at an altar. Hail Mary and Holy Mary. Flowers, incense, candles melting. Hide her blushes. (*U* 68)

If Joyce remains attached to the Marian aesthetics of Catholicism, Sade's cult of the goddess Reason induces him to vilify the Virgin as an adulteress, a Jew, and a whore. The violence of his language does not indicate indifference to Christian values or to the charms of the Madonna.

Bloom's scenario of adultery is based on a "little joke." The Libidinous God (dixit *Giacomo Joyce*) constructs a triangle by taking pos-

---

[13] See note 1. *La Philosophie dans le boudoir* in *Œuvres complètes*, vol. 3 (Paris: Pauvert, 1986) 408.

session of the Virgin. Language turns into the virile object, the bone or weapon: "Woman dying to." Molly dying for "it" is dying to talk about "it," the object of desire and rhetoric, the erotic encounter, and the ecstatic moment of carnal and mystical experience. On the sado-masochistic ground of eroticism, the pleasure principle and its beyond are the object of confession. Mystical love and the resurrection of the body are the subject of theology. In church, Bloom perceives aesthetic beauty "of all kinds" under the sign of the Virgin—immaculate, ashamed, blushing, adulterous, and lovely.

Encore

Joyce uses Molly as a vehicle for "talking dirty" or speaking the "French" of Anglo-Saxon slang, and since Joyce cannot overcome the taboo of this kind of talk in church, Molly uses those dirty words in bed. She remembers the priest's prying attempts to get her to confess her sexual experience, attempts that echo the questions that Joyce asked Nora. His interrogations move from one set of "French letters" (obscene and beautiful words) to the ones that he accused her of using in an affair with another man.[14] These French letters circulate in *Ulysses*, in Bloom's desire-filled wandering.

After her adulterous afternoon, Molly remembers Bloom's decep-tive manners. She does not understand his pleasure in "those words." "What a Deceiver then he wrote me that letter with all those words in it how could he have the face to any woman after his company man-ners" (*U* 615). Later she adds: "Ill see if he has that French letter still in his pocketbook I suppose he thinks I dont know deceitful men all their 20 pockets arent enough for their lies" (*U* 635). Bloom carries his "French letter" as furtively as the correspondence that he uses in the pursuit of sexual relations.

Other French letters and fictions of love emerge on the Joycean hori-zon, including the letters to Nora in 1909, a few notes that Joyce sent to Martha Fleischmann, and the detour of Flaubert's correspondence with Louise Colet. The erotics of writing leads through Joyce's Dublin "French" to Bloom's modest attempts at obscene letters to Mary and Martha (Molly and Martha Clifford), and to the productions of Shem

[14] See the letter dated December 9, 1909, in *Selected Letters* (New York: Viking, 1975).

the Penman. The impossibility of sending French letters to Amalia
Popper may have led to some of the beautiful words in the text of
Giacomo Joyce; their prolonged effects are written into *Ulysses* and
Finnegans Wake.

Giacomo Joyce is a kind of laboratory for the author's experiments
in identification, voice, rhythm, and the writing of seduction. When
Joyce concludes his quasi-fictional fantasmatic wrestling with sin,
conscience, a Jewish father, and a libidinous God, a new strategy
emerges. Fiction unfolds an erotic vocation, and the rejected Casanova
turns Eros into writing. The textual and stylistic relation of *Giacomo
Joyce* to *Ulysses* and *Finnegans Wake* offers evidence of the relation
between unwritten love letters and the deferral of seduction until
Bloomsday, the literary celebration of the first major favors for which
Joyce did not pay.[15] In this text, the relation between the fiction of
Ulysses and a hypothetical background for Bloomsday is worth men-
tioning for literary rather than biographical reasons. The experienced
effects of Eros can resonate within the scene of writing, but the biographical tendency to "explain" writing through an imaginary construction of a life cannot be justified in the terms of either psychoanalysis or literature. Freud's challenge to the biographical claim for
truth indirectly preserves the specificity of the literary object.

Eros is integrated in the ideal structure of Christian theology and its
family romance. The monotheistic focus shifts from the libidinous
Father (and even from the potential Trinity he composes with his
Spirit and the Messiah still suspended in time) to Christ the Son—the
Word born of a human mother. As a human creature who is (retroactively) born without sin, the Virgin becomes a non-menacing fantasmatic object, identified with the Church that continues to give birth
to him and to Christians. She nourishes them with beauty, sensual
presence, and feminine images that do not lead them into dangerous
waters. Catholicism preserves the cult images of a woman as an object of carnal love. It is significant that the figures of the feminine, rejected by Protestantism and Judaism, can return only in the margin-
alized figures of the mystics.

The *Transmagnificandjewbangtantiation* leads from Stephen to
Bloom.[16] The incarnation and the paschal sacrifice are repeatedly
echoed with bread and wine; transubstantiation occurs through the

---

[15] See Ellmann's preface to *Giacomo Joyce* (New York: Viking Press, 1968).
[16] See Schlossman, *Joyce's Catholic Comedy of Language.*

effects of language that bring the incarnation and sacrifice to the subject. Christ's human side allows for the erotic investment in a flesh and blood mother, the first and only woman in Judeo-Christian history who acts out the scenario that haunts the unconscious. She becomes the Sposa in Heaven, the mystical marriage partner, of the son she bore on earth. This act is consummated in the authentic turn of the son toward the Father (Lacan's Catholic reading of perversion). French letters encode the erotic turn of Bloom's imagination, his preoccupation with the writing of loveletters, and the lingering souvenir of sexuality. Molly has not forgotten that he carries it around all day. French letters translate the triangular predicaments of the Irish Catholic exiled in upon himself into the dark Nighttown of modernism.

Instead of the punishment that befalls Oedipus, whose sufferings for his involuntary act of parricide cannot obliterate the pleasure of incest, the union of the Blessed Virgin Mary and her son occurs as a belated consolation for the voluntary suffering of Christ's sacrifice of his body and blood. In psychoanalytic terms, this uniquely happy incest explains Mary's unique status as the "vergine madre." The Christian turn toward Eros prescribes a substitute for the sexual deadlock illustrated in hysteria: the hysteric repeats the stranglehold of the Oedipal scene. In *Studies in Hysteria,* Freud illustrates this stranglehold in Anna O.'s attempt to seduce Breuer, and Freud points out that the incident led Breuer to abandon psychoanalysis and his professional association with Freud. The terror of the triangle that psychoanalysis cannot elide seems to have only one alternative in the discontents of Western civilization—the "holy conversation" of God and his mother.

Because of the theological identity between father and son, there is no Oedipal violence in this family. It is not necessary to repress amorous foreplay or the figures of visual imagery that leave little to the imagination. Medieval and Renaissance iconography illustrates the *felix culpa* of Catholic liturgy. The before and after of Christian desire show a woman bringing sin into the Old Testament world, while the new couple of the New Testament present the Anointed Son of God and the "new Eve," his mother. The mystery of the Incarnation dissolves the knot of sin. The new recipe for love brings together a man who is God and a woman without sin. Joyce calls this combination "felix copula" in *Finnegans Wake.* Before the father appears in serialized form as HCE, Joyce inscribes Bloom's desire at the intersection of eroticism and religion.

Bloom's meditation on the Church's poetics of seduction occurs at a moment in *Ulysses* when his mind is on Molly's singing, her response to the seductions of a Don Giovanni figure, and Bloom's own attempt to play the Don with his correspondent, Martha Clifford. His thoughts include the "language of flowers" and the hummed version of the duet between Don Giovanni and Zerlina: "La ci darem la mano La la lala la la" (*U* 63). Bloom seems to be successful with Martha, "Weak joy opened his lips. Changed since the first letter." His seduction takes place on paper: "Could meet one Sunday after the rosary. Thank you: not having any. Usual love scrimmage. Then running round corners. Bad as a row with Molly" (*U* 64). Now that his correspondent is interested, Bloom prefers a literary relationship.

Joyce's "French letters" spell out the sexual relation of words that Bloom desires to obtain through the post from his Martha. Love letters to the Madonna emblematize the modernist encounter between religion and eroticism. Art knots them together in the two loves. Dante's virtual love letter to the Madonna in the final canto of the *Paradiso* resonates in modernism, but without silencing the language of the unnameable and of the obscene. Molly's four-letter words and her bedtime atmosphere do not diminish her parallels with the Virgin. These parallels include occasional moments of piety, recognition of the Madonna, mourning for her dead son, and another resurrection of the flesh, alluded to as love's old sweet song. Her lyrical ending exalts the first time: she remembers saying yes to Bloom's desire.

That Other World

Although the correspondences of Flaubert and Joyce were not intended for a public readership or for biographers, the texts of their letters resonate as essentially literary creations. As Flaubert pointed out to Colet, his "saltimbanque" character led to a certain autonomy of the pen. Epistolary form is open to the intrusive presence of fiction.

Biography displaces the impact of literature to the realm of confession, but the power of fiction over "life"—retroactively claimed by biography—eludes the biographer's scenarios. Flaubert criticism offers an illuminating example in the assumption that the character of Frédéric in *The Sentimental Education* is an autobiographical self-portrait of the author and his attachment to Elisa Schlésinger. This viewpoint allows for a seamless decoding of the novel, but it reduces the role of fiction and style to mere accessories. The risks of biographical criticism are anticipated at certain moments of Flaubert's correspondence with Colet. She demands that he write about their love affair, while he struggles to pry her away from her sentimental notions about writing. She persists in her fuzzy assertions that literature is a form of personal expression, while Flaubert puts distance between art and love. He encourages her to write poetry for the sake of art—a beautiful web of fiction and artifice.

Even Bloom's modest attempt at love correspondence illustrates the power of writing to elude the constraints and imaginary constructs of biography. Hypothetically obscene and perhaps conventionally romantic, the unseen letter to which Martha Clifford responds seems to be tame by most standards. It cannot compare to the highs and lows of Joyce's obscene and sentimental love correspondence. *Ulysses* indicates that the effect on Bloom of his correspondence moves beyond the question of the failure or success of his attempt to seduce his correspondent. Caught between reading and writing, "word" and "world" invade his thoughts after he receives Martha's letter on June 16, 1904. The writing of love letters takes him into an Other world.

Beyond the claims made for biography, love letters offer an intimate laboratory of fiction. The writer in the boudoir can do things with words, but perhaps it is what words do to him that is more to the point. This reversal is also evident in Flaubert's success at conducting an intense love affair, including scenes of jealousy, passion, reconciliation, and breaking off, almost entirely through the mail, or in Lacan's reading of "Joyce the symptom." The question of what words can do is explored in the crossroads of religion, poetics, and eroticism. These three versions of how the Symbolic and the Imaginary come to terms with the Real that tends to elude their capacity for representation are knotted together in love letters, the seductions that unfold on paper. It is not by chance that the page-long list of the verbal productions that "persianly literature" the floors and walls of Shem's house in *Finnegans Wake*, "the Haunted Inkbottle, no number Brimstone Walk" begins with "burst loveletters" (*FW* 182.31, 183.11).

Flaubert's double love of flesh and spirit is played out in the Christian poetics of seduction that haunt the early sketches for *Madame Bovary* as well as the characterizations of Saint Antoine, Salammbô, her eunuch priest Schahabarim, Frédéric Moreau, and Saint Julian. In an essay entitled "On the Universal Tendency to Debasement in the Sphere of Love," Freud discovers a similar dichotomy. He apparently

interrupts a commentary on modern subjectivity with the following
digression on the connection between asceticism and sexuality:

> In times in which there were no difficulties standing in the way of sex-
> ual satisfaction, such as perhaps during the decline of the ancient civi-
> lizations, love became worthless and life empty, and strong reaction-
> formations were required to restore indispensable affective values. In
> this connection it may be claimed that the ascetic current in Christian-
> ity created psychical values for love which pagan antiquity was never
> able to confer on it. This current assumed its greatest importance with
> the ascetic monks, whose lives were almost entirely occupied with the
> struggle against libidinal temptation.[17]

Freud's reading of love takes up the inheritance of modernity in the
Christian elaboration of desire. The connections between desire, asceticism, and spirituality shape Freud's concept of modern love. The
erotics of Christianity and the Christian poetics of seduction culminate in modernist love stories and figures.

Freud's account of sublimation in love recalls the Platonic origins of
Eros, in Poros and Penia. When sublimation has not yet taken effect,
the subject falls: sexual excess is associated with emptiness, debasement, and sin; excessive deprivation leads to a constant struggle with
repression. Joyce's *delectatio morosa* offers a strange condensation of
the sweets of sin and the blackness of hopeless obsession. The invisible theater of Flaubert's *Temptation of Saint Anthony* illustrates
Freud's comment and points toward the underground theater of sexual
difference in *Ulysses*.

The itinerary of *Ulysses* leads from morose delectation, familiar to
Freud and Lacan, to Molly's memories of letting it be done to her according to Bloom's will. She celebrates seduction, incarnation, and the
mystical roses of the Litanies to the Blessed Virgin Mary. The original
configuration of the two loves that permeate Flaubert's oeuvre is less
clear than the Joycean model, but the combined influence of Flaubert's childhood years in his father's hospital, the ambient Catholicism of Normandy, and an intense involvement with romanticism appear to determine the split between earthly and mystical love long
before Flaubert's famous breakdown. Flaubert's crisis of withdrawal

---

[17] Sigmund Freud, *Standard Edition of the Complete Psychological Works*, trans.
James Strachey, vol. 11 (London: Hogarth Press and the Institute for Psychoanalysis,
1953–74), 188.

turned the duality of love into a permanent instance of autobiographical alibi; his correspondence indicates that it became very useful for
keeping Colet at a safe distance. Letter-writing flourishes, in the space
that Bloom circumscribes for Henry Flower. The split became central
to Flaubert's writing about virgins and their seducers—Barbarians,
Carthaginians, Christians, and Don Juans.

Joyce's representation of Irish Catholicism is more in line with
Freud's portrait of extremes that meet on the terrain of love. Like
Joyce's other writings, his love letters subject the object of desire to
both extremes: the French talk of the underworld of the unconscious,
and the lyric tones celebrating beautiful virgins and the sublime.[18]
Joyce wants to have them both at once. His debased creature of sin is
also the holiest mother, the figure of the Virgin. When Flaubert writes
love letters to Colet, he maintains an even lyrical tone. He evokes her
sensual effects on him and his adoration of her as a Madonna figure
in the same paragraph. But Joyce alternates modes of discourse that
appear to be mutually exclusive. Like the many pages devoted to
Stephen's erotics and poetics in *A Portrait,* Joyce's love letters focus in
turn on the obscenity of "coarse words" and the "soft rose-like joy"
that he associates with heaven and the Virgin. "Are you too, then, like
me, one moment high as the stars, the next lower than the lowest
wretches?"[19] Sin and grace talk their way through Catholicism; the
language of obscenity alternates with the language of mystical ecstacy, like the worldly and the saintly realms that Flaubert inscribes
in his triptych of Saint Anthony. This clear separation veils the message that Flaubert revealed to Colet. Flaubert anticipates Freud in his
view that art and religion represent a break between the flesh and the
Other, but the artist cannot deny the intimate relation between the
sublime and the sexuality that sustains it.[20]

The Joycean connection between dirty words and beautiful ones
emerges in a love letter. "Write nothing else. Let every sentence be full
of dirty immodest words and sounds. They are all lovely to hear and
to see on paper but the dirtiest are the most beautiful." Obscenity alternates with the sublime in his vision of the feminine. "Or is love

---

[18] Here and in the paragraphs that follow I will be discussing Joyce's letters to Nora
dated 2 September, 9 December, and 31 August 1909. See *Selected Letters,* pp. 166–
67, 186, and 165.

[19] Letter to Nora dated 2 September 1909 in *Selected Letters.*

[20] See the discussions of the sublime in Schlossman, *Joyce's Catholic Comedy of
Language* and *The Orient of Style: Modernist Allegories of Conversion.*

madness? One moment I see you like a virgin or madonna the next moment I see you shameless, insolent, half naked and obscene!"[21]

The alternating images that emerge from the unconscious source of fantasy echo the discourse of sin and grace, hell and heaven. In the context of an interpretation of Joyce, Lacan claims that the true Catholic cannot be analyzed, since the symbolic structure of Catholicism competes with the framework of psychoanalysis. The rival discourse brings the sweets of sin into language. The Word takes on a human form and suspends desire in the talking cure of confession. Enter the Madonna. Singled out from the feminine bodies of paganism, she rises to prominence on the fertile medieval ground of asceticism, allegory, and the pedagogical seductions of visible form in iconographic art.[22] The doctrines of mystical and courtly love celebrate her as the ideal figure of the feminine. She is its model, its representation, and its aesthetic object. Like psychoanalysis, modernist representation of the insistence of desire unravels the subjectivity of eternity and damnation, purity and repression. That is why Dedalus refuses to kneel.

In Freud's analysis of the psychology of love, the prostitute-object is the counterpart of the mother-object. Desire can be satisfied only in the absence of love, while the purity of love can be sustained only in the absence of desire. The erotics of Christian asceticism offer a constellation that is even more perverse. The two categories threaten to run together in the endless permutations of a singular beautiful feminine image. It erases the boundaries between sensuality and purity, carnal desire and spiritual devotion, and pleasure and pain. This figure of Christian erotics and poetics is the image of the Virgin Mary. Joyce writes to Nora, "Every coarse word in speech offends me now (. . .) You have been to my young manhood what the idea of the Blessed Virgin was to my boyhood . . . One word of praise from you fills me with joy, a soft rose-like joy."[23] In a letter to Martha Fleischmann, Joyce writes, "rosa mistica, ora pro me! [mystic rose, pray for me!]"[24]

No wonder that Molly Bloom so badly wants a love letter! Miniatures of fiction, love letters transfer the world of seduction from one page to another and arrange the rendez-vous of the sublime and the

[21] Letter to Nora dated December 9, 1909, and letter dated September 2, 1909, in *Selected Letters.*

[22] See Régine Pernoud, *Le Visage de la femme médievale* (Paris: Flammarion, 1998).

[23] *Selected Letters,* 165.

[24] Letter dated 2 February 1919, *Selected Letters,* 238.

body. Bloom gives it a try with his Martha; Emma Bovary's correspondence with Rodolphe hovers in another register, and belatedly conveys its terrible message to Charles after her death. Like the message from the Commander that consigns Don Giovanni to his final struggle, the powers of seduction transcend the grave.

In Flaubert's theater of seduction, the message that contradicts Charles's notion about Emma's platonic relationship to Rodolphe comes from love letters that reach their final destination. They are received by the love-struck mourner after her death. Emma corrupts Charles from beyond the grave when the love letters that she received from another man reach Charles from the Other world.

Flaubert's sketch of Don Juan anticipates the posthumous supernatural dimensions of love in *Madame Bovary*. Donna Anna's encounter with Don Juan takes place in a temporary resurrection: she tells him of her illness and her death. The Other world takes over the task assigned to love letters in the words of this world. Because Flaubert's Salammbô cannot write a love letter, she envelopes herself in veils and slips under the tent flap to Mâtho's bed. This slip proves fatal, because it takes her over the edge of the sublime. Mâtho's passion for the Other is also fatal. Giscon, the hideous living dead, violently denounces her fall. Like Donna Anna, he is already posthumous; like her, he remains loyal to the Commander, the absent father. Love enters Flaubert's supernatural. It goes beyond limits of time, space, and the human heart's narrowness. The "going beyond" of the "inassouvissable" leads from desire to the Other, from earthly limits to the Other love of the mystics. Flaubert formulates the Other love as the love of Art that will resurrect the Past. Joyce's "retrospective arrangement" echoes it.

The infinite quality of the Other love goes beyond the limits of a romantic persona represented by an authorial voice. Flaubert bans sentimental expression—in the name of the author—of earthly love, sexual politics, jealousy, and self-pity. He proposes an alternative aesthetic of impersonality that translates the Other love into style. Rather than display the heart's passions, Flaubert's alternative strategy dissolves the heart in ink and hides it from the reader. The process of "dissolving" the "heart" disseminates passion in writing by depersonalizing, detaching, distancing, remembering, and reshaping. His use of allegory includes some traditional Judeo-Christian elements as well as baroque and romantic elements; this process allows the heart to enter the Other love, and the Other world.

Joyce's "rosa mystica" exclamation turns the Litany of the Virgin into a love letter. It wears the veil of modernist allegory. Seduction flowers on paper and renames its subject (like Bloom's Henry Flower) in an allegory of love. Joyce's brief but exemplary correspondence to Martha Fleischmann draws textual figures from Job and the dust of death: "the womb of a Jewess" in which Christ was conceived; Dante's "dark night"; Shakespeare and the "dark Lady"; and especially the Virgin Mary. Whereas the first known letter to Martha Fleischmann addresses her as a "Jewish woman" like the mother of Christ, the last letter invokes the Litany of Loreto. It is dated "Maria Lichtmesse 1919," the Feast of Lights for the Virgin, Joyce's Virginized birthday.[25]

Beautiful figures depersonalize the message. When writing is eroticized through the beautiful objects of literary tradition, the seductions of love letters enter the poetics that produce literature. The boundaries are blurred and the Catholic encounter of obscene and ideal, flesh and spirit, links Flaubert's configurations of the sublime to Joyce's Catholic comedy of language. Flaubert writes to Colet,

> Il y a chez toutes les prostituées d'Italie une madone qui jour et nuit brille aux bougies au-dessus de leur lit. L'épais bourgeois ne voit là qu'une jonglerie absurde . . . ça me touche, moi, cela, au contraire, je trouve cela sublime.

> [All the prostitutes of Italy have a madonna above their beds that day and night is illuminated with candles. The dim bourgeois sees only absurd farce in this. On the contrary, it touches me, I find it sublime.][26]

Theology meets popular culture in the aestheticization of the mother. Her beautiful flesh is made pure for the Father and turned into art, fetish, or kitsch—the fetish object that culture dismisses because it does not believe in it. Flaubert evokes as "sublime" the presence of that ideal beauty hovering over the commodity of the flesh. His letter to Colet echoes the sublime encounter between obscenity and the Madonna. Flaubert's tableau of the madonna of the prostitutes is filled with silence, like the most erotic (and "obscene") moments in his fiction.

Flaubert stages other encounters between sexuality and the figure

---

[25] These letters were first published in the *Selected Letters*, 232–38.
[26] Letter dated 5 September 1846, in *Correspondance I*.

of the Madonna. Like Rodolphe seducing Emma, he tells Colet: "je te regarde ... comme une madone [I look to you as a madonna]."[27] Flaubert broke off their tempestuous relationship between 1848 and 1851. Shortly before their reconciliation, she appears to him through a true Virgin, painted by Murillo. Like Baudelaire's ex-voto, Murillo's figure nursing the Child is in the Spanish style. Flaubert writes about the Virgin as an object of madness, love, obsession, and visionary hallucination: "J'ai vu une *Vierge* de Murillo qui me poursuit comme une hallucination perpétuelle [I saw a Murillo *Virgin* that pursues me like a perpetual hallucination]."[28] Flaubert's fantasy of being pursued by Murillo's Virgin returns, transformed, in *Salammbô* and *The Sentimental Education*. Mâtho and Frédéric are haunted and obsessed by images of the Virgin. Salammbô, the young protegée of the eunuch priest Schahabarim and the goddess Tanith, is desired by Mâtho, while Frédéric is haunted by a more motherly figure. His Marie is closer to Murillo's Virgin, to Colet, and to Elisa Schlésinger than Salammbô could be. At the moment of her belated return to Frédéric, he invokes her as a romantic version of the Madonna. "'C'était Mme Arnoux telle que vous étiez, avec ses deux enfants, tendre, sérieuse, belle à éblouir, et si bonne! Cette image-là effaçait tous les autres. [It was Mme Arnoux as you were, with her two children, tender, serious, dazzlingly beautiful, and so good! That image erased all others].'"[29]

Like Zerlina, Donna Anna, and Donna Elvira, the virginal objects of Don Giovanni's desire, and like their descendant Molly Bloom, Marie Arnoux sings beautifully in Italian.

> Ses lèvres s'entrouvrirent et un son pur, long, filé, monta dans l'air. . . . Cela commençait sur un rythme grave, tel qu'un chant d'église, puis, s'animant crescendo, multipliait les éclats sonores, s'apaisait tout à coup; et la mélodie revenait amoureusement, avec une oscillation large et paresseuse.

> [Her lips parted and a pure, long, drawn-out sound rose in the air . . . It began with a solemn rhythm, like a church song, then, crescendo, multiplied the bursts of sound, suddenly grew calm; and the melody was returning amorously, with a broad lazy oscillation.][30]

---

[27] Letter dated August 1846. Ibid.
[28] Letter to Bouilhet, 9 April 1851, in ibid.
[29] *L'Education sentimentale* in *Oeuvres*, vol. 2, Part 3, Chapter 6, 161.
[30] *L'Education sentimentale*, *Œuvres*, Part 1, Chapter 4, 26.

Frédéric is not quite ready to play the role of Don Giovanni at this
point, except, perhaps, with another virginal figure. As if by chance,
she borrows her Christian name from Louise Colet. When Marie
Arnoux sings, her admirer hears only the melody: "Frédéric ne com-
prit rien aux paroles italiennes [Frédéric understood none of the
Italian lyrics]."[31] Mozart's Don Giovanni, however, like Flaubert's
sketched-out Don Juan, seems to know all there is to know about lyric
and its potential for seduction. In and out of Nighttown, "Stephen-
Christ" awaits the Word from his phantom Madonna. Joyce places
Bloom somewhere in between Frédéric and Don Giovanni. He does
not know Italian, but when Molly sings Zerlina's duet he gets the
message. He sacrifices at the altar of the profane virgin: he adores the
Madonna in all her forms.

[31] Ibid.

6   Isolde at Sea: Jealousy, Erotics, and Poetics

He had written verses for her again after ten years.

—That's real poetry for you, he said. There's real love.

Asked me, was I writing poems? About whom? I asked her.
—Joyce, Portrait

The culture of love is channeled into the secularization that shapes modernity, and yet it continues to highlight the role of the Madonna. Faithful to its medieval origins, Renaissance art enthrones Mary, the Star of the Sea: she remains on a pedestal, and sits like a statue beneath the shell of Venus. Her aura of mystical virginity is preserved in the poetics of the Madonnas of Modernism. In contrast, the secularizing access to eroticism submits the Madonna figures to the debasement of the object. Identification and ambivalence characterize the triangular relationship of lover, beloved, and rival. The *Symposium*, and in particular the discourse of Alcibiades, foreshadows this configuration. In medieval Christian iconography and in Renaissance painting, Mary's melancholy husband, Joseph, is erotically displaced by the Father and then the Son. Bitter or resigned, he witnesses the love between his wife and the Son. In Carpaccio's *Flight into Egypt*, Joseph is spatially set apart, aand turns back to observe the Son's amorous gesture to Mary.

Beyond the boundaries of language, nationality, genre, folklore, and popular culture, the triangle haunts the culture of love.[1] Repeated

---

[1] See Peter N. Stearns, *Jealousy: The Evolution of an Emotion in American History* (New York: New York University Press, 1989). In the context of literature, see Rosemary Lloyd, *Closer and Closer Apart* (Ithaca: Cornell University Press, 1996).

10. Filippo Lippi, *Madonna and Child*, c. 1440–45, tempera on wood. Courtesy of the National Gallery of Art.

variations on certain literary figures indicate the powerful effects of the triangle. These figures range from the libertine Don Juan to Tristan and Isolde, the lovers who remain true to each other even after the effects of the herbed wine have worn off. Undisguised, the triangle of subjectivity shapes the medieval Tristan texts that feature Isolde as the object of desire. A genetically oriented interpretation of several texts focused on Isolde reveals the process that transforms a medieval figure of the feminine into a madonna of modernism.

The "Tristan and Isolde" sketch for *Finnegans Wake,* book 2, chapter 4, rewrites the Celtic legend of the adulterous triangle formed by King Marc of Cornwall, his Irish bride, the princess Iseult, and his nephew Tristan, who went in search of Iseult on behalf of his uncle. The triangular relationship develops during the sea voyage when Tristan brings Iseult to Cornwall to marry King Marc. Joyce's rendering combines a parodic narrative account of the philtre and kiss scene, a parodic dialogue between the lovers, and a lyrical poem. At first glance, the poem does not seem to be related to Joyce's parody of the Tristan literature, but Tristan's introduction and recitation of it in the sketch are unequivocal.[2] The poem in the sketch is very close to the version of the text that Joyce later published as "Nightpiece" in *Pomes Penyeach,* where he dated it "Trieste, 1915."

The poem (and the argument that follows its recitation) that forms the extension of "Tristan and Isolde" soon vanished from the manuscript version of Joyce's "Work in Progress". The main body of the sketch (the first large section, and a smaller one at the end) seems to have been central to Joyce's conception of the *Wake.* He transformed it extensively and preserved it in the published text. As David Hayman suggests, the sketch of "Tristan and Isolde" is unusual because false starts in the development of *Finnegans Wake* are rare.[3] In this case, a carefully reworked draft disappeared from the manuscript without a trace. The published text of the *Wake* does not allude to the poem or indicate its previous site. Its absence has been covered up with writing, and specifically, with the parody from "Mamalujo." The

---

[2] For a discussion of the status of the poem as an integral part of the manuscript, see Danis Rose's review essay on David Hayman's *The "Wake" in Transit,* entitled "The Beginning of all Thisorder of Work in Progress" in *James Joyce Quarterly* 28 (1990): 957–65 and David Hayman, "Transiting the *Wake:* a Response to Danis Rose", *James Joyce Quarterly* 29 (1991): 411–19.

[3] David Hayman, *The "Wake" in Transit* (Ithaca: Cornell University Press, 1990), 96.

collective voice of the chroniclers covers for the disappearance of Tristan's enigmatic lyric poem of seduction.

"Tristan and Isolde" plays a major role in the nodal system of the *Wake* and in the book's analogical and allegorical framework.[4] The focus on Tristan and Isolde raises the following question: what was at stake for Joyce in the "Tristan and Isolde" sketch and in the poem that he placed in its extension? Why did he first include (and carefully rework) the poem and then abruptly cut it, as well as the rest of the extension, from the sketch? Some tentative answers to these questions give insight into the sketch and its disappearance, in light of the triangle of subjectivity and the status of the feminine. Isolde's role as a madonna of modernism emerges from a reading of the erotic and lyrical connections between the figures Tristan and Iseult and the following elements of the Joycean corpus: (1) "Giacomo Joyce", especially Giacomo's "sindark nave"; (2) the poem in the "Tristan and Isolde" sketch and the nearly identical poem published as "Nightpiece" in *Pomes Penyeach;* and (3) the mariolatrous poetics of Gerty MacDowell in *Ulysses* and especially of Stephen Dedalus.

Stephen's poetic writing articulates the links between (1) Giacomo's sindark nave and (2) "Nightpiece". Stephen's writing in *A Portrait of the Artist as a Young Man* provides the basis for a reading of "Nightpiece" that indicates why Joyce covered its traces after inscribing "Tristan and Isolde" with it. The disappearance of the poem from the sketch can be interpreted only in connection with Joyce's interpretations of love, death, and the triangles of adultery. Because the extension is closely related to other manuscript material, and specifically with material that was not intended for publication or for parody, Joyce erased it.

In "Tristan and Isolde," something occurs after the philtre/kiss text, during the scene of stargazing, when Tristan speaks "in his girleen's ear" and recites a version of "Nightpiece" to her, that Joyce deliberately erased. The stargazing scene fades away, the voice of Tristan disappears in the *Wake* text, and the poem is nowhere to be found. From the act of speaking to the passive receptivity of the audience,

---

[4] See Hayman, *The "Wake" in Transit.* The theory of nodality is presented in chapter 2, and the question of analogy is treated throughout the book. The conceptualization of the nodal system responds to Joyce's revolutionary approach to narrative in his last work, since the *Wake* records narrative data within a framework that dissolves the metonymic continuity and the discrete elements (structural and morphological) of traditional narrative.

Tristan's poetic performance disappears. Like Isolde, he is instructed to listen ("Hear") with a command that in the *Wake* is often associated with the father, HCE: "Hear, O hear, Iseult la belle! Tristan, sad hero, hear!" (*FW* 398.29).

The quotation that follows is a transcription of the sections of the vanished extension that are relevant to a discussion of "Nightpiece" and the role of Tristan and Iseult in Joyce's novel.[5] The passage concerns "bellelettristicks" (*FW* 281.R3), a combination of eroticism and poetic style:

—I'm real glad to have met you, Tris, you fascinator, you! she said awfully bucked by the gratifying experience of the love embrace from a bigtimer with an interesting tallow complexion from whom great things were expected like him who was evidently a notoriety also in the poetry department for he never saw an orange but he thought of a porringer and to cut a long story short taking him by and large he meant everything to her just then, being her beau ideal of a true girl friend, handsome musical composer a thoroughbred Pomeranian lapdog, a box of preserved crystallized ginger clove cushions peppermint slices, satinette puffs, lime tablets and Nay even the Deity Itself—strewing, the strikingly shining, the twittingly twinkling, our true home and as he wranographically remarked, the lamplights of lovers in the Beyond.

Up they gazed, skyward to stardom, while in his girleen's ear that lovelier lover, sinless sinner, breathed:

> Gaunt in gloom
> The pale stars their torches
> Enshrouded wave
> Ghostfires from heaven's far verges faint illume
> Arches on soaring arches,
> Nights' sindark nave.
>
> Seraphim
> The pale stars awaken
> To service till
> In moonless gloom each lapses, muted, dim

[5] *FDV*, 209–11 (simplified). I have substituted several of the variant readings that appear in David Hayman, *The "Wake" in Transit*, 96–97. The passage quoted consists of approximately two thirds of the extension that continues with several paragraphs of dialogue (combined with some narration) between "Isy" and "her nephew."

Raised when she has & shaken
Her thurible

As long and loud
To night's nave upsoaring
A starknell tolls
As the bleak incense surges, cloud on cloud,
Voidward from the adoring
Waste of souls

As David Hayman has shown in *The "Wake" in Transit,* "Tristan and Isolde" draws on Joseph Bédier's popular version in modern French, on Wagner's libretto for the opera of "Tristan und Isolde", and on several passages of Pound's *Instigations* devoted to the poetics of Laforgue and to Pound's freely translated adaptation ("divagation") of Laforgue's "Salomé" ("Our Tetrarchal Précieuse").[6]

Both Bédier and Wagner suited Joyce's purposes in the writing of "Tristan and Isolde." Joyce's sketches indicate one of the ways that he was experimenting with new forms of irony, satire, and verbal art. Bédier provided a discreetly modernized rendering of the medieval texts. Wagner's opera, which Joyce knew well but no longer wholeheartedly revered, partially disfigured the source materials but translated Tristan and Iseult into a modern musical idiom and a much-admired poetic form. Given its fast-forward melodramatic style and the biographical connections that lead from the mythical Wagnerian persona to the legendary Celtic lover, Wagner's libretto presumably seemed fair game for parody. The connections between musical and verbal motifs in Wagner might have prompted Joyce to transform "kiss" into the German "kuss" in "the big kuss of Trustan with Usolde" (*FDV* 211; *FW* 383.30). The letter *u* takes the place of the *i/y* sound in the English word and the names of its protagonists.

The unexpected element in the background of Joyce's "Tristan and Isolde" is "Salomé," freely translated into a dazzling adaptation by Pound as "Our Tetrarchal Précieuse." Joyce's sketch frequently al-

---

[6] See Hayman, *The "Wake" in Transit.* The discussion of Joyce's debt to Bédier, Wagner, and Pound/Laforgue takes place in chapters 2 through 5. Hayman's study of these materials pursues the central questions found in his previous works on genetic development, parody, pantomime, French influences, and theories of literary style in Joyce within the new framework of a genetic study of *Finnegans Wake* and its focus on Tristan and Isolde.

ludes to "Our Tetrarchal Précieuse" and to Pound's commentary on Laforgue in *Instigations*.[7] Laforgue's parody of Flaubert's orientalism fits into Joyce's framework for several reasons. The Pound/Laforgue text lends itself to the pantomime stylization of *Work in Progress*, with its elements of farce and comic gestuality, dissolving plot-lines, sequences in repetition, and the alternation of song, dance, and farce with sustained dialogue and narration. Although Pound makes off-hand references to Flaubert, it is possible that Joyce was drawn to the text because of his own admiration for Flaubert.[8] It is also possible that "Tristan and Isolde" represents an attempt on Joyce's part to outdo Pound's accomplished version of Laforgue's parody. The reader of "Our Tetrarchal Précieuse" and the "Tristan and Isolde" sketch can draw her or his own conclusions.

In the discarded extension, Joyce's poem was accompanied by some dialogue that seems to be influenced by Pound's Laforgue and by Wagner's opera, as well as by Bedier's popular rewriting in modern French (rather than his editions of the Béroul and Thomas versions). Joyce's

[7] Hayman, chapters 3 and 4. After a brief introduction, Ezra Pound begins "A Study of French Poets" with Jules Laforgue, whom he quotes and praises at length; Pound begins "Part Second" of *Instigations* (Freeport: Books for Libraries Press, Inc., 1920, 1967) with his adaptation of "Salomé". Laforgue's "Moralité" is the only French text that Pound included in the translations found in "Part Second". Joyce's taste for quoting the beginnings of books appears to be overdetermined in this instance, since Joyce might have wished that Pound's praise for his work in the section entitled "In the Vortex" had appeared at the beginning of that section, in the space occupied by Eliot. It is clear from the tone of "A Study of French Poets" that Laforgue's place at the beginning of a long list of French poets is a deliberate reflection of Pound's admiration for the poet.

[8] Pound begins his commentary on Laforgue with the following remarks: "LA-FORGUE was the 'end of a period'; that is to say, he summed up and summarized and dismissed nineteenth-century French literature, its foibles and fashions, as Flaubert in "Bouvard and Pécuchet" summed up nineteenth-century general civilization. He satirized Flaubert's heavy "Salammbô" manner inimitably, and he manages to be more than a critic, for in process of this ironic summary he conveys himself, *il raconte lui-même en racontant son âge et ses moeurs*, he delivers the moods and the passion of a rare and sophisticated personality . . ." Toward the conclusion of the Laforgue sub-section, Pound writes: "Laforgue was a purge and a critic. He laughed out the errors of Flaubert, i.e., the clogging and cumbrous historical detail. He left *Coeur simple*, *L'Education*, *Madame Bovary*, *Bouvard*. His *Salome* makes game of the rest" (Ezra Pound, 7–8, 16). Pound's negative remarks about Flaubert's Orientalist works might include an implicit criticism of Flaubert's interest in Semitic cultures in addition to Pound's aesthetic condemnation of Orientalist allegory. I have analysed Flaubert's use of allegory in *The Orient of Style: Modernist Allegories of Conversion* (Durham: Duke University Press, 1991).

emphasis on the modern French novelistic version of the Tristan and
Iseult story locates the Bédier text in the category of the modern adaptation of a medieval legend and its literary developments. Bédier's attempt to combine several medieval texts into a single novelistic version produced a text that was in many respects remarkably faithful to
its sources, while Wagner's libretto discards most of the medieval material and emphasizes Wagner's personalized mythology.

Villanelle

The writing that articulates the connections between Giacomo's "sindark nave" and the published text of "Nightpiece" unfolds Joyce's
poetics of the Virgin. Fictionalized (or thinly fictionalized?), Joyce's
mariolatrous poetics inform the scene of Stephen's villanelle. Like
Giacomo experimenting with seduction, and like the temptress of the
villanelle, Stephen is weary. Four times, the villanelle asks, "Are you
not weary of ardent ways?" Simultaneously enchanted with an enjoyment of passion and "weary" of it, Stephen's subject is enjoined to
keep silent: "Tell no more of enchanted days." This paradox of sin anticipates Tristan as a "sinless sinner," reciting "Nightpiece," and it
prefigures the ghostly silence of the poem's first two stanzas. Sin's
paradox affects the seraphim who exercise their powers of seduction
after their fall ("Lure of the fallen seraphim"). Associated with the
stars through Stephen Dedalus' image of Lucifer, the seraphim occupy
the center of "Nightpiece" where they "awaken to service" and fall
("each lapses").

Their service occurs under the auspices of a nameless feminine subject, designated only by a possessive pronoun, who disseminates incense ("raised when she has & shaken / Her thurible"). The stars are
mentioned twice in the extension poem as "pale stars," possibly related to the "ghostfires" in the darkness of a twice-gloomy night.
Twice pale, the stars are described in words that echo the description
of Giacomo's beloved, "pale and chill, clothed with the shadows of the
sindark nave" (*GJ* 10).

The feminine subject, the seraphim in service, and the "sacrificing
hands [that] upraise / The chalice flowing to the brim" share a liturgical event and a set of allusions to anonymous lovers. The incantatory poetics of liturgical repetition also characterizes the villanelle.
The desires and falls of unnamed lovers occur in a depersonalized con-

text; their anonymity is protected under the cover of pronouns. In its multiplication of pronouns, Stephen's villanelle anticipates Molly's feminine flow. "Nightpiece" moves in the opposite direction by reducing the repetition of pronouns to a minimum. Prominently displayed in the villanelle, the lovers recede into the shadows of Night and the sindark nave in Tristan's "Nightpiece."

In the "soaring arches" that connect the architecture of "Nightpiece" with the Cathedral of Notre Dame in *Giacomo Joyce,* the lovers (like the stars) are "gaunt in gloom" and "enshrouded" in a faintly lit darkness. The seraphim, the stars as torches, the thurible and clouds of incense, and the souls in the void are figural elements that emerge from this shadowy atmosphere.

Less abstract in its diction than "Nightpiece" and less explicit than the didactic voice of the villanelle, Giacomo's erotic and lyrical recreation of the Passion at Notre Dame focuses on the same figural elements within the "sindark nave": the shadows of sindarkness that clothe (or enshroud) her; her paleness like the pale stars; the torches of the Passion that appear in "Nightpiece" as "the pale stars their torches" and as the "blaze" of passion in the villanelle; the cruel eyes recalled in memory, like the eyes of the villanelle temptress; the veils of mist from that morning, blending into the smoke of incense that rises "cloud on cloud" in Stephen's "instant of inspiration." Smoke also enters the eucharistic episode of the villanelle ("Smoke, incense . . . Smoke went up from the whole earth, from the vapoury oceans, smoke of her praise" [P 197]) and the service of the seraphim / stars in "Nightpiece" ("As the bleak incense surges, cloud on cloud"). An evocation of the soul begins and concludes the villanelle scene "while his soul had passed from ecstasy to languor"—and is echoed in the broken cries and the languorous atmosphere of the villanelle. In *Giacomo,* the sorrowful soul of the beloved ends the passage that begins with "the steelblue waking waters." "Nightpiece" ends with "the adoring / Waste of souls." Their clouds of incense surge toward the void, the favored trans-romantic space of terror and desire.

The "virgin womb" of the "priest of eternal imagination" conceives the fruit of sin and paradox as the "sindark nave," a vessel on the ocean or on "the steelblue waking waters." The scene of the villanelle ends with fire and water as "a glow of desire kindled again his soul." "Her nakedness yielded to him, radiant, warm, odorous and lavish-limbed, enfolded him like a shining cloud, enfolded him like water with liquid life" (P 201). The "liquid letters of speech" (P 201) resonate

in the "liquid letters" (l and r sounds, prolonged by nasal n and ng) of
the last stanza of the villanelle: "And still you hold our longing gaze /
With languorous look and lavish limb!" (*P* 202). The resonance of desire follows the same general pattern in "Nightpiece" in which it
stands out from the silent stanzas that precede it. The pale stars and
seraphim sound a "starknell" with liturgical (and eucharistic) overtones. The l, r, and nasal sounds ring bells among the clouds of
incense: "As long and loud / To night's nave upsoaring/ A starknell
tolls." These three texts unfold under the same trysting star of
"Bahnhofstraße."

Stephen's poetics in the *Portrait* is the ground of a reading of
"Nightpiece." This reading gives insight into the traces of "Nightpiece" that remained after Joyce had inscribed "Tristan and Isolde"
with it. Since "Nightpiece" includes a number of elements featured in
the *Portrait*'s villanelle (in addition to elements that originate in the
manuscript of *Giacomo Joyce*), the link between the two poems po-
tentially connects Tristan, the performer of "Nightpiece," with Stephen, who directs his lyrical–erotic ambitions toward the virginal
Emma. Given the articulation of the lyrical and erotic context in the
Portrait and the vocabulary that "Nightpiece" shares with it (as well
as with *Giacomo Joyce*), there were two good reasons for Joyce to cut
the poem from the sketch: (1) to avoid the possibility that its autobiographical resonances would appear in the explicit context of Tristan's adultery, and (2) to avoid the possibility that the fragile verses
produced in the sublime (the virgin womb of the imagination) would
fall prey to the pantomime atmosphere and the modernist parody that
dominate the sketch.

The *Portrait* does not make light of Stephen's villanelle, since its
aesthetic is not negotiable for the purposes of parody. Its combination
of liturgical resonances and the evil ardent ways of passion frames
desire in an anonymous framework that asks for silence, "Tell no
more . . ." Stephen's weariness resonates like Giacomo's weary voice
in an atmosphere of bitterness and despair, "Weary! Weary! He too
was weary of ardent ways" (*P* 200). Desire is inseparable from the Fall
into an abyss of terror that overwhelms the priest of eternal imagination. In Joyce's poems, terror and weariness motivate the frequent
supplications to a maternal and protective figure who resembles the
Virgin.

The virgins who inhabit Joyce's feminine fictions are figured in various states of seduction and fall. The "object" for whom Stephen

writes the villanelle is a white-gowned figure who moves through his thoughts in a dance of memory; he describes her as "giving herself to none" (*P* 199). Her bridal image of innocence and seduction is like the remembered object of Giacomo's desire. In *Ulysses*, Joyce recalls the imperfectly seduced object of Giacomo's strategies, the daughter of Jerusalem. At the threshold of *Finnegans Wake*, the figure of the Bride emerges from the dissolved night forms of the sacred and comic threads of Penelope's tapestry. The Bride is "vergina madre" and daughter of the new Bloomusalem, mother of Christ and bride of Bloom. In the *Wake* and its manuscripts, she is most easily recognizable in the guise of Iseult la Belle. Lyrical and obscene, Joyce's Bride speaks for the sirens, the whores, the coy and mincing girls with nothing under their hats but curls, and for the Beatrices of missed opportunity. Adulterous and lost forever, wanted dead or alive, sitting in the bar or on a rock, these feminine figures are pictured as brides, at the intersection of purity and adultery. They linger just out of reach, in the margins of doubt. Lost in the past, anticipated in the future, or present in the imagination, they are madonnas of modernism.

Gerty's connections to Stephen in *Ulysses* include allusions to the manuscript of *Stephen Hero*.[9] Suzette Henke points out the "private authorial joke" involved in Gerty's admiration of the sentimental poem entitled "My Ideal", attributed (in *Stephen Hero*) to the teacher, Mr. Hughes. But the joke is double-edged, since Stephen's negative reaction to the verses' images of the Madonna does not alter his mariolatry. The powerful presence of the Virgin resonates in the background of his verses for Emma. Images of the Madonna entrance Stephen even more than they affect Gerty, for whom the Madonna mediates between narcissism and idealization.

Gerty's version of the Madonna resolves the perils of feminine identity within a social framework that Stephen has decisively rejected. The unequivocal parody that Joyce presents in "My Ideal" suggests that the beautiful liturgy of the Virgin truly belongs to the poets and mystics who have flown past the nets of the institutions. The offensively stupid verse of "My Ideal" is produced as a kind of institutional poetry by one who has been "schooled in the discharging of a formal rite" (*P* 200). Joyce parodies Gerty's love of poetry in a context that combines weeping, sacrifice, and her disfigurement. "*Art thou real,*

[9] Suzette Henke, "Gerty MacDowell: Joyce's Sentimental Heroine" in *Women in Joyce*, edited by Suzette Henke and Elaine Unkeless (Urbana: University of Illinois Press, 1982), 132–49.

my ideal? it was called by Louis J. Walsh, Magherafelt, and after there was something about *twilight, wilt thou ever?* and ofttimes the beauty of poetry, so sad in its transient loveliness, had misted her eyes with silent tears that the years were slipping by for her" (*U* 298). This passage slips unobtrusively into "Tristan and Isolde" as Isolde's view of her lover. "He meant everything to her just then, being her beau ideal of a true girl friend" (*FDV* 210). Framed by the men's temperance retreat, the passage in *Ulysses* recalls Stephen's adoration of the Virgin as well as his scorn for the teacher's mariolatrous poem in *Stephen Hero*.

The link between beauty, poetry, and Stephen's passion for Emma (the virginal Young Lady) is already present in *Stephen Hero* in the context of Stephen's theoretical frame of epiphany, elaborated after an allusion to his "Vilanelle of the Temptress" (*SH* 188–89). The link between feminine beauty and poetic expression leads from the triangles of "Nausikaa" to the Tristan and Isolde sketch as it is transcribed in the *First-Draft Version*. Triangles leave their subject swooning in the regions of Joycean poetics: the "lure of the fallen seraphim" (*P* 202) connects the virgins to the whores in masculine desire. In Giacomo's attempt to win the daughter away from her father, he evokes his ideal love and the whores near the river in the same "dark love, dark longing," and in the same breath. The two loves converge in verse: "Mine eyes fail in darkness, mine eyes fail, / Mine eyes fail in darkness, love" (*GJ* 3). The motifs of falling and of failing vision, of darkness, night, and swooning, mark the moment of desire that Joyce articulates in the voice of Giacomo and in the portrait of Stephen. Stephen Dedalus swoons—like Gabriel Conroy, whose lyricism of desire in *The Dead* is modulated by Irish song; like Giacomo, alone among his fragments of verse; and like Bloom hearing the Virgin's service, on the strand with Gerty. Caught in a permanent triangle, Tristan and Isolde are the most spied-on pair of lovers in the courtly canon. Darkness and voyeurism evolve into the "Nightlanguage" that integrates them in its cast of motifs.

Joyce places the protean story of the love triangle "in the poetry department" (*FDV* 210). The seduction scene of Tristan and Iseult is presented in Tristan's elocution of a "lyrical bloom" (*FDV* 208) that turns out to be Joyce's "Nightpiece." Joyce's Isolde asks for "some but not too much" lyricism:

> She murmurously asked for some but not too much of the best poetry
> quotations reflecting on the situation smthng a stroke above its a fine

night and the moon shines bright and all to that for the plain fact of the matter was that by the light of the moon of the silvery moon she loved to spoon before her honeyoldmoon aat the same time drinking deep draughts of purest air serene. He promptly elocutioned to her a favourite lyrical bloom in decasyllabic iambic hexameter: Roll on, thou deep and darkblue ocean, roll! (*FDV* 208)

Tristan's "Isolde O Isolde" speech follows his "favourite lyrical bloom," his performance of "Roll on . . . ," borrowed from Pound's commentary on Laforgue. The ocean reference is overdetermined, since throughout Book II, chapter 4, Joyce emphasizes the elements of the kiss scene that takes place during the voyage. In Laforgue/Pound, Salome's poetic (and other) performances lead her ineluctably to the sea. In her formal recitation, she accompanies herself on the lyre that she breaks at the moment of conclusion. After she receives Jao Kanan's head on a platter in payment for her performance, she throws it into the sea, loses her balance, and falls in after it. As David Hayman points out, the "Isolde O Isolde" speech is reminiscent of Salome's incantatory performance in Laforgue/Pound. Salome's erotic and lyrical displays recall the lyric performances, accompanied on the harp, of Tristan and Isolde.

Between the sea and the stars, "the sindark nave" sets the scene for Tristan and Isolde; their "love embrace" is prolonged in "Nightpiece." Joyce's presentation of the lovers and their heavenly context takes the form of parody. "Nay even the Deity strewing, the strikingly shining, the twittingly twinkling, our true home and (as he wranographically remarked), the lamplights of lovers in the Beyond" (*FDV* 210). The comic-lyrical emphasis on the stars in this passage confirms the sublime context of the "beau ideal," and recalls the Laforgue/Pound parody of Salome as "the little astronomer."[10] She exults in the loss of her virginity:

Stars out in full company, eternities of zeniths of embers. Why go into exile? Salome, milk-sister to the Via Lactea, seldom lost herself in constellations. (. . .) Isolated nebulous matrices, not the formed nebulae, were her passion; she ruled out planetiform discs and sought but the unformed, perforated, tentacular. Orion's gaseous fog was the brother Benjamin of her galaxy. But she was no more the "little" Salome, this night brought a change of relations, exorcised from her

[10] The reference to lamplights is a subtle wave to "Nausikaa." See Suzette Henke.

virginity of tissue she felt peer to these matrices, fecund as they in gy-
ratory evolutions.[11]

She considers "the nebulae of her puberties . . . for ten minutes":
"What nights, what nights in the future! Who will have the last word
about it? Choral societies, fire-crackers down there in the city."[12]
Tristan's poem in the sketch for *Finnegans Wake* inscribes erotics in
the poetics of the Night: Joyce's investment in the text is reflected in
its striking resemblance to the published text of "Nightpiece" that appears with several minor changes in *Pomes Penyeach.* Joyce corrected
the repetition of "pale stars" in the second stanza to read "lost hosts."
"Nights' sindark nave" became "Night's sindark nave," parallel to
"night's nave" in the third stanza. At the beginning of the final stanza,
"As" was corrected to read "And," presumably to avoid the repetition
with "As" in "As the bleak incense surges."

Joyce's decision to cut the extension and to reserve the poem for later
use in a non-parodic context entailed several concomitant changes in
the text that developed from the "Tristan and Isolde" sketch. The entrance of "Mamalujo" on the scene of the cover-up introduces a new
emphasis on narrative repetitions that did not appear in the early
sketch, although it is essential to Joyce's approach to the Tristan material. Narrative covers for the compromising effects of poetry, "like
another tellmastory repeating yourself, how they used to be in leth-
argy's love" (*FW* 397.07). On the following page, Joyce substitutes
cinema for poetry. The *Wake* text subtly encodes an allusion to poetics
(and perhaps to the now-absent poem) with a possible allusion to
Pound's "A Study in French Poets" in *Instigations*. "In the poetry department" is replaced with "in the fulmfilming department" (*FW*
398.25). In the section of "A Study in French Poets" that Joyce found
most useful, Pound's remarks on Laforgue end with the following
words: "Laforgue is incontrovertible. The 'strong silent man' of the
kinema has not monopolized all the certitudes" (Pound, 19). The contemporary movie hero lends his presence to Joyce's Tristan under the
eager gaze of the four storytelling voyeurs.

The sketch of Tristan and Isolde brings together the connections
between poetry and love that Joyce portrays in Stephen and parodies
in Gerty. Joyce combines the serial story of Tristan and Isolde with the

---

[11] *Instigations*, 263–64.
[12] Ibid., 264.

poetics of eroticism. Nightlanguage uses Tristan and Isolde as a fictional disguise for the autobiographical elements of jealousy, adultery, and bitterness (evident in the characters of Gabriel, Dedalus, Richard Rowan, and Giacomo)[13] within the frame of a new serial language that reflects the cyclical rhythm of the "Arabian nights, serial stories, tales within tales, to be continued" and "desperate story telling."[14] While the sketch does not focus directly on the serial aspect of Nightlanguage, the manuscripts indicate that the serial qualities of the Tristan and Iseult texts suited Joyce's purposes in the *Wake*. In its published form, the *Wake* presents Tristan and Iseult as serial elements; the text isolates and repeats certain elements of their story (or stories) in a non-narrative setting.

The Sindark Nave

Joyce's images of the Madonna shape some of the genetic connections among "Nightpiece," the mariolatrous poetics of Gerty and Stephen, and the Tristan materials. Giacomo's "sindark nave" in the Cathedral of Notre Dame turns into the boat that brings the adulterous bride and her lover to the King, her new husband. Isolde's Nightprayer shapes the feminine into a context of sacrifice and sexual transgression. The Nightprayer focuses an early foray into Nightlanguage on the story of Tristan and Isolde. In *Portrait*, Stephen's poetics provides the basis for a reading of "Nightpiece" that demonstrates why Joyce covered its traces after inscribing "Tristan and Isolde" with it.

The Virgin is revered as the star of the sea. The metaphors of Catholic liturgy transform the vessel of her body (in which God took human form) into the body of the Church. The architectural usage of "nave" (or "nef") to designate the middle part of the body of a church deliberately recalls the womb/vessel images of the feminine body. The body that bore messianic fruit resonates in the etymology of the nave as a ship on the water. Joyce gathers these familiar images together in his version of "Tristan and Isolde." The "sindark nave"

[13] Although Ellmann suggested that Joyce might have been interested in having *Giacomo Joyce* published, its bitter subjectivity, its emphasis on adultery in an autobiographical context, and its rancorous tone cannot be assimilated to fiction. The Tristan story provides an adequate disguise for these elements.

[14] *Scribbledehobble*, 21.

includes the boat, the Church, and a virginal feminine body that bears sublime fruit.

The virginal Isolde succumbs to adultery in the boat, the sindark nave, that takes her from Ireland to Cornwall. In Joseph Bédier's composite version, Brangaene exclaims to Iseult and Tristan, "'vous avez bu l'amour et la mort! [you drank love and death!]'" (53). The philtre/kiss scene in chapter 4 of Bédier's *Le Roman de Tristan et Iseut* makes the connection between water and eroticism, "Et, quand le soir tomba, sur la nef qui bondissait plus rapide vers la terre du roi Marc, liés à jamais, ils s'abandonnèrent à l'amour [And, when night fell, on the nave that rushed more quickly toward the land of King Marc, forever tied together, they gave themselves over to love]" (54). The connection is strangely echoed when the second Isolde, Iseult des Blanches Mains, confesses to her brother Kaherdin that the water that splashes her above the knee is bolder than Tristan, who has not consummated their marriage (Bédier, 143–44).

The birdgirl of the *Portrait* is wading in the water when Stephen's voyeurism glides into ecstacy, Bertha in *Exiles* recalls her flight from Ireland and her lonely hours near the Tevere, and Molly in *Ulysses* is associated with the Gibraltar of her girlhood and with Howth Head where she seduced Bloom. Giacomo evokes morning in Paris near the Cathedral of Notre Dame; his revery on "the steelblue waking waters" echoes the Good Friday liturgy. His beloved "daughter of Jerusalem" is imaginatively recreated: "She stands beside me, pale and chill, clothed with the shadows of the sindark nave, her thin elbow at my arm. Her flesh recalls the thrill of that raw mist-veiled morning, hurrying torches, cruel eyes. Her soul is sorrowful, trembles and would weep" (*GJ* 10). The sindark nave turns the emblematic whiteness of the virgin into the darkness of the feminine—mourning and sorrow, shame and sexuality. The elusive dancing girl evoked in the *Portrait* is dressed in white. The darkness of Stephen's fantasy is erased, and the remembered image of her marketable virginity reappears (*P* 198). In Giacomo's disdainful words, "Take her now who will!" marks the moment of rejection that Stephen translates as Emma's preference for the "priested peasant." Giacomo's despairing and contemptuous arrogance maps out the moment when experience is preserved in the imagination. The *Portrait* shapes this moment in priestly terms: "To him she would unveil her soul's shy nakedness, to one who was but schooled in the discharging of a formal rite rather than to him, a priest of eternal imagination, transmuting the daily bread of experience into the radiant body of everliving life" (*P* 200). Stephen translates Emma's rejection of him into terms of Romantic nobility and Augustinian mysticism.

Joyce adapts Christian temporality and the glorious baroque art forms that celebrate the resurrection to the romantic imagination. The liturgy arranges commemorative time in a calendar that celebrates the Fall, original sin, and the death of Christ, followed by felix culpa and the resurrection. Experience is shaped by Roman Catholic cyclical time in the traditional calendar. According to Benjamin, modernity undermines this tradition linked to cult value. Joyce's interest in Vico's temporality is an attempt to salvage a traditional, repeating structure of time and to reshape it in modernist serial form. Vico's cycles generate history as a violent and erotic set of repetitions. Falls are redeemed, seductions are consummated, and deaths are absorbed into births. The sand, the coals, and the fleeting instant that are romantic figures of experience enter the field of resurrection—the repetition with a difference. Violence and eroticism turn an old story into a new one.

Joyce moves his theater of triangles from narrative style in *Ulysses* to the serial style of repeated motifs and the poetics of the word in *Finnegans Wake*. Joyce's modes of representation include the sacred and the comic, idealization and realism, lyricism and satire, and hyperbole and understatement. In *Ulysses*, the contrast between the highs and lows of these modes of representation reflects the confrontation with the "Other." This contrast can be understood as the tension (inherited from Flaubert) between the romantic sublime and the taboo formulations of obscenity. In the *Wake*, these modes are fragmented within the general process of dissolution that affects most of the Nightlanguage. The sublime almost seems to disappear into the taboo formula and the names, repetitions, jingles, and parodies that tend to cover its traces. Serialized motifs allow access to the newly constructed plurality of languages.

The new Nightlanguage conflates seduction and voyeurism in Book II, chapter iv. Facts, subjects, and identities melt, fuse, and reemerge in a form of writing that uses combinatory calculation to simultaneously reveal and hide the decisive events that occur in its stories. *Wake* language reshapes the triangles of story and history according to the libidinal fantasies of the Night. Moments of biographical, autobio-graphical, or erotographical confrontation with the Other (and other) of sexual difference are transfigured within this new

Night of modernist writing.[15] The Nightlanguage crystallizes the
erotic resonance of these moments and underscores their violence—
on one condition: the drama of triangles requires the opacity of disguise, the mask of Night, that covers both the sublime and the obscene. Within the Tristan sketch, Joyce's fragile "Nightpiece" exposes
the connections between Eros and style to the bright lights of parody.

Joyce's sublime brides of art and corruption end *Ulysses*, mark its
opening scene, and structure a crucial mid-point in "Nausikaa." This
chapter echoes the strand scene of the *Portrait* and the "Proteus"
chapter earlier in *Ulysses* when Stephen broods among the images and
questions associated with desire and the Blessed Virgin Mary. "Nausikaa" marks the peak of Bloom's desire and ends with Bloom writing
fragments about identity in the sand among pools of reflecting water.
The characterization of Gerty in this chapter and the simultaneous
accompaniment of the Roman candles and the Blessed Sacrament
parody Stephen's erotic visions in the fourth and fifth chapters of the
Portrait.

As Joyce's profane Virgin, the modernist madonna figure of Molly
Bloom completes the series. Gerty's bridal aspirations introduce
Molly's monologue and the mother in *Finnegans Wake*.[16] The reflections and desires of "Nausikaa" also connect Gerty with the daughter
figures of Issy, Nuvoletta, and especially Isolde. Gerty's triangles of
seduction link her to the Tristan and Isolde story that was central to
Joyce's conception of his *Work in Progress*.[17]

Gerty is an alternative siren who disappoints the voyeur when
she stands and walks away. As a pre-text of Isolde, Gerty recalls the

[15] I am alluding to Lacan's theory of the unconscious in which the Other (Autre) is
the other sex, as well as the site where Lacan locates the divine authority or agency
of the Symbolic. The other (autre) appears in two forms that are both relevant for the
contexts of Joycean triangles: (1) the other as the "objet petit a," or the partial object(s)
of the drives and (2) the other as a double or a rival.

[16] The important connection between Gerty's discourse and Molly's monologue
has been made by Jean-Michel Rabaté in *Joyce: Portrait de l'auteur en autre lecteur*
(Petit-Roeulx: Cistre, 1984), 79–91.

[17] See *Scribbledehobble* in addition to suggestive remarks in the *Exiles* notes about
Celtic women. David Hayman points out that Joyce planned to make "Tristan and
Isolde" the central parody of the *Wake* until 1923. "Reading Joyce's Notebooks?!
Finnegans Wake from Within" in *Finnegans Wake: Fifty Years*, ed. Geert Lernout
(Amsterdam: Rodopi, 1990), 10. See also the introduction to David Hayman, *A First-
Draft Version of Finnegans Wake* (Austin: University of Texas Press, 1963), 3–43.

similarly-named Gretta of *The Dead*, the unnamed Italian figure of the *Giacomo Joyce* manuscript, and Bertha and Beatrice in *Exiles*. Like Dedalus, she bears the marks of Joycean castration. Joyce's effective combination of parody and pathos in the portrayal of Gerty is foreshadowed by *Giacomo Joyce* and the fifth chapter of the *Portrait*. It anticipates the mixed genres and tones of the Wake's approach to young women. As a source for them, the fictional creation of Gerty complements the family structures that occupied much of Joyce's energies during the construction of *Work in Progress*. In particular, Joyce's rendering of Gerty provides a freely parodic and pathetic representation of the type of the young woman (and Pop's daughter) that connects the persona of Issy/Isolde to Joyce's complex observations of his daughter Lucia.[18] Gerty is a siren of images and silence. When she presents herself to Bloom's gaze, seduction occurs at a distance.

In Gerty's intermittent monologue, Joyce's performance of style includes elements of stereotyped preciosity, narcissism, a keenly self-deluding awareness of the opposite sex, and a strong sense of a Catholic sublime. These elements move through Gerty's memories and anticipations; they merge with her obsessive thoughts about being "arrayed for the bridal" on one of two altars. Joyce represents a perverse virginal perspective on Eros and the feminine in Gerty's text. From the advertising clichés and homilies of domesticity to the lyrical evocations of clean underwear, Gerty's discourse translates the language of the Other into something that might have arrived just now from the laundry.

Joyce attributes the negative qualities displayed in Gerty's thoughts to the feminine. Molly's self-portrait confirms Gerty's flaws designated within the projected feminine discourse of "Nausikaa." Both characters are obsessive, false, self-serving, vain, ignorant, trivial, wanton, and calculating. Gerty's adolescent characteristics lead away from Molly, however, into another terrain of Joycean aesthetics, erotics, and poetics.

[18] The thesis that Lucia informs the character type of Issy is proposed and developed by David Hayman, most recently in *The "Wake" in Transit*, chapters 4, 5, and 6; Hayman refers to the question again in "Transiting the *Wake*." See also Hayman's essay, "Shadow of His Mind: The Papers of Lucia Joyce" in *Joyce at Texas*, ed. David Oliphant and Thomas Zigal (Austin: Humanities Research Center, University of Texas, 1983), 65–79; "I Think Her Pretty: Reflections of the Familiar in Joyce's Notebook VI.B.5," in *Joyce Studies Annual* (Austin: University of Texas Press, 1990), 43–60. For a biographical discussion of family life, see Brenda Maddox, *Nora* (New York: Houghton Mifflin, 1988).

The feminine stereotypes that characterize Gerty include saccharine sentimentality, a denial of sexuality, and an extreme form of idealization. Symptoms of castration in feminine discourse echo Stephen's rather precious moments of reform in *Portrait*. Gerty's sentimentality and Stephen's idealizations meet retroactively in Stephen's bad faith and falsification during this brief period. The dangers of castration lead back to the denial and self-delusion that are engaged in the repression of sexuality. Stephen the sinless priest and ladylike Gerty are briefly united in a moment of mawkish sentimentality. "The old love was waiting, waiting with little white hands stretched out, with blue appealing eyes. Heart of mine! She would follow her dream of love, the dictates of her heart that told her he was her all in all, the only man in all the world for her for love was the master guide" (*U* 299).

These parodic lines echo the *Portrait*, especially the motifs of the fourth chapter ("On! On! his heart seemed to cry" [179]) and the "unrest" passages of the second chapter: "He did not want to play. He wanted to meet in the real world the unsubstantial image which his soul so constantly beheld . . . a premonition which led him on told him that this image would, without any overt act of his, encounter him" (*P* 68). Restless, passive, dreamy, convinced that she too is "different from others," Gerty's portrait parodies the Stephen who is inspired by Mercedes in *The Count of Monte Cristo*. Joyce underscores Gerty's connection with Stephen at the end of the paragraph: "Nothing else mattered. Come what might she would be wild, untrammeled, free" (*U* 299). In the fourth chapter of the *Portrait*, Stephen experiences an ecstacy of erotic and poetic fantasy, couched in lyrical terms that will return in the following chapter to Stephen's "dewy wet soul." On the strand, Stephen decides, "He would create proudly out of the freedom and power of his soul (. . .) He was unheeded, happy, and near to the wild heart of life. He was alone and young and wilful and wildhearted, alone amid a waste of wild air and brackish waters" (*P* 179–180).

This suprising parallel between the beached Gerty and Stephen on the strand in the *Portrait* is duplicitous. Stephen's self-proclaimed new freedom is the effect of his celebrated return to life (namely, the repeated fall into Sin), and his decision to fly past the social nets of Ireland, while Joyce's parody of it in Gerty's thoughts has a more somber side. In addition to the "typically feminine" self-serving delusions and illusions that permeate her discourse, Gerty's notion of freedom is all that women get, and according to most of Joyce's portraits, all that they deserve. Gerty's small freedom leads her fantasies in the direction of erotic service to a master, "the only man in the world." Stephen Dedalus, however, artfully transforms his early investment in the worship of the Blessed Virgin and his erotic reveries into poetry. He writes the villanelle, immodestly announced in the *Portrait* by the angel Gabriel.

Ambered Wines

"Nausikaa" virtually includes the absent Stephen Dedalus in its parody of the strand scene in the *Portrait* and in its repetitions of the motifs of voyeurism and desire that invade Stephen's thoughts in "Proteus." The parody in "Nausikaa" is double-edged. While Gerty's language of hyperbolic idealization echoes Stephen's ecstatic consummation of voyeurism on the strand in the *Portrait*, her access to the mariolatrous heights of the sublime is limited. The "namby-pamby jammy marmalady drawersy" style of the chapter is an example of the arch, cute, and brainless sentimentality that Joyce associates with young women, especially daughter figures. Desirable young women do not have access to the Penelopean boldness of Molly, ALP/Mum, and other motherly figures. The "namby-pamby" stylizations of Gerty's discourse return in a similar comic and sexual frame in the Tristan and Isolde sketch. A note in Joyce's draft notebook published as *Scribbledehobble* is illuminating. "Man— who the hell took that bloody comb Cf. woman— now where on earth has that little brat of a comb disappeared to?"[19] The contrast between verbal violence and 'womanly' use of euphemism to circumvent sacrifice and blasphemy is related to the Joycean emphasis on castration, virginity, and blood sacrifice as the definitive characteristics of femininity.

In Joyce, men curse and evoke manly violence, while young women simper (or lisp) and infantilize their object. Masculine and feminine styles in the manuscripts and in the *Wake* indicate that Joyce is consistent in his treatment of the question of gender. The libidinal relation to the Virgin produces poetic eloquence on the part of Stephen

---

[19] *Scribbledehobble* (*Penelope*), 902. The note seems to have been related to Molly Bloom; on the following manuscript page, a separate entry in a different context includes the name of the anonymous object of Giacomo's erotic vision. "J.J. was caudele for O. G. Tripcovich, Miss Popper, Miss Luzzatto, B[aron] R[alli] Nora, Mr Sauter, Schaureck," 903.

Dedalus (as well as moments of self-parody that repair the damages of sentimentality), but in Joyce's portrait of the worshipper of Mary as a young woman, neither eloquence nor self-parody is possible. Gerty is by turns mawkish and comical, but she is incapable of self-parody. Joyce's gender split never seems to work to the advantage of female characters.[20] Joyce's parallels between Gerty and Stephen are private, as are the potential connections between her and an autobiographical allusion to the Fleischmann affair.[21]

Joyce's parodic portrait of Gerty indirectly recalls the virginal son's visual ecstacy of "profane joy." Dedalus will come down from his lyrical heights into the sea of abjection, where sexuality and sacrifice threaten him. The language of *Giacomo Joyce* sets the scene: "Here are wines all ambered (. . .) kind gentlewomen wooing from their balconies with sucking mouths, the pox-fouled wenches and young wives that, gaily yielding to their ravishers, clip and clip again" (*GJ* 9). This passage resonates in Stephen's thoughts in the *Portrait:* "And he tasted in the language of memory ambered wines . . ." (*P* 210). The passage is echoed in the roguewords of "Proteus," where the "white flesh of the she fiend" (*U* 47) connects the pale beauty of Giacomo's beloved with the pale young women in *Ulysses.* In English, Iseult la Belle becomes Isolde the Fair; the "vin herbé" of the love philtre lends its powers to the "ambered wines" that Stephen attributes to the courtly love contexts (obscene and sublime) of John Dowland's Renaissance songs. Nausikaa's libidinal triangles bring the mysterious and fatherly Bloom to Gerty's attention during the men's service to the Virgin. Joyce pursues this suggestive context and its resonances of *fin'amor* in the writing of *Work in Progress.* "Nausikaa" prefigures an important manuscript passage concerning Isolde. The two consecutive versions of her "Patternoster" recreate the "Pater Noster" in the voice of the daughter. Her turn toward the Father first takes this shape: "Howfar wartinevin / alibithenem / kingthecome / wilbydun / nerth tisnevin / Giveusday dailybread / gives dresspass / sweegivethem dresspss /

---

[20] In "Gerty MacDowell: Joyce's Sentimental Heroine" in *Women in Joyce,* ed. Suzette Henke and Elaine Unkeless (Urbana: University of Illinois Press, 1982, 132–49), Suzette Henke makes the very different claim that Gerty's characterization is elusive and ambivalent. Mark Schechner claims that Gerty is both a "virginal villain", albeit an absurd one, and a professional whore in Nighttown. *Joyce in Nighttown* (Berkeley: University of California Press, 1974), 161–65. Fritz Senn describes her as an "avatar of the temptress" in "Nausikaa." *James Joyce's "Ulysses,"* ed. David Hayman and Clive Hart (Berkeley: University of California Press, 1974), 283–90.

[21] See Fritz Senn.

genstus leesnot / tootentation / liversm / evil men." The following entry includes some revision: "Isolde's Patternoster / Howfar wartnevin alibithe / name, kingcome, wibedun / nerth tisnevin. Givensday / dailybread, givesdresspss / sweegivethem dresspssa / gensts leesnot / tootentation livresm / evil men."[22] The prayer is an early experiment with Nightlanguage.[23] It plays out the effects of echos and repetitions, of whispers, slurred pronunciation, and lisping, that will shape some of the verbal patterns of Issy/Isolde.

Isolde's Patternoster probably has at its source a passage from Bédier's third chapter, "La Quête de la Belle aux Cheveux d'Or [The quest for the beauty with the golden hair]". After having killed Morholt and returned to Cornwall, Tristan sails again to Ireland. He hears the dragon's horrible roar and asks a woman where the "voice" comes from. She explains that the monster waits at the city gates and demands a continual supply of virgins. "Nul n'en peut sortir, nul n'y peut entrer, qu'on n'ait livré au dragon une jeune fille . . . il la dévore en moins de temps qu'il n'en faut pour dire une patenôtre [No one can leave, no one can enter, without delivering a young lady to the dragon . . . he devours her in less time than it takes to say a Pater Noster]" (Bédier, 39). According to the narrative patterns of the motif of sacrifice, the young lady sacrificed to the dragon substitutes for Iseult. Tristan addresses her twice as "young lady," and defends himself when she threatens to kill him: "Ah! C'est pour toi, jeune fille, que j'ai combattu le dragon [Ah! young lady, it was for you that I fought the dragon]" (Bédier, 44).

During his conversation with the woman at the port, Tristan learns how he will win "Iseut the Blond." Her father the King has proclaimed that he will give his daughter to the slayer of the dragon. Isolde's Patternoster refers to sacrifice and the father's crime in a suggestive frame that combines HCE with "the king of Ireland," and superimposes the sacrifice of the daughter to the father on the sacrifice of the virgins to the horrible dragon. In the Tristan texts, either the Princess will die as a victim of the dragon's excessive appetite for virgins, or she will enter into the sublime and impersonal arrangements of Romance by becoming the bride of the heroic dragon-slayer.

---

[22] Notebook VI.B.3 : 58. My thanks to David Hayman for showing me his richly annotated transcriptions of some of Joyce's notebooks including material on Tristan and Isolde.

[23] Notebook VI.B.3.

The first and the last women to appear in *Ulysses* are the mother whose virginity is denied by her son Stephen and the profane Virgin who will take her place, May Dedalus and Molly Bloom. In the *Wake*, Anna Livia Plurabelle takes up the maternal virgin roles, while Isabel/Isolde as the daughter incarnates the adulterous brides. In *Ulysses*, Gerty anticipates the role played by Isolde. She poses on the strand in full hearing of the Blessed Sacrament, "the fragrant names of her who was conceived without original sin" (*U* 292). She broods about the same questions that obsess Stephen. At one point in the novel, Joyce lends Gerty's style to Stephen: "But he said very entirely it was clean contrary to their suppose for he was the eternal son and ever virgin" (*U* 321). Gerty's Oedipal foot connects her worry over menstruation and other forms of sexual sacrifice with Stephen Dedalus' Oedipal difficulties, in spite of Father Conroy's view of femininity "that that was no sin because that came from the nature of woman instituted by God, he said, and that the Blessed Lady Herself said to the archangel Gabriel be it done unto me according to Thy Word" (*U* 294).

When Gerty watches Bloom and fantasizes about his "wounds that wanted healing with heartbalm" (*U* 293), the link between her and Molly is mediated by the erotically suggestive "balm" that Zerlina offers to Masetto in Mozart's *Don Giovanni*. Zerlina too is a virgin. Don Giovanni attempts to seduce her during her wedding celebration, and "Là ci darem la mano" is a love duet that illustrates Don Giovanni's seductive persuasion and Zerlina's weakening resistance to him. Zerlina's "balsamo [balm]" consoles Masetto, her jealous bridegroom. She advises him to be less jealous in the future. Within the Joycean contexts of adultery, Gerty's "heartbalm" connects her fantasy to Molly and Boylan, Zerlina and Don Giovanni. Tristan and Isolde might be implicated in this passage, since the love philtre and its magical powers are evoked in the Wagner libretto as "Balsam," "Balsamsaft," "Balsamtränke": "Für Weh und Wunden Balsam hier; für böse Gifte Gegengift [Balm for pain and wounds; antidote for evil poisons]." It is possible that Joyce alludes to Wagner's series of "balm" neologisms in Gerty's "heartbalm."

Joyce's interest in the Tristan material may have originated in the connection between Tristan, the idealized lover of *fin'amor*, and melancholy, inscribed in Tristan's fate (and name) by his mother. Soon after his father dies in violent battle, Tristan's mother gives birth and

names her son for the sadness of death. She utters the threefold etymology of "Tristan," kisses him, and dies: "Triste j'accouche, triste
est la première fête que je te fais, à cause de toi j'ai tristesse à mourir.
Et comme ainsi tu es venu sur terre par tristesse, tu auras nom Tristan [Sad am I giving birth, sad is the first celebration for you, because
of you I am so sad that I will die. And because you arrived on earth in
sadness, your name will be Tristan]" (Bédier, 18).

The melancholy sadness inscribed in Tristan's name contrasts with
the "joie d'amour" that he enjoys with Isolde in their sad "lovestory."
Joyce plays on the name of Tristan and its contrast with his own name
in a Tristan-centered passage of the *Wake*. "Between his voyous and
her consinnantes! (. . .) Are we speachin d'anglas landage or are you
sprakin sea Djoytsch?" (*FW* 485.10). English land and the joys of love
at sea are contextualized in the French-sounding vowels and consonants of the text of Tristan the "voyou" (delinquent) and his partner
in sin. His name is split and reversed ("Tantris") in the original Old
French text of the "Folie Tristan" from which Bédier takes several epi-
sodes. The name of "Tantris" is not emphasized in Bédier's modernized text, but Wagner's libretto uses the name of "Tantris" to refer to
Tristan's repeatedly disguised identity (especially when he appears in
disguise before Isolde).

Heard repeatedly in the *Wake*, Tristan's name is linked to the vicissitudes of love. The Tristan story is serialized, possibly in the form of
Viconian recirculation. Modern readers continue to be puzzled by the
circular impetus of courtly love discourse in the Tristan texts. The
story of perfect love ("fin'amor") paradoxically continues even after
the three-year (1001 nights?) period of the philtre is over. In the Béroul
text from which Bédier borrowed extensively, "fin'amor" continues
after Iseult returns to King Marc, even though the time limit of the
philtre has expired. Intrigued by this paradox of perfection, Maurice
Blanchot includes Tristan and Iseult among the conversations that
form *L'Entretien infini*. He writes:

> They leave each other and each goes back into common existence. It's
> all over? Not at all; on the contrary, it all begins again. They have
> separated to come together anew; far apart, but they unite in this dis-
> tance, across it they do not cease to call each other, to agree and to re-
> turn to each other. The chroniclers and poets have been burdened with
> this contradiction without daring to resolve it: as if passion had to be

fleeting and simultaneously to remain the site of the indefinite and the movement of the interminable.[24]

In the medieval Tristan poems, Tristan and Isolde mistakenly drink the love philtre that had been prepared for Iseult and King Marc to guarantee their love for the first three years of marriage. Neither Bédier nor Wagner includes the three-year limit of the philtre's effects, although Bédier knew of it from Béroul. The fatal philtre turns King Marc into a violent and jealous voyeur, tricked by his wife and her lover. In a variation of the Celtic Tristan myth that also plays a role in the *Wake*, Finn MacCool receives a philtre from his bride Grainne (Grania), engaged in an adulterous love affair with Diarmaid (Dermot). In the French versions, the love philtre is mixed by Iseult's mother. Some of her magical powers of mixing potions are transmitted to her daughter Isolde, who healed Tristan's incurable wound following the slaying of Morholt and cured him of the dragon's venom. She discovers his identity after curing him for the second time. Isolde threatens to kill Tristan to avenge her uncle, but Tristan convinces her of his chivalry by revealing that he killed the dragon to win her hand.

Brangaene (or a servant girl) mistakes the "vin herbé" for ordinary wine and gives it to her mistress and Tristan during their voyage. She later laments, "'par mon crime, dans la coupe maudite, vous avez bu l'amour et la mort! [through my crime, you drank love and death in the cursed cup!]'" Tristan is returning to Cornwall from Ireland for the second time, after he has won the golden-haired Iseult la Belle for his uncle. In all of the versions, the philtre is instrumental in the consummation of adultery. The first paragraph of the *Wake* alludes to the decisive moment of the journey of Tristan and Iseult from Ireland to Cornwall: "Sir Tristram, violer d'amores, fr'over the short sea, had passencore rearrived from North Armorica on this side the scraggy isthmus of Europe Minor to wielderfight his penisolate war" (*FW* 3.16). The Iseult who arrives with Tristan in Cornwall is not a

---

[24] Blanchot writes: "Ils se quittent et rentrent, chacun de leur côté, dans l'existence de tous. Tout est donc fini? Nullement; au contraire, tout recommence. Séparés, c'est pour à nouveau se rejoindre; éloignés, mais ils s'unissent dans ce lointain à travers lequel ils ne cessent de s'appeler, de s'entendre et de revenir l'un près de l'autre. Les chroniqueurs et les poètes ont été embarrassés par cette contradiction sans oser la lever: comme s'il fallait à la fois que la passion fût passagère et qu'elle restât le lieu de l'indéfini et le mouvement de l'interminable." *L'Entretien infini* (Paris: Gallimard, 1969), 286.

virgin any longer; after their voyage from Ireland, Joyce wrote that Nora was "pas encore vierge." "Pas encore" is incorrect French or a slip of the tongue; it recalls Joyce's reversed temporality of innocence and the fall in *Exiles* and elsewhere.[25]

Quand le Soir Tomba, Sur la Nef

In the evolution of Joyce's oeuvre, the bitterness and violence of jealousy and adultery that are related to an obsession with the Fall are masked in a range of disguises. These disguises begin with the Catholic worship of the Virgin that is inscribed in Stephen's poetry long before it is parodied in "Nausikaa." The ultimate form of Joycean disguise is developed in *Finnegans Wake*, where identity is fluid. At all times, every 'character' evoked by name has the alibi of being 'someone' else. The innocent man is guilty. "Felix culpa" insures that the guilty man is innocent, as Anna Livia's letter (and her signature) proclaims in a passage related to Tristan and Isolde: "Yours very truthful. Add dapple inn. Yet is it but an old story, the tale of a Treestone with one Ysold" (*FW* 113.17).[26]

In Book 2, chapter 4 of the *Wake*, the love scene between Tristan and Isolde is combined with the voyeurism scene that focuses on Mamalujo. Three evil barons and a dwarf arouse King Marc's jealousy; they enter the *Wake* identities of the voyeur-chroniclers who write the gospel of adultery. In a passage that may allude to Finn's sleep after drinking Grainne's philtre, the jealous King Marc is spying on the lovers: "When here who adolls me infuxes sleep. But if this could see with its backsight he'd be the grand old greeneyed lobster. He's my first viewmarc since Valentine" (*FW* 249.01).

Seduction turns into history played on Tristan's harp, played out in disguises (Tantris), trysts, and separations, and the sea Djoytsch of poetry: "—History as her is harped. (. . .) Tantris hattrick, tryst and parting, by vowelglide! I feel your thrilljoy mouths overtspeaking, O dragoman, hands understudium" (*FW* 486.07). Isolde the beautiful virgin is conjured up and dissolves again when "the triptyck vision passes" (*FW* 486.32): "a cathedral of lovejelly for his . . . *Tiens*, how he

---

[25] See chapter 2, "Love's Bitter Mystery: Edenville and Nighttown."

[26] The parallel between Isolde and ALP anticipates this passage: "And she has a heart of Arin!" (*FW* 112.33).

is like somebodies! (. . .) What sound of tistress isoles my ear? I horizont the same, this serpe with ramshead, and lay it lightly to your lip a little. What do you feel, liplove?—I feel a fine lady . . . floating on a stillstream of isisglass . . . with gold hair to the bed . . . and white arms to the twinklers . . . O la la!" (FW 486.18).

The adulterous lover ("violer d'amores") disguises himself as a "jongleur," adept at song: "my tristy minstrel" (FW 521.22). On FW 466, Tristan is linked to other *Wake* cycles in the context of song, with allusions to "coloraturas" and the singer's voice (heard in Book 2, chapter 4, singing the seaswans opening song and the parodic "come all ye" that closes the chapter.) Tristan and Isolde (the "courting cousins!") take the philtre that was meant for the King and his bride: "love potients for Leos, the next beast king" (466.04,06). Tristan is familiar with the vocal traditions associated with the troubadours, who provided the pre-texts of courtly love. In the *Portrait,* the Renaissance forms of the alba, aubade, or Tagelied are recalled by Stephen's contextualization of the villanelle as a dawn piece. From Stephen's poem to the Temptress, the evocation of an enchanted night enters the Joycean contexts of "Nightpiece." Shaun accuses Shem, "The froubadour! I fremble!" (FW 462.26). Writing and singing come together in the indictment of a *Wake* version of Giacomo Joyce when the lover's sensibility is mocked: "If you doubt of his love of darearing his feelings you'll very much hurt" (FW 466.11). The Joycean lover's display of doubt and Dedalean bitterness seems to enter the character of Tristan, who dies when the second Iseult falsely convinces him that Iseult la Belle is not coming to heal him.

The warfare of adultery that Joyce evokes in contexts other than the Tristan myth yields results that are noticeably different from the erotic achievements of Don Juan or of Giacomo Casanova. "It will never be," laments the narrator of the Ulyssean pre-text that Richard Ellmann published in 1968 as *Giacomo Joyce.* From "A Little Cloud" and "The Dead" to *Exiles* and the later works, Giacomo's "end" resonates in this context of mourning and defeat: "Youth has an end: the end is here. It will never be. You know that well. What then? Write it, damn you, write it! What else are you good for?" (GJ 16). This bitter ending comes on the heels of the object's resistance to seduction, translated via Brunetto into "black basilisk eyes," "darting at me for an instant out of her sluggish sidelong eyes a jet of liquorish venom" (GJ 15). The monster's venom follows an earlier wearied ending, evoked according to figures of the Annunciation. "Her eyes have drunk my thoughts: and into the moist warm yielding welcoming darkness of her womanhood my soul, itself dissolving, has streamed and poured and flooded a liquid and abundant seed . . . . Take her now who will! . . . . ." (*GJ* 14). This passage seems to echo in the *Portrait,* where an allusion to Gabriel enters the lyrical-erotic scene of the villanelle. "O! In the virgin womb of the imagination the word was made flesh. Gabriel the seraph had come to the virgin's chamber" (*P* 196).[27] The correspondence between desire and writing occurs through figures of virginity, defloration, and mysticism. The villanelle scene temporarily softens the bitter dismissal of Giacomo's "end" by emphasizing the doubled and mutual dissolving of body and soul, woman and man, that conflates erotics and poetics in a single text.

Giacomo and Tristan, the failed lover and the adulterer of courtly love, are blended together as "Mr Jinglejoys." Giacomo's bitter comment at the end of the text ("Write it damn you, write it! What else are you good for?") is evoked as "a staveling encore" that echoes the "passencore" at the beginning of the *Wake.* "That's the side that appeals to em, the wring wrong way to wright woman. Shuck her! Let him. What he's good for. Shuck her more! Let him again! All she wants! Could you wheedle a staveling encore out of your imitationer's jubalharp, hey, Mr Jinglejoys?" (*FW* 466.14). Shaun's attack on "Mr Jinglejoys" combines Mr James Joyce, author, with Shem, brother/ rival and brother/double of Shaun, writer-in-progress of the letter that Shaun is slowly in the process of delivering.

The Giacomo narrator curses his mirror-image double, to whom he utters the command of writing. Shaun/Jaun describes it in alliterative form as "the wring wrong way to wright woman." The poetic context has been underscored earlier in the paragraph. "Turn about, skeezy Sammy, out of metaphor, till we feel are you still tropeful of popetry" (*FW* 466.09). The turn, the trope, and metaphor designate the figures of poetic transports. Shaun pronounces "poetry" with an extra letter p to parody Shem's rhyming efforts in "trope" and "pope." In the same way, "he never saw an orange but he thought of a porringer" parodies

---

[27] For a discussion of the theological context in this passage, see Schlossman, *Joyce's Catholic Comedy of Language* (Madison: University of Wisconsin Press, 1985). The name of Gabriel in "The Dead" is also relevant to Joyce's allusions to the Annunciation.

Tristan's big-shot status as "a notoriety also in the poetry department" (*FDV* 210).

The name of "Jinglejoys" continues the references to the lyric tradition of the troubadours and its combination of musical and written
poetic performance. A jingle is a rhyme; Cain's descendant Jubal was
associated with music. The opposing images of the names of Joyce and
Tristan the singer-harpist reappear in Shaun's denunciation as the
Latin "jubilare" (rejoice) with a potential echo of the Hebrew origin of
"jubilee" (a trumpet blast). "Skeezy Sammy" and the other repetitions of initial consonants produce stave rhyme, an alliterative meter
common in old Germanic poetry. A stave is a set of verses, a stanza,
or the lines of a poem or song. Shaun's insinuations about Shem's
erotic and poetic activity may combine the poetics of "stave" with the
word's other definitions—thin stripwood, a stick, or a staff.

To shuck means to remove like a husk or shell, or in slang usage,
to fool or to hoax. Shem the lover is sarcastically urged to undress
"her" (or to fool "her") and to take "her" over the edge of roman-
ticized troubadour poetics to the obscene command encoded by a
switch and a displacement of letters from "The froubadour! I fremble!"
to "Shuck her! . . . Shuck her more!" Shaun/Yawn will mirror his
brother's exquisite sensibility and lyrical expression at the beginning
of Book 3, chapter 3, when he swoons and "semiswoons" in the best
Dedalean fashion: "Lowly, longly, a wail went forth. Pure Yawn lay
low. . . . Yawn in a semiswoon lay awailing and (hooh!) what help-
ings of honeyful swoothead (phew!), which earpiercing dulcitude!"
(*FW* 474.13). Yawn as the swooning "chubby boybold love of an angel" in the third watch of Night echoes the contexts of swooning,
seraphim, and "sweet music" (repeated as "the faint sweet music"
and the spirit "sweet as dew") of the birdgirl and villanelle scenes in
the *Portrait*.

Joyce first wrote two separate sketches (*FDV* 208–19) that he later
combined in Book 2, chapter 4 of the *Wake*. The merging of "Tristan
and Isolde" and "Mamalujo" is accompanied by the disappearance of
the version of "Nightpiece" that Joyce used in the early draft. Autobiographical traces of the subjectivity of adultery vanish into the woods
of the *Wake* text. Joyce's precautions include several stratagems:

1. The scene from the "Tristan and Isolde" sketch is obliquely presented in the *Wake* through the confused and imperfect observations of the four libidinal voyeurs who chronicle the love-death

on board "la nef qui bondissait plus rapide vers la terre du roi Marc [the ship that moved more quickly toward the land of king Marc]."[28]

2. As Tristan's lyrical utterance in the extension, "Nightpiece" connects the "sindark nave" of Tristan and Isolde's fatal love with the "sindark nave" of Giacomo's fantasy, and the connection (and its autobiographical resonances) does not occur in later drafts of the *Wake*, since the poem disappears.[29]

3. The poem and its accompanying text in the sketch of "Tristan and Isolde" echo the service to the Virgin in "Nausikaa," the lyrical constructions of Stephen Dedalus, and the seducer-temptress relations that Joyce elaborates in both texts. But these echoes disappear with "Nightpiece," and the poem is not replaced. The passage about Tristan's "love embrace" and his "notoriety also in the poetry department" (*FDV* 209–10) is transformed into a passage on *FW* 398. It leads into the verse from the "Mamalujo" sketch that is introduced by a call to the lovers: "Hear, O hear, Iseult la belle! Tristan, sad hero, hear!" (*FW* 398.29). Lyric verse is replaced with the parody that begins "Anno Domini nostri sancti Jesu Christi" (*FW* 398.32).

4. The scene of adultery circulates throughout the *Wake*, where its serial quality integrates it within the Viconian structures of circulating motifs: "There are sordidly tales within tales, you clearly understand that?" (*FW* 522.05). A few lines later, King Marc's repeated fits of jealousy and attempts to catch Tristan and Iseult in the woods and castle gardens are evoked as the serial motif of spying on the lovers. "Besides (and serially now) bushes have eyes, don't forget. Hah!" (*FW* 522.12).[30] Joyce's parody of the refined intoxications of courtly love turns the Tristan story into one more version of the events that occur at the wake. These events are evoked in the *Wake*'s most important literary document—the mother's letter, the manuscript that implicates all the members of the Wake family in its vicissitudes. At the meeting point between parody and poetics, between Eros and style, Tristan and Isolde are featured in the "bellettristicks" (*FW* 281.R3) of *Finnegans Wake*.

---

[28] Joseph Bédier, *Le Roman de Tristan et Iseut* (Paris: UGE, 1981), 54.
[29] See Hayman, *FDV*, 210, n. 9.
[30] *FW* 522 is related to notes on Tristan and Isolde in *Scribbledehobble*.

7 Writing and Erasing the Feminine: Sappho's Eros, Modernist Poetics, and the Madonna

Eros weaver of myths,
Eros sweet and bitter,
Eros bringer of pain.
                —Sappho

From the Christian perspective on Eve, the snake, and the losing of paradise in chapter three of *Genesis* to the liturgical and popular traces of the Blessed Virgin Mary, eroticism in Western culture is mediated by a discourse of feminine desire, transgression, and original sin. Translated into feminine form, Eros enters the scene of modernity. Attentive to the resonances of antiquity, Modernism rearticulates the impact of Eros the bittersweet on the poetics of love. Joyce inscribes his fictions with a leitmotif of desire that begins with a self-portrait in the first paragraph of *Stephen Hero* (the "small feminine mouth" in the "face of a debauchee"). Tragic and comic, the leitmotif of desire develops into "love's bitter mystery" in *Ulysses*. The final development of Joyce's writing of desire coincides with the *Wake*'s sacred and comic war on language. The Virgin's balm of mercy becomes an urban paradise in the sea of Joyce's French, English, and German, "*Notre Dame de la Ville,* mercy of thy balmheartzyheat!" (*FW* 102.18). Desire turns the page back to the Roman Catholic liturgy with the "happy sin" that shapes the dark Night and the luminous resurrection in *Finnegans Wake*.

Beautiful Allegories of Desire

In the paschal liturgy of Holy Saturday, the treatment of original sin
as the "felix culpa" shapes the overturning of bitter sin into the
sweetness of redemption. The Old Testament becomes literature;
Eve is a figure for Mary. Eve's tears are sweetened by Mary's tears,
shaped like almonds. In the iconography of European painting, the
Virgin frequently crushes the snake that led Eve to the downfall of
original sin. In the "Allegory of Faith," Vermeer pushes the snake
into the foreground, where it leaves traces of blood on the black and
white checkered floor not far from the apple, the bitter fruit of
knowledge. Eve does not appear, but the Virgin is present in a painting of the Deposition, behind the figure of Faith as a beautiful and el-
egant young woman. She sits on a pedestal near a draped altar and
she ecstatically contemplates a glass globe hanging from the ceiling.
In the room that contains many of Vermeer's musical scenes of love,
the painter portrays his feminine allegory. The accessories are borrowed from the Garden of Eden and from the Church. A tapestry curtain with Oriental motifs, opened to show the room, alludes to
Christian revelation.

Mary the Virgin mother is a uniquely idealized feminine object of
Christendom and the highest lady addressed by the poetic discourses
of courtly love and *fin'amor*. She is crowned with the seductive shell
of beauty borrowed from Venus, the powerful goddess of love; with the
desire and melancholy of Psyche, the allegory of the soul and the mortal beloved of Amor; and with the cultic knowledge of the enigmatic
priestesses of antiquity.[1] Her role is passive, maternal, and ancillary;
her femininity is defined by Christian doctrine in precisely these
terms.[2] Christian mysticism reflects the femininity of the Virgin. The

[1] See the statue of Aphrodite and Canova's "Amor and Psyche" in the illustrations
of chapter 1. See the Carthaginian "Winged Priestess" later in the present chapter.
[2] See Leo Steinberg, *The Sexuality of Christ in Renaissance Art and in Modern
Oblivion* (New York: Random House, 1984); John W. O'Malley, *Praise and Blame
in Renaissance Rome: Rhetoric, Doctrine and Reform in the Sacred Orators of the
Papal Court, c. 1450–1521* (Durham: Duke University Press, 1979); Jaroslav Pelikan, *Mary through the Centuries* (New Haven: Yale University Press, 1996); Marina
Warner, *Alone of All Her Sex: The Myth and Cult of the Virgin Mary* (New York: Al-
fred A. Knopf, 1976); Els Maeckelberghe, *Desperately Seeking Mary: A Feminist Ap-
propriation of a Traditional Religious Symbol* (Kampen, Netherlands: Pharos, 1991);
Alvin J. Schmidt, *Veiled and Silenced: How Culture Shaped Sexist Theology* (Macon:

11. Johannes Vermeer, *The Allegory of the Faith*. All rights reserved, The Metropolitan Museum of Art.

subjects of mystical experience articulate it in the terms of self-portrayal.

The familiar figure of Mary as the tree or rod of Jesse links her to Old Testament genealogy. This figure invests Mary's image with a phallic power that seems odd in the context of her humility and the construction of her femininity through dogma and popular culture. The beauty of the Virgin's cult images and her mysteriously virginal condition do not threaten men with the potential dangers that Freud observed in beauty and virginity, nor is the figure of her identification with the rod seen as threatening. In the unique case of the Virgin, idealization suspends the dangers of desire. The figure of the rod is not the image of the "phallic mother/phallic woman," the female figure who has a phallus and threatens the subject in dreams and phantasms. Otto Fenichel's equation of "girl = phallus" identifies the feminine figure with the phallus; the girl appears in the form of a phallus that identifies her without implying that she possesses a phallus. This equation is relevant to an understanding of the figure of the Virgin.[3]

The rod of Jesse gives a phallic form to the body of the Virgin in the antiphon of a prayer to the Virgin in honor of the Immaculate Conception: "Haec est virga in qua nec nodus originalis, nec cortex actualis culpae fuit [This is the rod in which was neither knot of original sin, nor rind of actual guilt]."[4] In the Versicle, an apostrophe to the Virgin ("virgo") echoes "virga:" "In conceptione tua, virgo, immaculata fuisti [In thy conception, O Virgin! thou wast immaculate]". From the rod to the Virgin, from "virgo" to "virga," something like the Other *jouissance* slips into the text. "Vergare," to write, is also present in the wordplay that celebrates the beautiful figure of the Virgin. Like the tower of ivory from the Litany of Loreto, the rod without sin or guilt presents its image of mystical jubilation in an explicit phallic form. This Roman Catholic form of "girl = phallus" celebrates the love of Virgin and Son in precisely the terms of sex without sin that Renaissance art reveals in representations of Christ.

Mercer University Press, 1989); Jean Pétrin, *Le sens de l'oeuvre de Saint Luc et le mystère marial* (Ottawa: Séminaire Saint Paul, 1979).

[3] Otto Fenichel, "Die symbolische Gleichung: Mädchen = Phallus" in *Collected Papers* (London: Routledge and Kegan, 1955), 3–18.

[4] See the prayerbook by Reverend F. X. Lasance, *Manna of the Soul* (New York: Benziger Brothers, 1917), 384–85. The prayer is assigned the indulgence of "100 days, every time.—Pius IX, March 31, 1876" and is followed by the Memorare.

The figure of Psyche as a young woman resonates within the Christian scenario that stages desire and repression through the immaculate virginity of the beloved maternal figure. The attribution of beauty renders the Virgin secretly desirable while it underscores her appropriateness as an object of sacrifice, implicated through her sorrows and her purity, in the destiny of her Son, the lamb who takes away the sins of the world. Her maternal bliss is illustrated in gestures of amorous *jouissance* that Leo Steinberg has explored from the perspective of Christ's sexuality. In *The Sexuality of Christ in Renaissance Art and in Modern Oblivion*, Steinberg draws attention to the central role of masculine sexuality in sacred art. Christ's victory over violence, torture, crucifixion, and death is explicitly figured in phallic terms.

Leo Steinberg's exploration of Christ's sexuality originates in a vast repertory of visual images of desire. The portrayal of the Virgin focuses another series of sacred images of desire on the figure of a beautiful young woman who sits or stands erect. Many of these images, including Italian renderings of the Assumption and the Spanish Virgin of the Column (an iconographic theme that combines a vertical figure of Mary with a pillar), seem to anticipate Fenichel's equation. Giovanni Battista Piazetta's *Madonna and Child Appearing to Saint Philip Neri* is a late example that recalls Eros the bittersweet, and the combined motifs of love and death. In Piazetta's rendering of the saint's vision, the Madonna stands erect and is accompanied by *amoretti* cherubs and a death's head.

The phallic quality of the Virgin's beautiful feminine image in sacred art is confirmed by the iconography of the rod or tree of Jesse that identifies her through the male lineage of genealogy. The Virgin's impact on the worshipper (and viewer) occurs through her feminine role, through the poetics of courtly love, and through the tradition of the imitation of Christ. The Virgin is the theological figure of the mother, a pagan import foreign to Judaism; she is Notre Dame, Our Lady, queen of heaven, and the adored figure of joy, sorrow, and glory; she belongs to you as she belongs to Christ her son/father, both man and God.[5]

---

[5] See Schlossman, "L'Ecriture joycienne: juive ou chrétienne?" in *James Joyce, Cahiers de l'Herne 50*, edited by Fritz Senn and Jacques Aubert (Paris: L'Herne, 1985), 318–333.

12. Giovanni Battista Piazzetta, *Madonna and Child Appearing to Saint Philip Neri*, c. 1725, oil on canvas. Courtesy of the National Gallery of Art.

The Virgin is a focus for Christian desire and a model of the sacrifice of desire. In a scenario that resembles the "perverse phenomenology" evoked by Lacan's discussion of Psyche, the Virgin's beauty mingles with repression, chastity, and purity. Lacan evokes the elements of the equation girl = phallus through the figure of Psyche in relation to Amor: "I have taught you for a long time that the gracile form of the feminine, at the borderline between puberty and girlhood, is the phallic image for us."[6] Lacan's interpretation of the equation emphasizes the image of the phallus reflected in the narcissistic form of the body.[7] Lacan's allusion to Psyche's scimitar, an emblem of castration that threatens her lover, recalls the earlier myth of Venus emerging from the sea at the scene of a castration. Like Psyche, Venus on the shell is the phallus presented as the sign of the desire that she arouses.[8] Lacan describes the projection of the form of the phallus onto the feminine object in the form of "girl = phallus": "The signifier is not simply sending a sign *to* someone, but at the moment of the signifying mechanism, sending a sign *of* someone . . . the someone becomes a signifier."[9]

The Madonna is the mother-daughter object of mariolatry, who replaces sensual transgression and sin with a complex distantiation of desire. Projected onto the son of God and imitated through Christ's suffering, the subject's desire has a divine alibi. The Madonna masters libidinal transgression, and illicit desire appears as the serpent crushed beneath her feet. Eve fades away, aging and cast off as an Old Testament figure: enthroned, the Virgin remains eternally young and beautiful. The shell of Venus risen from the sea curves above and behind her like a crown. In Renaissance and Baroque art, the Virgin often appears erect on a pedestal of clouds. Beneath her feet are the crescent moon and the serpent. In a style typical of seventeenth-century

---

[6] Jacques Lacan, *Le Transfert* [Séminaire 1960–61] (Paris: Seuil, 1991), 287. See also *Ecole Lacanienne de Psychanalyse, Le Transfert dans tous ses errata* (Paris: E.P.E.L., 1991).

[7] Ibid. Lacan, *Le Transfert*, 287.

[8] Lacan writes: "Le phallus se présente au niveau humain, entre autres, comme le signe du désir. (. . .) Nous constatons, dans la phénoménologie, la projection plus facile du phallus, en raison de sa forme prégnante, sur l'objet féminin par exemple, et c'est ce qui nous a fait maintes fois articuler, dans la phénoménologie perverse, la fameuse équivalence Girl = Phallus dans sa forme la plus simple, la forme érigée du phallus. (. . .) le signifiant, ce n'est pas simplement faire signe *à* quelqu'un, mais, dans le même moment du ressort signifiant, faire signe *de* quelqu'un . . . le quelqu'un devienne lui aussi ce signifiant" (*Le Transfert*, 306).

[9] *Le Transfert*, 306.

13. Anonymous, *Madonna and Child*, seventeenth century, polychrome on wood. Antwerp, Belgium. Private Collection. Photograph, Paul Stuyven.

Flemish sculpture, a polychrome wooden figure of the Virgin holds the serpent under her left foot. The sculptor emphasized the head of the serpent biting the apple. Vermeer refers to this tradition in the "Allegory of Faith," a painting that takes the hieratic pose apart. He alludes to Eve in the Garden through a painting within a painting—a visual *mise en abyme*—of the Virgin who appears on the wall, behind the allegory of Faith. Vermeer's allegory shifts the time frame away from Eve and the serpent as the New Testament replaces the Old. Christian Virtue kills the serpent, lying in the foreground of the painting.

In the modernist portrait of *The White Girl* (known as *Symphony in White*), Whistler includes a witty allusion to the tradition of portraying the Madonna crushing the fanged serpent. The woman dressed in white stands on an open-mouthed bear rug, strewn with cut flowers like an altar. Her left foot is closer to the bear's head; in her left hand, she holds a flower pointing down to the strewn flowers on the two rugs. Behind her, the background is covered with a curtain; it hangs in elaborate folds that might allude to the veils and curtains of Christian revelation, frequently found in religious painting. Whistler's curtain is covered with a pale stylized floral motif that appears in different contexts throughout Whistler's career. The motif echoes the tonal detailing of the dress as well as the floral motif on the two rugs. The bow of her high-waisted dress attracts the viewer's gaze to the site of conception, emphasized in countless representations of the Annunciation. The simplicity of the model's pose and the detailing of her sleeves and bodice emphasize the vertical quality of the composition. The anonymous figure stands, almost suspended, on a fluffy-textured bear skin that recalls the clouds of the Madonna's pedestal. Instead of the serpent's fanged head, the open-jawed face of the bear confronts the viewer. In contrast to its pathos as a figure of desire, the face of the young woman is neutral, without affect or expression, and her mouth is closed. Inscribed in a visual vocabulary of emblematic purity that recalls idealizations of the Virgin, this figure is also secular and modern. The woman's thoughts cannot be read through theology, and although the identity of the model is well-known, the figure in the painting remains enigmatic and unnamed. She is a stranger who confronts the viewer. The power of her gaze is representative of the erotic impact of the madonnas of modernism.

With the influence of Christianity, Eros (or Amor) loses his prestige as a god or daimon. He becomes the companion of a feminine figure. Love is distributed among figures of Eve, the Virgin, Mary Magdalen

14. James McNeill Whistler, *Symphony in White Number 1: The White Girl*, 1862, oil on canvas. Courtesy of the National Gallery of Art.

and other female saints, and goddesses borrowed from paganism. At a cultural crossroads, a Carthaginian sarcophagus represents an unknown goddess or priestess of love as a full-length figure of a beautiful woman. She wears a Greek gown, and has the wings of the soul's immortality that are evoked in Plato's account of love and in depictions of Psyche, the beloved of Amor.[10]

In the Renaissance, love is represented by the allegorical figure of Venus. The winged Eros of antiquity reappears in a somewhat trivialized form as a sweet-faced cherub or as an assembly of *amoretti*. The Eros of antiquity represents desire, whereas the angelic Renaissance version is a winsome decorative accessory for the goddess.[11] When the painter Caravaggio rejects the Renaissance domestication of Eros, he returns to the tradition of antiquity that Edgar Wind describes. His figures of Amor sleeping on a black background allude to Death as well as to Love.[12] With his eyes closed, without a blindfold, the boy Love is a body lying on the ground. In tone, Caravaggio returns to Sappho's blackest renderings of Eros the bittersweet.

Represented in beautiful feminine form, elaborate draped clothing, and tender amorous gestures exchanged with her son, the Madonna enters the scene of early Italian Renaissance painting. Byzantine influences indirectly connect her with the idealized form and the exquisite carved drapery of classical sculpture of the goddess of love. The Italian Church portrays the Madonna in beautiful poetic images ranging in content from physical purity (and the celebration of her unique femininity) to precious materials and architectonic abstractions. In European Renaissance painting, the image of the Madonna offers and arouses love without inviting the transgressions associated with Eve and the serpent or with the pagan culture of Eros and Amor. Her feminine body is unique, virginal, and without desire of its own. The only woman who escapes Eve's sin is Christ's virgin mother. The Blessed

[10] The marble sarcophagus is identified as the sarcophagus of the winged priestess, fourth to third century B.C., Carthage, National Museum. The Egyptian coiffure and the wings that enclose her body recall images of Isis and Nephtys. *Carthage, numéro spécial de "Connaissance des Arts,"* Paris (1995), 10.

[11] The cherubic Amor in Botticelli's "Primavera" is suspended and maintains some individuality; he hovers almost like a halo or a cloud over the beautiful figure of Venus. In his study of this important painting, Charles Dempsey points out that Botticelli does not take up emblems of the Virgin in his rendering of Venus. See *The Portrayal of Love* (Princeton: Princeton University Press, 1992).

[12] Edgar Wind, *Pagan Mysteries of the Renaissance,* revised edition (New York: Norton, 1968).

15. *Sarcophagus of the Winged Priestess*, c. Fourth to Third Century, B.C. Museum of Carthage, Tunisia.

Virgin Mary appears in a feminine form that is as young and beautiful as the prestigious figures of Aphrodite inherited from antiquity. In medieval and Renaissance art, saints and goddesses frequently are connected with the Virgin through the iconography of mystical love. The Virgin is portrayed in idealized representations of the feminine: her sensual and visible beauty is modified by delicacy of expression, by her acceptance of divine will in the Incarnation, and by the Christian rendering of the bittersweet in Mary's joyous, dolorous, and glorious mysteries. Ideally modest, passive, and tender, she says Yes, and conceives of the Holy Spirit. Her love is pure, maternal, and mystical, and she is untainted by desire or by original sin. Prayers are said in the Virgin's chapel. In *A Portrait of the Artist as a Young Man*, it is to her rather than to her Son that the sinner turns for solace. Across a range of cultures, centuries, and schools of painting, her theologically unique presence allows her to slip past the taboos on femininity and to represent desire and love for the Church. Because the New Testament places her beneath the divine shadow, she enters a secret erotic space that cannot be painted. This space is figured in the tender melancholy that shades the Virgin's eyes and in the enigmatic expression of her gaze—it appears to wander to love and death, to joy and sorrow.

Sappho's Eros and the Blessed Virgin Mary

In a poem-fragment saved from the flames, the poet Sappho launched "Eros the bittersweet" on the sea of black and white. Her poems give an account of the two realms of passion, the hell and heaven of love:

> It seems to me that he is similar to the gods, that man who is sitting next to you, and who, close to you, listens to the sweet sound of your voice, and how you, full of charm, smile toward him: but in my chest, this has taken away the calmness of my heart when I look at you, it happens suddenly that I become mute, for my tongue lies motionless, a subtle fire instantly trickles through my skin, with my eyes I see nothing, there is a dull thunder that rushes in my ears, and sweat breaks out, a trembling seizes all my limbs, I am more pale than dry grass, and I seem to myself not far away anymore from having died. But one must bear everything.[13]

---

[13] *Sappho: Lieder.* Greek and German edition by Max Treu (Munich and Zurich: Artemis & Winkler Verlag, 1991). First Book of Sappho, Fragment 31 (Lobel-Page).

Simultaneously analytic and intimate, Sappho's account of desire reveals the complex resonances of amorous passion. Her image of desire presents the effect of Eros as bitter and sweet; it includes the shining-forth of beauty and the suffering of passion. The early Church will shape its figures of Christ along these lines of the extremes of Eros.

The Renaissance associates Sappho's figure of bittersweet Eros with Plato, especially with the *Symposium*. The intuition that shapes the currents of Neoplatonic thought seems to indicate that the identity of Sappho was unknown to Marsilio Ficino and his followers. Renaissance confusion over the Platonic identity of the Sapphic Eros ("dulce amarem") has lingered into modernity. In indirect tribute to Sappho, the ambivalence of suffering and bliss that she evokes appears as compelling to present-day readers as it did to Ficino, Lorenzo de' Medici, and Michelangelo.

In his studies of Renaissance art and letters, Edgar Wind breaks the long silence of art historians on the connection between love and death. He highlights a tradition derived from antiquity that emphasizes their combined representation in the love of a god for a mortal. In its most extreme forms, Amor is presented as a god of Death. These forms are portrayed on Roman sarcophagi, in Italian Renaissance painting, and in Renaissance emblems. Wind's hypothesis is based on his reading of the effects of Sappho's bittersweet love in the philosophy, art, and poetry of the Italian Renaissance. The love of a god slips toward the representation of mortality. Wind suggests that a figure of Leda found on Roman sarcophagi connects Michelangelo's source for his statue of *Night* with his 1529 design of a *Leda* figure for Alfonso d'Este.[14] Through Eros the bittersweet, these figures combine allusions to desire and love, rendered inseparable from mourning and death.

The literature of courtly love and the products of Renaissance Neoplatonism preserve Sappho's bittersweet Eros until the modern period rediscovers her and begins to unpeel the mummified translated texts and fragments.[15] Sappho's Eros is violent, shaking, and driven; Eros, she says, is the servant like herself, of Aphrodite. In Fragment 31,

---

English translation by Rainer Nägele. I have consulted many translations of Sappho in English, French, and German. Epigraph quotations of fragments are quoted from Guy Davenport, *Seven Greeks* (New York: New Directions, 1996).

[14] Wind, *Pagan Mysteries of the Renaissance.*

[15] See Edgar Wind, 73 for relevant remarks about troubadour culture, emblems, and Platonic love; see Joan de Jean, Appendix, on fragment 31.

Sappho's most famous poem, Eros is 'inside' the desiring narrator (or speaking I). Eros brings this speaker close to death. The gender of the object hovers in the undecidable, because Sappho inscribes it or renders it indeterminate. The object is beautiful and desirable. Its shape is unknown. Normative heterosexual readings declare it male, and homosexual readings borrow from other Sapphic poems to read it as female. In sacrificial opposition or in narcissistic reflection, these readings tamper with Sappho's rendering of a passion that takes subject and object over the edge, beyond the cultural contours of gendered identity. Sappho uncovers desire in the suspension of identity and the extreme experience of the bittersweet.

In her portrayal of the subjectivity of love, the poet Sappho sets the stage for modernism. Eros the bittersweet haunts Sappho's representations of love and shapes the discreet, enigmatic presence of her poetics in some literary works of modernity. In part through Sappho's literary influence, the madonna figures lead the reader beyond the dichotomies of male and female, of artist and subject, to the resonance of voices in silence. These figures speak from the outside in, or from the inside in. The voice of the Poet locates love inside an unnatural space, in a courtyard or a garden of artifice. Love is inscribed with the oxymoron of the bittersweet, suffering and pleasure, that courtly love tradition and Renaissance neo-Platonism preserve and recirculate. The voice of the Poet is dramatically altered in the framework of modernism, but Eros the bittersweet takes on modern shapes that echo its lyrical origins.

Several late descendants of Sappho's figure of Eros appear as literary figures of desire and the feminine. They take shape as madonnas of modernism. The inscription of Eros the bittersweet in modernism implicates these feminine figures within a representation of love that incorporates elements of classical culture in a secular framework of post-classical and post-religious culture. The Renaissance writers and artists who transformed "Eros the bittersweet" into their own images of love did not (or could not) acknowledge their debt to Sappho, but modern scholarship has revealed the literary identity of Ficino's Platonic Eros in Sappho's epithet. Sappho's transformation of Eros into "the bittersweet" portrays passionate love in the context of the writing of a subjectivity of excess. Sappho makes the connection between eroticism and poetics.

When Sappho's figure of Eros reaches modernity, it confronts an inheritance of courtly love rhetoric that originates in the twelfth century. Christianity reshapes desire in light of a form of idealization of the love-object that is foreign to antiquity. "Romantic love" is a late cultural product of the Christian ideology of love. For this reason, a reading of the impact of Sappho's figure of Eros on modernist representations of love must take into account the Christian revision of desire and the enigmatic traces of original sin. The source of these traces is the narrative account of the Fall in chapter three of the book of *Genesis*.[16] The Fall and, especially, Eve's encounter with the seductive serpent in the Garden, are constantly evoked in European medieval and Renaissance art and literature, as well as in religious and theological writings. The doctrine of mariolatry evolves in reference to Mary as the second Eve; as the mother of Christ, immaculately conceived, Mary undoes original sin.[17] The figure of the madonna becomes the most important feminine figure in the religion of love. As the human vessel of the Incarnation and a feminine object of cultic devotion, she replaces the goddesses of antiquity. Her relation with her Son represents a kind of successful incest.[18]

Modernism and Eros the Bittersweet

The madonnas of modernism are feminine love objects who incarnate desire in a literary construction; they inhabit a space of sensuality and renunciation. Modernist representations of love raise the question of the status of the feminine in traditional cult value and in exhibition value, in love and in desire. Urban modernity, inscribed in modernism,

---

[16] Biblical quotations are taken from the King James version. I have consulted the revised and annotated edition of the *Bible de Jérusalem* (Paris: Editions du Cerf, 1973) and *La Bible*, translated by André Chouraqui (Paris: Desclée de Brouwer, 1989). The concept of original sin and the explicit parallel between Jesus and Adam are generally attributed to Paul in chapter 5 of *Romans*.

On original sin, see *Nouvelle Histoire de l'Eglise*, vols. 1–2 (Paris: Seuil, 1963–68); Henri Rondet, S.J., *Le Péché originel dans la tradition patristique et théologique* (Paris: Fayard, 1967); Jacques Turmel, *Histoire des dogmes* 6 vols. (Paris: Rieder, 1931–36); Henri de Lubac, *Méditations sur l'Eglise* (Paris: Aubier-Montaigne, 1968).

[17] For a cultural history of mariolatry, see Marina Warner, *Alone of All Her Sex*, and Jaroslav Pelikan, *Mary Through the Centuries* (New Haven: Yale University Press, 1996). For the image of Christ and his Mother in Renaissance art, see Leo Steinberg's magistral work, *The Sexuality of Christ*, op. cit.

[18] See Schlossman, *Joyce's Catholic Comedy of Language* (Madison: University of Wisconsin Press, 1985) for the resonances of successful incest in Joycean mariolatry, with a focus on the *Portrait*, *Ulysses*, and *Finnegans Wake*.

shocks the traditional taboos and idealizations of love into a confrontation with commodification and perversion. Yeats and Joyce illustrate the tensions of this confrontation in their inscriptions of Eros.

While Yeats explicitly integrates his reading of classical texts within his recreation of a Celtic sensibility, he is more discreet on the subject of Christian tradition. His investment in the construction of an Irish political identity absorbs the tensions between the revived nostalgia for paganism and the continental literary canon of modernism. Joyce rejects the Yeatsian blend of Irish politics and druidic mysticism, but he retains the modernization of classical love that Yeats presents in his poetry. For Joyce, the central focus of love shifts to theology. The modernist source of his approach to desire and original sin is the trans-romanticism of Flaubert and Baudelaire, and in particular their evocations of antiquity.

The role of love in modernism is shaped by the impact of a literary figure, a fragment, Eros the bittersweet, on a secularized modern literature that derives its conception of love from Christian religion. For Sappho, death is not far from the power of love; Eros plays a leading role in the staging of the extremes of love from Greek antiquity to the Renaissance. Eros/Amor appears to the Romans as a god of Death. In Western culture, the religion of love begins with punishment inflicted by a jealous god, in *Genesis*, when desire leads to transgression. The desiring subject goes too far and turns the sweetness of paradise to the bitterness of expulsion. Eve is blamed for all the evils that beset mankind; the Church's emphasis on the doctrine of original sin structures a discourse of sin and grace. Sappho and the daimonic Eros imperceptibly fade away, but Eve's encounter with the snake is branded onto art and letters for centuries to come.

The figure of Eros the bittersweet is divided. He speaks for the masculine and the feminine. The figure of Eros represents love as sensual desire and beauty celebrated in the beloved, and as a powerful passion that transforms (and threatens) the lover from within. Since the Renaissance, Sappho's Eros of pleasure and pain has been associated with Plato's *Symposium*, where the same split is evident. Diotima presents Socrates with "the ladder of Eros," and she claims to lead her pupil from the desire for pleasure derived from beautiful bodies to the interior shining of virtue. Her discourse is undercut by the speech of Aristophanes, who claims to suffer from the pain of passion before he declares that Socrates himself is split like a Silenus, and his seductive shining of inner beauty is composed of divine images, philosophical

16. Bernard van Orley, *The Marriage of the Virgin*, 1513, oil on panel. Courtesy of the National Gallery of Art.

knowledge, and virtue. Eros the bittersweet and the Silenus-like split of Socrates locate the oxymoron of love within Eros, offspring of Poros and Penia, and within the subject who is transformed by love.

In Christianity, desire takes on form according to the images of *Genesis*. The snake is a menacing phallic creature who attacks Eve and whom God condemns to lodge beneath the heel of man (and especially woman). The snake sometimes appears as a dragon. The Tristan and Isolde story discussed in chapter 6 features a dragon who devours virgins; religious art inserts snakes and snakelike dragon figures under the Madonna's heel, or discreetly frames her inviolate space. Bernard van Orley's *The Marriage of the Virgin* contains obvious references to the biblical snake; Carlo Crivelli's *Madonna and Child Enthroned with Donor* is more subtle. Snakes and apples appear in the ornamentation of the Virgin's throne. In his French translation of the Bible, André Chouraqui indicates a pun linking the serpent's "nakedness" with his "cunning" or "ruse."[19] In the legends of Saint Michael, Saint George, and the Celtic Tristan, dragons replace the snake, and pure images of the Virgin require salvation from them. The doctrine of mariolatry takes up God's condemnation of the serpent in Genesis 3 and places it under the heel of Eve's replacement, the Madonna.

The visual and textual reference to Eve seems to become less frequent as secularization progresses. From early modernity to present-day popular culture, the Madonna continues to resonate as a model for love and art. At the threshold of modernism, Balzac's *Human Comedy* illustrates the enduring influence of the image of the Virgin in its repeated use of the Madonnas of Raphael as a model of artistic representation and portraiture.[20] In the first major novel of early Modernism, Flaubert borrows from his own love-letters to Louise Colet when he places the epithet of "madonna" in the persuasive rhetoric of a small-time Don Juan courting Madame Bovary. Baudelaire is even more explicit in "Le Flambeau Vivant;" the speaking I of the poem invokes the Madonna at the crossroads of love and writing. These canonical references lead to Yeats's poetic inscriptions and epitaphs for desirable young women, and to the figures of Isabel and Nuvoletta as daughter, sister, or bride in Joyce's *Finnegans Wake*.

[19] Paris: Desclée, 1984.
[20] See Schlossman, "Balzac's Art of Excess" in *Modern Language Notes* 109:5 (1994), 873–896.

17. Carlo Crivelli, *Madonna and Child Enthroned with Donor*, 1470, oil and tempera on panel. Courtesy of the National Gallery of Art.

Staging the Drives: Literature and Psychoanalysis

Based in part on the insights of literature, Freud's theoretical writings on psychoanalysis appear to lay the foundations for twentieth-century modernism. The work (and the working through) of analysis constructs a new discourse in the process of undoing repression. When Freud alludes to the return of the repressed in theatrical terms, the figures of desire appear on the stage of subjectivity. In the process of analysis, graphic and dramatic renderings of desire unfold from the traces of the distant days of childhood. Modernist evocations of Greco-Roman antiquity, the pagan Orient, and the bible explore the traces of a distant culture. Yeats isolates figures of antiquity within a modern focus on the poetic voice of an individual speaker, and Joyce uses Vico's structure of returns to reinforce the analogy between individual experience and periods of culture. The importance of love and sex, Adam and Eve, Christ and Mary, and a new language repeating the same old story of the obscene incident and the sublime letter shape *Finnegans Wake* into a dramatic narrative of desire. In the staging of the drives, modernity focuses on the distant days of the pre-Christian past. Freud's critique of courtly love appears in his concept of the debasement of the love object. Joyce's writing plays out the debasement of the object through a rejection of romantic sentiment and an emphasis on parody, obscenity, and sin. Joyce represents desire by turning back the clock of Freud's "progress in repression" to antiquity: the Wake confronts Christ with Eros at the celebration of Issy's "erosmas".

In the wake of early modernism, emerging from romantic culture in the mid-nineteenth century, the discourse of psychoanalysis challenges the overvaluation of the love object and its corollary, the taboo on an explicit discourse of sexuality.[21] Freud makes the connection between the object and the drive (translated by Strachey as "instinct"): "The most striking distinction between the erotic life of antiquity and our own no doubt lies in the fact that the ancients laid the stress upon the instinct itself, whereas we emphasize its object. The ancients glorified the instinct and were prepared on its account to honour even an inferior object; while we despise the instinctual activity in itself,

---

[21] In this context, certain writers who are considered to be romantic—e.g. Nerval and Keats—anticipate the modernism of later writers. The impact of Keats and the other great English romantic poets is widely recognized, whereas Nerval, arguably the most important nineteenth-century influence on Baudelaire, is neglected in favor of the larger-than-life romantic writers like Lamartine, Chateaubriand, and Hugo.

and find excuses for it only in the merits of the object."[22] In another text, Freud returns to the repression of the drives in Christianity and the resulting values attributed to love.

> The fact that the curb put upon love by civilization involves a universal tendency to debase sexual objects will perhaps lead us to turn our attention from the object to the instincts themselves. (. . .) It can easily be shown that the psychical value of erotic needs is reduced as soon as their satisfaction becomes easy. An obstacle is required in order to heighten libido; and where natural resistances to satisfaction have not been sufficient men have at all times erected conventional ones so as to be able to enjoy love. This is true both of individuals and of nations. In times in which there were no difficulties standing in the way of sexual satisfaction, such as perhaps during the decline of the ancient civilizations, love became worthless and life empty, and strong reaction-formations were required to restore indispensable affective values. In this connection it may be claimed that the ascetic current in Christianity created psychical values for love which pagan antiquity was never able to confer on it. This current assumed its greatest importance with the ascetic monks, whose lives were almost entirely occupied with the struggle against libidinal temptation.[23]

These remarks shed light on Freud's interpretation of modernity as progress in repression. In the first passage quoted above, the modern valorization of the love object appears to disguise desire in the trappings inherited from courtly love. In the second quotation, Freud reveals that the valorization of the love object is Christian. This valorization disguises the inevitable debasement of the object produced by a repressive culture that limits its subjects' access to sexual satisfaction. The comment that "we despise the instinctual activity in itself" locates modernity itself under the shadow of ascetic disgust and mortified temptation.

Eros in Ireland: Yeats and Joyce

Modernism counters the repression that marks Christian culture by staging a return to figures from antiquity: Eros reappears. The

---

[22] Sigmund Freud, *Three Essays*, "I. The Sexual Aberrations," footnote added 1910.
[23] Sigmund Freud, "On the Universal Tendency to Debasement in the Sphere of Love," 3, *SE* volume 11, 177–190.

inscription of desire in Modernism leads from Sappho's Eros the bittersweet to Yeats and Joyce. The gestures of weeping, descending, and writing accompany the key references to Sappho in Yeats. In "A Woman Young and Old," XI: "From the 'Antigone,'" he writes:

> OVERCOME—O bitter sweetness,
> Inhabitant of the soft cheek of a girl— (. . .)
> Pray I will and sing I must,
> And yet I weep—Oedipus' child
> Descends into the loveless dust.[24]

The bitter sweetness of love is in Antigone's face: the speaker's singing and weeping express the grief of her descent, banished from love.

In addition to "Fergus' Song," "The Gift of Harun Al-Rachid," a long poem on love that Joyce echoes throughout *Ulysses*, evokes the mystery of love as the bittersweet, explicitly borrowed from Sappho.[25] Yeats first conjures Eros the bittersweet near the beginning of the poem, with its program of "how violent great hearts can lose / Their bitterness and find the honeycomb" (440). Joyce borrows the gift (a young woman, offered by the prince to his courtier) to link the dreams of Stephen Dedalus and Leopold Bloom in anticipation of their meeting. Bloom's writing in the sand in "Nausikaa" also alludes to the poem through the writing of the feminine. The final Joycean form of the girl's midnight writing in the sand appears in the letter that is written and circulated in *Finnegans Wake*.

In the poem, the "gift" of love brings beauty, truth, and possibly death to the courtier. His story is told in a letter written by a chronicler called "the wild Bedouin," and the question of where to hide the letter is answered in an evocation of Sappho:

> And pause at last, I was about to say,
> at the great book of Sappho's song, but no:
> For should you leave my letter there, a boy's
> Lovelorn, indifferent hands might come upon it
> And let it fall unnoticed to the floor.
> ("The Gift," 439)

[24] W. B. Yeats, *Collected Poems* (New York: Macmillan, 1956), 272.
[25] "The Gift of Harun Al-Rachid" (1923) in W. B. Yeats, *Collected Poems* (New York: Macmillan, 1956), 439–44.

Harun, the mightiest of princes, offers the girl to the least considered of his courtiers (440). The courtier wonders: "Yet was it love of me, or was it love / Of the stark mystery that has dazed my sight, / Perplexed her fantasy and planned her care?" (442). The Bedouin narrator says that a Djinn speaks truths through the girl. Her sleepwalking leads to her writing in the sand:

> I wrapped her in a hooded cloak, and she,
> Half running, dropped at the first ridge of the desert
> And there marked out those emblems on the sand
> That day by day I study and marvel at,
> With her white finger. I led her home asleep
> And once again she rose and swept the house
> In childish ignorance of all that passed.
> (443)

The Djinn's "midnight voice" of truth has been transformed by her "woman's beauty" and by Eros the bittersweet. The voice takes wisdom from her mysterious and unspoken love. Vaguely phallic, wisdom "stands" under the "storm-tossed banner" of feminine beauty. Beauty and love are inseparable: wisdom combines the poetry and philosophy of antiquity with something reminiscent of neo-platonic mystery. This mystery is revealed at the end of the poem as Eros:

> All, all thoses gyres and cubes and midnight things
> Are but a new expression of her body
> Drunk with the bitter sweetness of her youth.
> (444)

At the beginning and again toward the end of the poem, the narrator pairs Sappho's poetry with Parmenides. The "midnight things" of mysterious "wisdom" are revealed to "the wild Bedouin" as the writing of feminine beauty.

Joyce's turn to Sappho's Eros occurs in part through the mediation of Yeats, the source for Stephen's brooding on "love's bitter mystery" in *Ulysses*. In "The Gift of Harun al-Rachid" the bitter sweetness of love is linked to gestures that remain unconscious; the gestuality of love that marks the poetry of Yeats represents desire through a theatricality of form. The stylization of gesture is linked in Modernism to the caesura that breaks continuity, and to the process of fragmentation that threatens the idealized wholeness of the body.[26] Gesture in writing eludes some of the taboos on spoken language by returning to pre-symbolic forms of representation. Without directly attacking repression, gesture is a progress in the undoing of repression. It takes hold of the repressed materials and brings them to light. Gesture gives form and representation to the writing of desire.

Joyce's motifs of gesture portray love through comedy, farce, and the gesture-based lazzi derived from the commedia dell'arte and disseminated in European theater: these motifs emphasize violence, low life, and the obscene.[27] Other motifs that appear in Joyce's work are derived from the Church, the Passion, and the sublime associated with baroque tragedy. Joyce's articulation of a gestuality of love in modernity begins with the bittersweet contrast of beauty and death in Yeats but moves away from the lyricism of the speaker in Yeats's poems. The extreme contrasts of the comic and the sacred allow Joyce to depersonalize the bittersweet and to mask the lyrical voice he associates with writing, singing, and Irish identity.

From *Giacomo Joyce* and "Exiles" through *Ulysses* and the *Wake*, the experience of love—or of falling in love—appears in repeated gestual forms, including the exchange of glances, the mirroring of the subject in the feminine identity of the object (or her feminine and Jewish identity), the swooning of the moment of conception (the Annunciation), weeping and dissolving in tears, the kiss (sublime and obscene), the Fall, and gestures related to the snake in Genesis. This includes the poisoning glance and the coiling movement, related to the seduction of the beloved. Modernist gestures of love appear in the rise and fall of virility, morality, going to bed, and dying. Writing love letters, melancholy introspection and retrospection, and dreaming also enter the context of gesture. In *Finnegans Wake*, Shem illustrates Joyce's self-styled combination of 'low' (seductive and obscene) behavior, desire, and writing. Obscenity and beauty add up to an aesthetic of desire—Eros bitter and sweet.

[26] See the interpretation of gestuality in Modernism in Rainer Nägele, *Theater, Theory, Speculation: Walter Benjamin and the Scenes of Modernity* (Baltimore: Johns Hopkins University Press, 1991), especially chapter 7, "From Aesthetics to Poetics: Benjamin, Brecht, and the Poetics of the Caesura," 135–66.

[27] Much of David Hayman's work represents the gestural qualities in modernism, and especially in Joyce's writing. See "Language of/as Gesture in Joyce," *Ulysses: cinquante ans après*, ed. Louis Bonnerot (Paris: Didier, 1966), 209–21, reprinted in *James Joyce: A Collection of Critical Essays*, edited by Mary T. Reynolds (Englewood Cliffs, N.J.: Prentice-Hall, 1993), 37–47.

Gesture shapes the expression of Gabriel Conroy's eroticism at the
end of "The Dead"; his fiasco leads to a doubled mirroring of desire.
Following his initial incomprehension, Gabriel gives himself over to
the figure of dissolving that brings the ghosts of the dead among the
living. "His own identity was fading out into a grey impalpable world:
the solid world itself which these dead had one time reared and lived
in was dissolving and dwindling" (D 200). In a Joycean virtual triangle,
Gabriel loses his wife to the boy who sang "The Lass of Aughrim" and
died for her. Her mourning overcomes his desire. Gretta weeps, and
Gabriel feels tears in his own eyes. The figure of swooning in the last
sentence confirms Gabriel's mirroring in the feminine: "His soul
swooned softly as he heard the snow falling faintly through the universe and faintly falling, like the descent of their last end, upon all the
living and the dead" (D 201). Translated into erotic terms, Gabriel's
mirrored reflection in the feminine is a sign of his love for Gretta.

Love triangles, real and virtual, are essential to Joyce's erotic com-
binations. The role of the reflection that mirrors the lover in the feminine is less apparent. This doubling or mirroring adds apparently poetic repetitions to the verbal formulations of desire. An example from
a letter to Nora portrays her through the doubled formulations of talking about her and observing her: "I spoke of you today to my aunt and
told her of you—how you sit at the opera with the grey ribbon in your
hair, listening to music, and observed by men,—and of many other
things (even very intimate things) between us." [28] Joyce repeats "I
spoke of you" as "told her of you," and he repeats "many other things"
in "even very intimate things." The beloved at the opera is "observed
by men": he observes her being observed by men. The triangle enters
the configuration of his self-reflection. The parallel scene in *Giacomo
Joyce* contains a similar repetition that imaginatively captures the
view of the object of desire. "All night I have watched her, all night I
shall see her" (GJ 12). Unlike the description of Nora, the lyrical passage that evokes the narrator's pupil idealizes her, and places her beyond the vulgar crowd of the loggione. She appears dressed in green,
the color of nature's illusion and the color of graves. Like the conva-
lescent Beatrice in *Exiles*, the pupil is idealized: her unsensual, anti-
septic virginity and God's possession of her through sickness and
death appear as conscious appropriations of Dante's figure of Beatrice.

---

[28] Letter to Nora dated 21 August 1912. Letters quoted in this essay refer to Richard Ellmann's edition of *Selected Letters of James Joyce* (New York: Viking, 1974).

When Giacomo's advances are rebuffed, the pupil loses some of her idealized qualities and reveals the animal side of the debasement that Freud describes as universal. Joyce quotes Brunetto on the basilisk's visual attack, but the object of desire refuses to return his greeting or his gaze. Giacomo's violent language transforms her into a mythic monster, while her attack is a negative one. "She answers my sudden greeting by turning and averting her black basilisk eyes. *E col suo vedere attosca l'uomo quando lo vede.* I thank you for the word, messer Brunetto" (*GJ* 15). The monstrous image of attacking vision is repeated within the context of a snake's venom in which "she greets me wintrily and passes up the staircase darting at me for an instant out of her sluggish sidelong eyes a jet of liquorish venom" (*GJ* 15). The basilisk with its eyes that spurt venom becomes the coiling snake of the dream sequence that alludes to the terror of sin: "Adultery of wisdom. (. . .) Soft sucking lips kiss my left armpit: a coiling kiss on myriad veins. (. . .) A starry snake has kissed me: a cold nightsnake. I am lost!—Nora!—" (*GJ* 15). The gestures of the snake include coiling movement, a coiling kiss, the burning of venom and of desire. The positions are reversed: Giacomo is passive, and the "nightsnake" that burns him with its kiss is "cold," like the pupil herself. The dream with its cry to Nora contains an exchange of roles. "Adultery of wisdom?" "No." The wish that seems to be disguised by the dream narrative is that if only the pupil had tried to seduce Giacomo, adultery would not have culminated in resignation and failure, or wisdom evoked as the end of youth: "Youth has an end: the end is here. It will never be. You know that well. What then? Write it, damn you, write it! What else are you good for?" (*GJ* 16).

Giacomo's adulterous eroticism misfires, but his observation of his object leads him to fantasize the penetration of feminine interiority: "Her eyes have drunk my thoughts: and into the moist warm yielding welcoming darkness of her womanhood my soul, itself dissolving, has streamed and poured and flooded a liquid and abundant seed . . . . Take her now who will! . . . ." (*GJ* 14). The narrator's "soul" has entered her through her eyes, and has poured seed into the darkness of the feminine. "Itself dissolving," the soul bearing the seed of virility is absorbed in the feminine element that surrounds it. The contemptuous exclamation that ends this doubling and dissolving expresses bitterness about the fiasco and leaves her, no longer quite virgin, to the fate of the feminine object, the debasement that all the idealization in the world cannot erase.

One of Joyce's letters to Martha Fleischmann, dated early December 1918, explicitly evokes the Virgin, the black madonna of volcanic passion, as well as the debased animal-like female creature observed by the literary voyeur. This seductive letter is refined and literary, unlike the letters to Nora, but it includes the same doubled verbal formulations of desire that result from the mirroring in the feminine figure:

> Ma première impression de vous. Voilà. Vous étiez vêtue de noir avec un gros chapeau aux ailes flottantes. La couleur vous allait très bien. Et j'ai pensé: un joli animal. (. . .) Puis, en vous regardant, j'ai observé la mollesse des traits réguliers et la douceur des yeux. Et j'ai pensé: une juive. Si je me suis trompé il ne faut pas vous offenser. Jésus Christ a pris son corps humain: dans le ventre d'une femme juive. J'ai 35 ans. C'est l'âge que Shakespeare a eu quand il a conçu sa douloureuse passion pour la 'dame noire.' C'est l'âge que le Dante a eu quand il est entré dans la nuit de son être.

"I thought," Joyce writes, "a pretty animal" and again, "I thought: a Jew." "Looking at you" is mirrored in "I observed." Her features have a softness, her eyes a sweetness: she is dressed in black. The reality of anti-Semitism leads him to apologize for his fantasy of her Jewishness. He compares her to the Jewish woman whose belly gave human form to Jesus, to Shakespeare's Dark Lady, and to Dante's mystical Night in the dark wood, at the beginning of the *Commedia*. Shakespeare connects Christ to Dante "when he conceived his dolorous passion for the Dark Lady." The "conception" anchors the mystical mirroring in the feminine in the scene of the Annunciation, when desire and writing unite in the imagination. While Joyce's letters to Nora proclaim his own suffering and announce her identity with the Virgin and with the Madonna, this stylized letter to Martha Fleischmann elaborates an image of her within a scene of literary identification. From Christ's mother and the Dark Lady to Dante, the feminine reflection leads into the Night. He enters it, and she seems to disappear.

The contexts of Joyce's Italian experience, with explicit overtones of time past, of the Middle Ages, and of Dante, are prominent in *Giacomo Joyce*. The lightness of earlier failed attempts at seduction (in *Stephen Hero* and even in *A Portrait*) has disappeared; Eros appears to the semi-fictional character of "Giacomo"/"James"/"Jim" in Trieste in a deepening bitterness. "Love's bitter mystery" from "Fergus'

Song" recalls the combination of love and death. In Sappho's epithet of Eros the bittersweet, and again, in the Renaissance adaptation of it, exemplified by an emblem of Amor as a cherub crowning a death's head, love and death mingle together through the blackness of mourning, jealousy, incest, libertine desire, intrigue, and revenge.[29] Joyce echoes the Passion. His inner staging of tragedy or, more precisely, of a baroque mourning play shapes love's bitter mystery in the terms of modern allegory.

In *Giacomo Joyce*, the tragic approach to love's bitter mystery leaves the virginal Beatrice-like figure cold. The Narrator (figured as Giacomo, but not named in the text) feels angry and rejected. He turns his pupil into Brunetto's figure of a basilisk (a lizardlike monster, hatched by a serpent from a cock's egg) that appears before him only to poison him. Instead of her desire and her affirmation in response to his desire, he is confronted by negation, denial, and bitterness. His own conscience appears to be afflicted with guilt, the mainstay of Joycean love. His object of desire is transformed into a basilisk that glares at him from her dark liquid eyes. Into them, he has poured the seed of his seductive soul. Pseudo-Beatrice and the cockatrice are a thin cover-up for Eve and the serpent. The snake-like figure reappears in the Narrator's dream as a counterpoint to his black lamentation about loss and the end of youth. Dissolved in bitter sarcasm and despair, the voice reemerges in a dream account of seduction. The narrator is approached by a snake-like woman. The dream narrative ends with his supplication to a virginal and maternal Nora, who appears briefly to save the son of Eire from the snake. Nora's one-time role in *Giacomo Joyce* anticipates the *Wake*'s repeated emphasis on Saint Patrick's historical-hagiographical accomplishment of ridding Ireland of snakes.

The self-conscious Troubadour figure of Stephen the would-be poet and lover is absorbed in brooding on death, sin, and the obscene. Love's bitter mystery, a reminder from Yeats about Sapphic Eros, emerges in the replay of the mother's death. "Fergus' Song" is the motif of Stephen's guilty and mournful repetition of the deathbed scene. His mourning is mirrored in the weeping of the dying mother who listens to him play. Stephen puts the accent on irony and bitterness, on the Fall, and on loss. Joyce's important shift from Dedalus to Bloom puts away the preciousness, the Victorian prettiness, and the "deeply

---

[29] Edgar Wind, *Pagan Mysteries in the Renaissance*.

deep" self-dramatization that rule Stephen's aesthetic. In the realm of love, the shift dissolves the tragic tone that limits Stephen's range within a new articulation of love—in comedy and violence, in pleasure and obscenity—that leads through Bloom, Nighttown, and Molly into the corrosive mode of comic violence and disguised lyricism of the *Wake,* where the obscene (like the staging of original sin) is present on every page.

In any order desired, the names that are dropped in the left margins of the *Wake* allude to original sin as well as to the mysteries of love in Greek antiquity: "Adam, Eve./ Socrates./ Alcibiades./ Plato./ Dionysius./ Sappho" (*FW* 306–307). Between Plato and Sappho, the name of Dionysos evokes the divine madness that tears its subjects to pieces. The name of Sappho follows Dionysos with the extremes of Eros. Venereal disease combines with the alphabet of love in Shem's riddle, "and offering the prize of a bittersweet crab, a little present from the past" (*FW* 170.07). The tenth question combines the high and the low with an evocation of smoke, fire, and Eros the bittersweet: "10. What bitter's love but yurning, what' sour lovemutch but a bref burning till shee that drawes dothe smoake retourne?" (*FW* 143.29). Bitter and sweet, love is gestualized in the fire that draws smoke from its object.

Lacan's reading of Joyce focuses on the symbolic rendered in the obscene. The scene of language becomes a ladder of desire that structures an approach to beauty. This is the "eaub-scène," where the dirtiest words are the most beautiful, according to Joyce's long-censored correspondence to Nora in 1909. These words and gestures choreograph the ups and downs of *Finnegans Wake.* In Lacan's perspective, it might be the most beautiful book of modernism. Diotima's ladder of desire in Plato's *Symposium* reveals beauty from within the interiority of Socrates and from within the conjured image of the feminine voice. Virtual, sublime, and idealized, or cold, bestial, and debased, the feminine translates into modernist gestuality. The lover sees his own reflection in the beloved who leads him into the dark night of being. "Beautiful" translates Sappho's Eros into an aesthetic of desire, from the medieval Tristan texts and the spectral amalgamations of Sappho, Plato, and Orpheus in the Renaissance to the returns of modernism.

CONCLUSION
Virgin or Madonna

Eros makes me shiver again
Strengthless in the knees,
Eros gall and honey,
Snake-sly, invincible.
    —Sappho

Freud sees the moment of erotic union as the end of the exaltation of the feminine object. The non-courtly lover's enjoyment is followed by the universal tendency to debasement of the object of love. But Freud's vision of erotic disaster goes beyond the loss of virginity. Not only is the beloved seen as devalued, she is filled with bitterness against the man who has deprived her of her "chaste treasure." Only ideal objects like the Madonna escape debasement. The madonnas of modernism are represented as having it both ways. They fit the images of the ideal, but also the imaged of the debased. Writing preserves them as desirable objects, and maintains the two sets of images.

Written, erased, and repossessed, Sappho's insight into love figured as Eros the bittersweet confronts the condemnation of the drives that Freud interprets as the key to the erotic life of modernity and the modern focus on the object of desire. In Strachey's translation of Freud, "instinctual activity" refers to the drives. Freud's 1910 footnote to "The Sexual Aberrations" points out the modern emphasis on the object in contrast to the ancients' glorification of the "instinct." In "On the Universal Tendency to Debasement in the Sphere of Love," Freud observes that "the ascetic current in Christianity created psychical values for love which pagan antiquity was never able to confer on it."[1]

---

[1] Sigmund Freud, *SE* 2:178.

Sappho's poems evoke passion and invoke its powers. They analyze desire and its effects. Her writings sometimes give the contours of a relation to a particular love object, but frequently, the identity of subject and object are suspended. Sappho never allows the identity of the object to erase the impact of sexuality on the subject who speaks. In other words, when Eros speaks through the subject, the ramparts of identity dissolve. The poetry of Sappho articulates the power of desire—its truth and its beauty, but also its illusion, pain, and "snakesly" cunning. The sophist priestess Diotima displaces the poetics of desire into philosophy when she teaches Socrates that beyond the dissolving edges of identity the Form of the Beautiful unfolds. Diotima's Eros does not run into conflict with gods, humans, or laws. It could be claimed that Diotima's Eros represents only one side of Sappho's story. The appearance of Alcibiades in Dionysian form in the *Symposium* illustrates Sappho's darker side. Alcibiades responds to the Diotima in Socrates as Don Juan cuts the ground from under the brothers of Donna Elvira. Libertine desire denounces the impossible idealization of courtly love.

Libertine desire erases the taboo and consumes virginity: the debased feminine object loses its status. Molière uses the veil to identify Elvire first as a lady and then as a specter. She loses her honor and her life in the world. Louis Jouvet staged her conversion by including a figure of the Virgin as the counterpart of the skeleton bearing the scythe of Death.[2] Mozart's Donna Anna loses her father, delays her wedding with an undesired fiancé, and is consumed with mourning for the pleasure she did not receive. Unlike the angry ex-virgins who punish the consumers of their virginity, according to Freud, Don Juan's victims are under his spell. They forget everything else in their attempt to possess him. Their lust for vengeance is a veil for their unavowable response to his seduction. Molière's Elvire and Mozart-Da Ponte's Donna Elvira illustrate the shift from anger and revenge to Christian charity, a disguise for tenderness and love. Don Giovanni's "affected tenderness" in his response to Donna Elvira indicates his recognition of her feeling for him. Christian solicitude does not fool him; her love cannot save him. In the end, she will return to the convent and take the veil.

---

[2] Louis Jouvet directed *Dom Juan* and played the title role at the Theatre of the Athénée, in Paris, in 1948.

The veil hides identity. The Lady and the Specter wear it like a mask. In Christian rhetoric, the veil figures the body as the incarnation, but it also figures the revelation of the invisible in the Other world. Behind the veil, the madonnas of the past and the future bid farewell to the world of vain illusions. They await their betrothal to Christ the bridegroom. Renaissance painting uses the veil as an erotic figure of beauty. Its translucence simultaneously hides and displays the body.

The veil signals beautiful form and insubstantial illusion—the incarnation and the resurrection, but also the shadow of a dream. Lacan reads the veil as the idolization of the nothingness that is beyond the love object. The veil covers the object of desire in different ways, but always in the context of desire. The Giotto Madonna is artfully connected to her son; Lippi's delicate Madonna wears a transparent veil; Vermeer's opulent tapestry curtains are open only for the viewer's intimate view of Faith in ecstasy; and Whistler's "Symphony in White" sets the girl's body in relief against the damasked folds of the drapery, white on white. She floats against the veil-like background and above the bear rug, an object of hallucination.

In a pre-modernist reading of love, the romantic poet John Keats accentuates the feminine when he takes up the Sapphic and Platonic figure of Eros. The "still unravish'd bride" addressed in the "Ode on a Grecian Urn" by Keats remains a virgin because she is frozen in time, caught at the moment before her lover possesses her. The speaker of the poem limits knowledge to the Platonic identity of Beauty and Truth—but the "Bold Lover" is deprived of pleasure, since the two are frozen in timeless representation. Keats writes:

> 'Beauty is truth, truth beauty,'—that is all
> Ye know on earth, and all ye need to know.

The Platonic closing sounds strange in light of the premises of the long poem entitled "Lamia," with its subject borrowed from *The Anatomy of Melancholy*. The agent of love is a woman and a "serpent rod:" like the phallic form of the young woman in modern psychoanalysis, she is a virginal object of desire. Lamia is described as

> A virgin purest lipp'd, yet in the lore
> Of love deep learned to the red heart's core.

She possesses the snake's knowledge—the knowledge that leads Adam and Eve to expulsion from Paradise and original sin—but at the moment of her wedding celebration, the bride is unmasked as an illusion by the Philosopher. Like the Grecian bride, she disappears into a cloud of representation. Original sin hovers in the shadows; the paternal agency of the Christian God the Father is occupied by the Philosopher, who frowns like Baudelaire's Plato. Classical antiquity, the Christian tradition of the Renaissance, and the romantic interest in melancholy culminate in the philosopher's destruction of illusion— the bitter "snake-sly" and mysterious truth that erases the illusory sweetness of desire. In Keats, the search for the feminine does not have a happy ending: the idealization of the object and its debasement are irreconcilable.

Keats exposes the virgin's limitation as an object of desire; only at the price of non-satisfaction can the object remain a virgin. Once "married," as Don Juan puts it, her value goes up in smoke and the no longer virginal object fantasizes about turning the clock back to the first time, like Joyce's heroines. With his life slipping away almost before his eyes, Keats holds fast to the identity of Beauty and Truth; the virginal object of desire slips out of reach and then disappears. These poems articulate the impossibility of satisfying desire.

Modernism gives evidence of idealization and betrayal, of sublime virgins and shameless temptresses. Idealization comes at a high price. Repression and the debasement of the object accompany it. The result is bitterness, jealousy, and melancholy. Love gets lost, through betrayal, illusion, or death. Modernity is haunted by the erasure of love. The Madonna frequently says no, and refuses the lover. In an alternative scenario, explored by Freud, desire and love cannot coincide; they are fatally separated, like the divided figures of Aristophanes' fable in the *Symposium*. The would-be lover is put on hold in the disjunction between desire and love.

The cult of love sends us in search of some answers. Christianity proposes a model of a sublime and successful incest between a son-god and his pure mother—daughter of her son, in Dante's account, echoed in *Ulysses*. Art replaces the rules of religion with images and figures. The post-romantic sublime reaffirms Sappho's Eros the bittersweet and empties out the space where the Greek gods held court. Sappho's poetic fictions of lover and beloved are played out under their eyes. Modernity turns out the lights.

Contemporary mass culture plays it both ways, divine and human. Every day, we encounter religious institutions and cults that absorb individual suffering in the name of a superior agency, but we also encounter materialist answers to the search for love and its values. Flaubert's sketch of a Don Juan figure who ultimately desires the Virgin combines the two approaches, divine and human. Don Juan's last object of desire leads him beyond the fleeting pleasures of seduction to a union, a fusion. Only this blending of the two loves survives the pleasures of the moment: like Flaubertian memory, it endures beyond death.

Mediated by romanticism, Plato's *Symposium* takes us on an elaborate detour around the question of Judeo-Christian morality. With its configuration of Beauty and Truth, Eros leads us imperceptibly toward art. The ends of passion are undecidable. They run the gamut from the fairy-tale wish ("they lived happily ever after"), the fall, and the constructions of memory. When seduction goes wrong, only the figure remains. The arabesque of writing preserves the image of the madonnas of modernism. The finalizing declaration in *Giacomo Joyce* ("write it . . . what else are you good for") conflates erotics with poetics: Yeats's dancer merges with the dance. The lost object is found in the sublime.

For Flaubert, this precarious fusion occurs in the encounter between desire and mystical love. European painting repeatedly illustrates this encounter in the beauty of the Virgin. Flaubert's mystical Madonna figure talks to her lover after her death. Realism is suspended and the mystical virgin makes a fantastic return. In the same suspension of belief, a 1997 billboard over a highway announces to people going downtown to work or a movie that the Virgin talks to America. A phone number is provided. The Virgin reigns over a virtual theater of desire; in it, our solitude shimmers with a projected dialogue. We look for love on the phone and in the dark of the unconscious, where, as Lacan pointed out, something does not stop turning into writing, and something keeps on talking.

Innovation in love and in writing is inseparable from the belatedness of something that happened in the distant past. Plato's mix of love and virtue is central to the secret knowledge of the mysteries that modernism ultimately inherits from Sappho's Eros and from the *Symposium*. Socrates claims to have learned about love "long ago" from the priestess Diotima. Baudelaire's speaker in "Lesbos" echoes that

18. Jacopo Tintoretto, *The Madonna of the Stars*, c. 1550–1600, oil on canvas. Courtesy of the National Gallery of Art.

"long ago," in reference to the secret knowledge granted to him in childhood. In a playful allusion to these Mysteries, Wallace Stevens's "Homunculus et la Belle Etoile" evokes a sexually satisfying mistress. Her appearance as the most pointedly Platonic madonna of modernism allows Sappho's poetics of desire and Plato's ultimate Eros to shine, bitter and sweet, through the illusions of modernity.

Reminiscent of the dark-haired Murillo Virgin who haunted Flaubert and anticipating the Beautiful Star of the poem by Wallace Stevens, a Tintoretto Virgin connects the Renaissance and baroque revisions of Sappho's Eros to trans-romanticism and modernism. Strikingly modern in appearance and in expression, Tintoretto's *Madonna of the Stars* presents a sensual and enigmatic figure under a sky filled with yellow light and cherub-stars. Like the Tintoretto Madonna, "Homunculus et la Belle Etoile" dismisses the dead bodies and fleeting ghosts that haunt representations of the feminine. In their place, Stevens proposes a secular and ideally beautiful version of Mary, Star of the Sea. The poem's speaker evokes her luminous presence in Platonic terms.

> It is a good light, then, for those
> That know the ultimate Plato,

The light shines through her jewel-like translucence. Dedicated to desire, her image appears on the coastline of modernity, where the poem ends:

> Tranquillizing with this jewel
> The torments of confusion.

Index

Numerals in italics indicate illustrations.